Wages
Against
Artwork

Wages Against Artwork

Decommodified Labor and the Claims of Socially Engaged Art

Leigh Claire La Berge

DUKE UNIVERSITY PRESS *Durham and London* 2019

Designed by Matthew Tauch
Typeset in HelveticaNeue Std. and Garamond
Premier Pro by Copperline Book Services

Library of Congress Cataloging-in-Publication Data
Names: La Berge, Leigh Claire, author.
Title: Wages against artwork : decommodified
labor and the claims of socially engaged art /
Leigh Claire La Berge.
Description: Durham : Duke University Press, 2019. |
Includes bibliographical references and index.
Identifiers: LCCN 2018055384 (print) |
LCCN 2019010348 (ebook)
ISBN 9781478005278 (ebook)
ISBN 9781478004233 (hardcover : alk. paper)
ISBN 9781478004820 (pbk. : alk. paper)
Subjects: LCSH: Social practice (Art) | Art and
social action. | Art and society. | Art—Study and
teaching—Social aspects. | Art—Economic aspects. |
Artists—Political activity—History—21st century. |
Artists and community.
Classification: LCC N7433.915 (ebook) | LCC N7433.915
.L34 2019 (print) | DDC 701/.03—dc23
LC record available at https://lccn.loc.gov/2018055384

For Caroline

Contents

The Argument

The past twenty years have seen a rise in the production, the circulation, and subsequently the criticism of new forms of socially engaged art. This kind of art authors a demand for societal reorganization, for economic equality, and for access to the power to transform social relations. The turn of socially engaged art toward such functions offers a site at which to consider historical changes to the realm of the aesthetic itself.

Concurrently, since the mid-1970s, real wages—the price for which workers sell their labor—have increased only little or not at all. Many people, particularly those in the culture industries, now work longer days for more years, and they receive a steady reduction in the money they are offered in return. I call this slow diminishment of the wage alongside an increase in the demands of work *decommodified labor.*

I argue that the turn of socially engaged art toward function, this art's seeming abandonment of autonomy, is grounded in the decommodification of labor. I orient my readings of such art within the hermeneutics of the commodity form, its constitutive obfuscation of labor in particular, and I suggest that decommodified labor has reconstituted what kind of claims can be made on the aesthetic and what kind of practices may be understood as art practices.

Acknowledgments

This book got its genesis from a series of conversations with and encouragement from Imre Szeman and Caroline Woolard.

A curatorial grant from the Elizabeth Foundation for the Arts enabled Laurel Ptak and me to curate in 2012 a show called "To Have and to Owe," which was in many ways the beginning of my experience of working with artists and thinking about art as an object of scholarly investigation. Critics including the late Randy Martin as well as Andrew Ross, Annie McClanahan, and Richard Dienst generously contributed to that show through both insights and conversations.

Research support for this book came from the City University of New York (CUNY) in the guises of various centers, granting agencies, and organizations: the Professional Staff Congress–CUNY Research Award; the Center for Place, Culture and Politics; the Provost's Office at Borough of Manhattan Community College; and the CUNY Office of Diversity's Faculty Publication Program.

Audiences at the University of Sydney, the University of Cambridge, the University of Minnesota, Princeton University, California Institute of the Arts, the University of Alberta, the University of the Arts, Saint Mary's University, Wellesley College, Dartmouth College, the CUNY Graduate Center, Mildred's Lane, the University of St. Gallen, Goldsmith's College, Duke University, and Kingston University have offered many challenges and provocations over the course of my writing.

Several conferences were also crucial, particularly Princeton's "The Contemporary" and the Zentrum für Literatur-und Kulturforschung's "The Politics of Form: What Does Art Know About Society?" Such conferences take time and money and all forms of energy to organize. I am grateful to Joshua Kotin, Sarah Chihaya, and Kinohi Nishiwaka at Princeton, and to Ulrich Plass at Wesleyan University and Matthias Rothe at the University of Minnesota, for their efforts. The University of Sydney's "Rethinking Money" conference introduced me to two critics who have changed the way I understand political economy: Dick Bryan and Bob Meister. I thank Melinda Cooper,

Martijn Konings, and Fiona Allon for inviting me. I also thank Melinda and Martijn for originally bringing this book to Duke University Press.

At Duke, both Courtney Burger and her assistant, Sandra Korn, have been available, encouraging, and wonderfully supportive. Sandra was beyond helpful. Courtney was not only a supporter of this project; she also located for it two wonderful anonymous readers, one of whom stated in their report that "a book like this needs a reading of Adorno." I don't know whether I have risen to that challenge, but I certainly had fun trying—"fun" in the context of Adorno's insistence that any concept is in necessary, dialectical entanglement with its opposite. The other reader motivated my conclusion. I hope both readers will see their generous and incisive comments reflected here.

Colleagues who have read parts of the book include Max Haiven, Christian Haines, Teresa Heffernan, Mathias Nilges, Matt Tierney, Eyal Amaran, Imre Szeman, Michael Hardt, Miranda Joseph, Bob Meister, Quinn Slobodian, Daniel Harvey, Arne De Boever, Jason Schneiderman, Tracy Bealer, Keridiana Chez, Adele Kudish, Jennifer Bajorek, Sianne Ngai, Keston Sutherland, Silvia Federici, Laurel Ptak, Mathias Ropke, Fiona Allon, Stephen Best, Nicholas Brown, John Munro, Peter Osborne, Phanuel Antwi, Anita Chari, Anna Kornbluh, Jane Blocker, Maria Luisa Mendoca, Neil Argawal, Sooran Choi, Annie Spencer, Richard Dienst, Marcia Kay Klotz, Marina Vishmidt, Michelle Chihara, Jasper Bernes, Phoebe Stubbs, and Andrew Weiner.

Doug Barrett has been a consistent interlocutor throughout this project; I can't overstate his help. Likewise, so much of my thinking about what it means to make aesthetic claims has been motivated by Dehlia Hannah and our conversations about Kant's continued relevance, still.

One of the fantastic things about working with artists who themselves are interested in questions of the relation between economy and culture is that they are open to ongoing conversations with critics. Many of the artists I write about here have shared their thoughts with me, offered their own critiques, and given me permission to reproduce their images. I thank for their time and their art Cassie Thornton, Thomas Gokey, Caroline Woolard, Renzo Martens, and the collective Mammalian Diving Reflex. Caitlin Berrigan not only shared her thoughts with me but also discussed many aspects of children at work. Dave Sinclair gave me permission to use some of his images and made the Thatcherite 1980s come alive for me through conversation. Duke Riley, Koki Tanaka, Tania Bruguera, Sun Yuan, and Peng Yu generously allowed me permission to reprint their images.

My mother, Ann La Berge, has—as always—been a reader, re-reader, proof-reader, and interlocutor of this and all my work. A great lover of animals, she has been particularly interested in thinking through how various of our family cats might have responded to chapter 3, "Art Worker Animal."

Finally, to "acknowledge" one artist in particular is simply not enough. This book and my love are for Caroline.

Socially Engaged Art
and Decommodified Labor

Artists and their artworks circulate in strange economies. When artists desire a wage, payment often seems elusive; when they reject the payment system, their rejection offers no guarantee that money will not be attracted to their work. In this book I examine socially engaged artists and their relationships to the wage form. I assemble a collection of artists who address their own or other artists' lack of a wage to ground their method of artistic social engagement and, indeed, to critique our economic present. Sometimes this art thematizes its economic concern: Cassie Thornton, an artist who works on debt, invites other artists to construct "debt visualizations," verbal and imagistic collages of the consequences of a wageless life. Sometimes the art effects a change: Renzo Martens creates artist-run institutions that attempt to transform wageless Congolese farmers into moneymaking artists. At still other times such art allegorizes the lack of a wage: Duke Riley's pigeon-based performances and Koki Tanaka's child-oriented enactments both use as their subjects those among us who cannot be waged: animals and children.

Two anecdotes from contemporary art illustrate well how artists themselves understand their own economic possibilities and limitations. The first concerns Caroline Woolard, an artist I write about in chapter 2. While speaking at a panel on artists' pay during Bushwick Open Studios in 2015, Woolard was asked to comment on the possibility of "artists' resale rights." An almost century-old idea, such rights enable artists to continue to make money if their artwork is resold after its initial purchase, much as authors retain the right to new editions and translations of their texts through copyright protection. The audience nodded in seeming agreement at the idea; it was the first concrete proposal of the event, after all. Woolard then responded: "I've never sold any art. I don't know many artists who have ever sold anything. Most art will never sell and most artists won't make money from their art." If one does

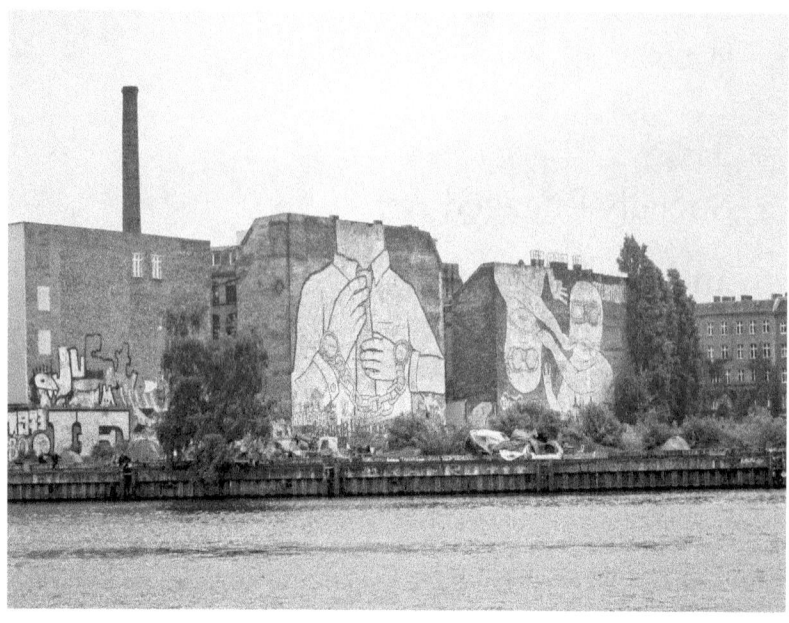

I.1 Kreuzberg Mural by Lutz Henke and Blu. Photograph by Leigh Claire La Berge.

not sell one's art the first time, then "resale rights" are a modest proposal, indeed. The *Guardian* newspaper recently reported that 71 percent of artists in the United Kingdom are paid no wages for their work; we can only assume a higher number in the United States.[1]

Artist Lutz Henke recently recounted a related, if inverse, scene in Berlin's Kreuzberg neighborhood. Along with the Italian artist Blu, Henke produced two of Berlin's most famous murals (figure I.1). As murals that have graced a thousand postcards and social media posts, these site-specific pieces had begun to star in a well-known story of urban spatial availability transformed into displacement.

As the Kreuzberg neighborhood has begun and no doubt will continue to host a revolving slate of ex-pats, as apartments have been transformed into investment properties and remediated back to an international, culture-consuming public through *biennales* and Airbnb, Henke and Blu made the decision to withdraw their images from public circulation.[2] They covered the building-wide murals with black paint, all the while being booed by onlookers who were unaware of their identity and who no doubt thought they were real estate developers. One of their images (left) presents the so-called golden handcuffs of bourgeois existence. Here those handcuffs are accentuated by the capitalist temporality of the wristwatches. Too discomfited to be satisfied with their lot in life, yet too comfortable to risk changing it, those wearing the golden handcuffs wait and hope passively for a different scenario. The pieces were created in 2008 as an antagonism and provocation; by 2014 Blu and Henke understood that their art anchored "a [Berlin] art scene preserved as an amusement park for those who can afford rising rents."[3] As anyone with a rudimentary knowledge of the avant-garde knows, the path from artist-based rejection of commodification to artistic commodity is a well-worn one, and Henke describes perhaps the only available assurance that their murals would not continue to travel down it: the work concludes through its destruction, and who better to conclude it than its creators?

These stories make reference to an ill-defined moment in the social life of artistic commodities—namely, the gap between making art and making money. Sometimes the first leads to the second, but often by a circuitous route and not the one intended *by* the artist, let alone *for* the artist. In the first anecdote, Woolard interrupts a certain fantasy of possibility: that with the right proprietary arrangements in place, artists will support themselves through their art. In the second, Henke interrupts someone else's fantasy: that his and Blu's murals, made free, could be the mise-en-scène for an increase in property values and the consequent scarcity and constriction of public space. In the first moment, money cannot be made; in the second, money is being made, but not for the artists, as the public-ness of the pieces is transformed into a private, appropriative gaze. In Woolard's case, the artist desires the commodification of her labor—who among us doesn't want to get paid for our work?—but that commodification is not available. In Blu and Henke's case, the artists desire that the decommodification of public space match their own decommodified labor, a process only able to be located by removing the art object from circulation. Both anecdotes illustrate the moment in which value embodied in the art object as a result of labor has limits placed on its ability to circulate as a commodity. I want to suggest that artistic labor enters a scene of decommodification in both.

The subject of this book, then, is the realization and the artistic representation of a kind of everyday, unwaged, yet formal and professional work that I call *decommodified labor* as it manifests in contemporary socially engaged art mostly, but not entirely, in the contemporary United States. I understand work as a local action in which we all engage in order to make our lives both meaningful and possible, and labor as an abstraction through which our work is organized. What I mean to capacitate with the term "decommodified labor" is a kind of work that is not compensated through a wage or available through a market purchase. Nor does decommodified labor primarily derive from or circulate through the intimate settings of family, care, and love, a kind of work increasingly recognized as "affective labor."[4]

Even the famous artists, the ones who do get paid, repeatedly turn to the themes and instances of which decommodified labor is composed—namely, those who cannot or are not paid to make art. The Russian conceptual artists Vitaly Komar and Alexander Melamid train chimpanzees to take and sell photographs in Red Square; Martha Rosler stages a garage sale in *Meta-Monumental Garage Sale* at the Museum of Modern Art; the *New York Times* publishes Tino Sehgal's pay rates, which include nothing for the young children who populate his performance installations. Yet while the fact and representation of decommodified labor predominate, artists position themselves in different relations to it. Sometimes the nonwage of decommodified labor in the arts is chosen: the person working does not desire a wage, as in the case of a barter or trade, two activities present throughout contemporary art and which I address in chapter 2.[5] Other times the nonwage is enforced: the person working cannot garner a wage, as in much student and amateur work, because their efforts are not recognized as work, which I address in chapter 1. Because most artists begin their careers as students, and because many will work as amateurs for much of their careers, this wage limitation, too, is important to my archive. Finally, other times still, because the worker is an animal or child—two new populations visible in work by artists such as Jannis Kounellis and Carsten Höller and addressed in chapters 3 and 4—they categorically cannot be waged.

Before artistic labor could be decommodified it had to be commodified. And indeed, the 1950s through the 1970s saw an incredible expansion of the possibilities for artists to sell their artistic labor through "a deluge of grants and array of agencies which led to a rapid expansion of the art-labor force."[6] That expansion was followed by a contraction. Decommodified artistic labor might be novel, but decommodified labor itself does not constitute a historically new phenomenon; it has been realized before and it now is available again in our contemporary moment.[7] Yet while we are quite accustomed to an analysis of how labor or any object becomes a commodity, we are less used to a critique of how things cease to dwell in that state. Nonetheless, we do have a repertoire of cognate terms on which to draw. For example, "deskilling" designates the devaluation of a certain task, and because any task takes time to acquire, deskilling is also a reorganization of a worker's time and life possibilities. And as critics such as Harry Braverman have argued, skilling, deskilling, and reskilling reveal a dialectic unto themselves; historically they emerge and recede with new technologies. "Deindustrialization" meanwhile marks the devaluation of a certain place and its built environment. Deindustrialization is often positioned as local to the 1970s and cities such as Detroit and Manchester loom large in its imaginaries, but in fact deindustrialization has been a recurrent feature of urban life since the eighteenth century.[8] Yet we do not currently have a term for the state in which our formal labor is devalued to the point of wagelessness while we are still doing it, and this process too ebbs and flows through modernity.

The larger concept of decommodification has been developed almost exclusively, if not broadly, in political science and legal studies, where it designates a certain independence from market forces. That independence, on the whole, is understood as a salve against whatever particular injuries an actor, or asset, might face were it to remain in the market.[9] My aims in this book diverge from those of social science. I move the problem of decommodification into the realm of arts production and the "imaginative cogency" of art's circulation, what I will further define as "the aesthetic." There, I train my focus on the central commodity of labor. Yet "the aesthetic," however defined, has since Immanuel Kant been theorized as outside the market: as antidote, as opposition, as compensation—what Terry Eagleton calls its "ideology." And for me, the double displacement from the market that the aesthetic and decommodified labor together provide produces a surprising optic for the analysis of contemporary art. This combination becomes the lens through which to situate and analyze what many critics have considered our new avant-garde: "socially engaged art," sometimes called Social Practice art. This kind of art aims to make a useful intervention.[10]

I locate decommodified labor both as it is *used to produce* and as it is *represented in* socially engaged art.[11] As a consequence I use decommodified labor as a device to tell a story about the rise of this moment in art history as it develops from aspects of institutional critique, conceptual art, performance art, and community arts traditions. What differentiates today's socially engaged art from its predecessors is that it attempts both to represent forms of social inequity and to amend those forms through the artwork itself.[12] We might say, then, that socially engaged artwork is a bit like social work: it is the craft of transporting people to a more supported place—be that support economic or affective, durational or immediate. But socially engaged art is also like artwork, too: it encourages its participants to contemplate a different place and perhaps to take pleasure in that contemplation, even if only for a moment and even if no action derives from the contemplation.

I find scenes of decommodified labor in the training of the art student; in the artistic deployment of animals and children as well as in artist-run institutions of barter and exchange; and indeed, in the kind of "socially engaged" business practices that are often conflated with art practices. What is important for me is that each iteration of decommodified labor functions without reliance on a wage. Animals were for centuries considered crucial workers in multiple industries. Indeed, it was only with the rise of a broad-based wage system that they were disbarred from such work. Children, too, have long been important economic agents and only recently were they stripped of that status in the Global North. That those members of our social world who were once workers now appear in artwork *as artwork* without remuneration is an important constituent of my argument. It is important that those bartering and exchanging activities, which might be waged or thought of as either work or an adjunct to artwork, appear here both as unpaid and as the artworks themselves. Together such formations constitute but do not exhaust my class of decommodified labors.[13] This approach may seem overly restrictive to some readers—what about slavery? what about indenture? what about the Global South?—and yet, as I argue throughout this book, the ability to limit a wage to certain times, places, and people is a crucial feature of accumulation and therefore deserves some conceptual adherence. The wage renders the nonwage productive. As Marx himself says: "Capital . . . is not only . . . the command over labour. It is essentially the command over unpaid labour."[14] He consequently affirms that "the secret of the self-expansion of capital resolves itself into having the disposal of a definite quantity of other people's unpaid labour."[15]

My primary archive derives from contemporary socially engaged art, but as I exfoliate the term "decommodified labor" throughout the book, one will see how it has become a cultural discourse and practice unto itself. Of course, the "internship" has long been placed outside the bounds of "suffer or permit to work" since it has been interpreted as being "for the educational benefit of the intern . . . [because] the employer derives no advantages [from it]."[16] That logic is transformed in a scene of decommodification: now the work *is* work and it is unpaid. Much of reality television, for example, runs on decommodified labor: those "real" people we see on television often forgo a wage in exchange for "exposure."[17] It was recently reported that the corporate-hipster company Urban Outfitters asked its employees to "volunteer" for six-hour holiday shifts. Such volunteerism would be like work but without the wage.[18] In an episode of the popular HBO series *Girls*, one character notes to another that he has taken "a new job as an assistant to a curator of dance. It's unpaid, but it could lead somewhere."[19] Whether in cultural production, in cultural consumption, or in the content of various cultural texts, decommodified labor limns our present.

As a site to translate between theories of labor and capital, of art production and art criticism, I believe decommodified labor is the missing term in contemporary discussions about art and value, as those conversations relate to socially engaged art.[20] While Shannon Jackson and Claire Bishop have written incisive treatments of this art, they have not offered an economic basis for it. When, for example, Shannon Jackson claims that Social Practice art orients itself around a "de-autonomized aesthetic," I would add that decommodified labor governs such an "aesthetic"—by which she here means "style."[21]

Two remarkable recent books by John Roberts and Dave Beech do offer such a basis for that economic specificity, yet they do not use their economic terms heuristically to analyze art. Decommodified labor has more precision and conceptual specificity than John Roberts's term "second economy."[22] It organizes a historical process in a manner that Dave Beech's "commodification without commodification" only hints at as a category. I use decommodified labor as both an object of an analysis and a site for interpretation. It denotes a dialectical process that may be located at the level of capitalist production and in daily life, in critical theory and in the next DIY gallery show. Within critical theory, I understand decommodified labor to be a pivotal term between the two narratives and idioms that we use to understand our current economy: Marxist theories of an intensification of labor under a regime that is sometimes called the "real subsumption of labor to capital," and neoliberal theories of an end of labor and its replacement with "human capital." Decommodified labor provides a material and conceptual site to investigate how the shifting composition of value and the structure of surplus appropriation finds a potentially critical form in arts production.

This book's title, *Wages Against Artwork: Decommodified Labor and the Claims of Socially Engaged Art*, alerts us that I will be tarrying with the long opposition between various ideologies of the aesthetic and the corresponding understandings of the economy; the subtitle itself indicates more precisely the matter of intercourse: how socially engaged artwork incorporates and critiques decommodified labor. The phrase "wages against" artwork is taken from Silvia Federici's 1970s pamphlet, "Wages Against Housework." In an odd and perhaps utopian bit of historical misremembering, Federici's essay has often been explained as a demand that women's home-based labor, from sex to mothering to all varieties of care—what would now be grouped under the rubric of affective labor—be monetarily compensated. This sentiment has been colloquially inscribed through a modified title, "Wages *for* Housework," after the feminist movement of the same name. And indeed, one often hears Federici's text inaccurately called "Wages for Housework." But as Federici herself explains, "I actually titled [that] essay 'Wages *Against* Housework,' because it was very clear for us that wages for housework was at the same time wages against housework."[23] Wages are needed and wages are not enough, a historical contradiction that Peter Linebaugh notes has been present since the inception of wage form.[24]

Commodification is likewise needed and commodification is likewise not enough. Decommodification points to another space that portends the arrival of another time. Like its theoretical root, commodification, decommodification should not be ethically categorized as good or bad; it should not be categorized ethically at all. Certain artists whom I critique herein seize a space of decommodified labor as liberating; others paint it as ironic; still others understand it as constricting and delegitimizing. Some understand it as historical, a lineage to another past, and some see it as novel, a gateway to a different future. Using examples from socially engaged artwork, I identify a reconfiguration of both commodified labor and a transformation of some of the concepts used for the analysis and periodization of art that derive from art's fraught relationship with the commodity, including autonomy, purposelessness, and medium. Decommodified labor will denote in this book multiple social and artistic forms, but its most basic conceit is the nonwage or the nonmonetary remuneration of formal labor.

My claims are twofold, and I hope they will resonate in art criticism, cultural studies, and critical theory. First, I argue that those writing about socially engaged art have yet to produce an economic concept to buttress their criticism. Because such art is devoted to working on all that can be redistributed, this economic concept is of signal importance. Second, I suggest that decommodification be understood as a complimentary trend to that word we hear so often: "commodification," a process memorialized in the pejorative phrase "that's so commodified." We must also begin saying, "that's so decommodifed." And then we must ask two questions: Why does decommodified labor seem so prominent now? and, Why has it been so forcefully distilled in the arts?

I suggest that the pervasive decommodification of cultural labor today may be interpreted as one response to what various critics have understood as the late-twentieth-century shifting composition of value, whether that moment is diagnosed as the end of the Keynesian compact, or the rise of financialization, or the neoliberalization of the state. An emergent financial infrastructure has allowed for the increase of the price of assets without either a wage increase or an inflationary currency adjustment—both of which could have transformative social effects. In my last book, *Scandals and Abstraction: Financial Fiction of the Long 1980s*, I explored the financial aspects of this economic transformation as they were mediated through American literary texts and what I called financial print culture.[25] Here I continue that work by exploring the flipside of the problem, as it were. I investigate the changing composition of labor and the changing artistic production that this reconstitution engenders. When money's price is too high, labor's price will suffer, and that suffering has left a trace in contemporary arts practices.

Approaching Decommodification:
Aesthetics and Labor, Art and Work

To produce a theory of decommodified labor suitable for the arts, one has to begin with the centrality of the commodity in organizing our understanding of the concepts of art and work, and our understanding of the more philosophical terms that organize and critique such content—namely, aesthetics and labor. In this section I demonstrate how central the commodity has been in structuring our thinking about how and why we work, and how and why we create spheres of social life seemingly antagonistic to work, such as art. In the subsequent two sections I then derive from political economy and art criticism a theory of decommodified labor.

We all know what a commodity is: a trivial thing, a thing outside us, and a thing whose looks are deceiving. Marx uses the language of vision, first glances, and awkward impressions to introduce what he calls the commodity form. He explains that "a commodity is, in the first place, an object outside us, a thing that by its properties satisfies human wants of some sort or another. The nature of such wants, whether, for instance, they spring from the stomach or from fancy, makes no difference." And famously, for Marx, "a commodity appears, at first sight, a very trivial thing, and easily understood. [Yet] its analysis shows that it is, in reality, a very queer thing."[26] Likewise, we all know how the commodity's armature will unravel and unwind. Its simplicity and easy apprehension will soon transform into "metaphysical subtleties and theological niceties" whose hermeneutics and historical disposition will become the sine qua non of the capitalist mode of production. Central to its subtleties is the fact that while anything may take the form of a commodity, only one action may generate the value found within it: the expenditure of human labor power.

According to Marx, capitalism's uniqueness is found in the fact that everyone has to sell her labor to someone else as a commodity. This ceaseless, global exchange of labor power generates the social world of modernity in which we are all connected locally, nationally, globally through our commerce. This is a world in which all things, services, and actions may be and will be commodified, or purchased by someone who has paid for the right to our labor for a certain amount of time. When I speak of the commodity, as I will do throughout this book, I mean to emphasize human labor. Yet even as it comes to define our lives, the selling of labor power produces a fundamental misrecognition; namely, the value of commodities seems to be located in the things, not in the labor of the people who made them. Marx notes that such a scenario produces a world governed by "material relations between persons and social relations between things."[27] Such a worldview may seem totalizing, and it is. Yet in the history of critical theory, one possible and tenuous exception to this regime has been continually noted and returned to: the capacious sphere of the production of and reaction to natural and artful stimuli known as "the aesthetic."[28] Simultaneous to the emergent eighteenth-century capitalist reality that all goods and services, that some people and most property, could be sold, the category of the aesthetic emerged to circumvent commodity relations. "In a notable historical irony," Terry Eagleton writes, "the birth of aesthetics as an intellectual discourse coincides with the period in which cultural productions [begin] to suffer the miseries and indignities of commodification."[29]

As with "commodity," "aesthetic," too, is a term in need of definition and specification. Its use varies widely across critical theory, art criticism, and philosophy where indeed it denotes radically different problems. Sometimes it is a freestanding noun—"the aesthetic"—meant to designate a social sphere of historical experience. More often though, it is used as an adjective to qualify a type of response to external stimuli: "aesthetic category," "aesthetic experience," and "aesthetic judgment" all hint toward this usage. At its most generic, "aesthetic" has come to mean something like "style" or "artfulness," a use that reminds us of the term's link to sensuousness as encountered in time and space. I will use the term rather normatively. For the sake of clarity and argumentation, I will avoid using "aesthetic" to mean art or style. I am less concerned with aesthetic response, aesthetic judgment, and the manner in which we reflect on stimuli and synthesize those reflections as individuals, but I do refer to the literature related to this idea. My primary engagement is to understand "the aesthetic" as a sphere of cultural production and consumption that offers a fleeting respite—even for a moment, even if contingent—from the capitalist imperative to buy and sell labor, and from the philosophical imperative to think concept-based thought. A collective "horizon of imaginative cogency," I will use "the aesthetic" as it constitutes a sphere of shared historical experience in which "serious play sublimates purposeful activity or where an illusory freedom from function provides a necessary critique from praxis."[30] That may seem unfashionable, perhaps too Kantian, or indeed *wrong*—"contemporary art is post-aesthetic art," argues Peter Osborne.[31] Yet despite its varied usage, its seeming obsolescence after conceptual art, the aesthetic remains an "irreducible dimension" of modernity. To be organized by the aesthetic is to be shepherded by what Eagleton calls "the ideology of the aesthetic," for better—one can realize an otherness to capitalism—or worse: the realization likely won't be realized, but rather it will be subsumed.[32]

In a different, perhaps more practical idiom, we may speak of the relation between waged work, the result of labor power sold as a commodity, and artwork, one site that prompts aesthetic judgment taking the place of nature from Hegel on. As aesthetic judgments refer to art—that to which people have a particular and a not moral or rational response—and as art often contains noncommodified labor, art gradually came to represent the autonomy contained in the aesthetic. Those characterizations are quite ideal, but we will let them stand for the moment as they allow us to enter a long historical and philosophical conversation about what it means to work for oneself or to work for someone else in order to complete the tasks that carry us from one day to the next—what critical theorists have termed "social reproduction."[33] The making of artwork is a kind of labor that is usually taken to be qualitatively distinct from social reproduction. Marx himself specifies that "works of art are not taken into consideration [in his study of capitalism] for they are of a special nature."[34] In Dave Beech's contemporary language, art is an exceptional economic object—one that doesn't follow economic logics.[35]

What distinguishes this special nature of art? According to philosophical aesthetics, in a world in which we are compelled to make ourselves useful to others by selling our labor, the artwork distinguishes itself by being useless. Here we see art's relation to "the aesthetic," a site divorced from praxis and that can be used to critique praxis. What can one actually *do* with art? It does not have an immediately realizable purpose. When individuals make an aesthetic judgment about art, they do so for their own reasons. Nonetheless, as anyone who has ever appreciated an artwork knows, at that moment of subjective impingement, the moment when the artwork means something to someone, it does offer a *sense* of purpose. Thus an aesthetic judgment produces, in Kant's words, a sense of what is "purposeful without purpose."[36] Theodor Adorno proffers that in a society where everything must have an instrumental purpose—namely, the making of money through the exchange of labor—only objects without such purpose may offer a critique of that system. Adorno claims that "insofar as a social function may be predicated of works of art, it is the function of having no function." Indeed, he insists: "Only what is useless can stand in for stunted use values."[37]

To understand what the aesthetic is differentiated from, to understand why theorists continue to view it as perhaps decreasingly autonomous but autonomous nonetheless, one only has to compare it to the world of work. Unlike the freedom and particularity involved in aesthetic judgment, and unlike the refusal of art to be useful, almost everyone has to work in order to get their needs met. Some of us choose the work that we do, but few of us may choose not to do any work, and many of us would select other jobs were the choice a truly free one. As Michael Denning correctly notes, "the workplace remains the fundamental unfree association of civil society."[38] It is through that site of unfreedom, however, that most of us meet our basic needs; find our friends and our partners; and indeed orient our lives. Kathi Weeks argues more expansively that "Waged-work remains today the centerpiece of late capitalist economic systems . . . . It is not only the primary mechanism by which income is distributed, it is also the basic means by which status is allocated . . . . After the family, waged-work is often the most important, if not sole, source of sociality for millions."[39] For whom we work, with whom we work, for how long, and under what conditions impart dimensions of the experience that rarely fall within the scope of a worker's own agency. The world of work as an imperative and a need, as a seemingly chosen structure that ultimately comes to structure us, acts in concert to compose something no longer reducible to work, but rather better conceived of as the social form of labor.[40] There is waged work and there is artwork, and the two have been long opposed in our divided social world in which art and work, labor and aesthetics, confront each other. We can now understand this binary as a constitutive disassociation: the aesthetic with its freedom and labor with its unfreedom have been long understood as oppositional categories.

That does not mean that those who produce the experiences and objects we often reflect on through aesthetic judgment (art, food, nature even) do not work or that such products cannot be purchased; rather, it means that histories and criticism of labor and histories and criticism of the aesthetic must be mapped on divergent theoretical—if not practical—trajectories, even while they follow the intimate contours of careful disarticulation and opportunistic trespass. Work conducts the worker toward an end: finishing the hour, finishing the day, perhaps even retiring, if one is lucky. Work's end-oriented and time-based structure, memorialized in Marx's famous chapter of *Capital*, "The Working Day," is too necessity-bound, too organized, and too determined to be aesthetic.[41] Work has a purpose and the aesthetic produces a feeling that is "purposeful without purpose"; the working world is codified by a whole series of regulations and laws, whereas the aesthetic provides a sense of "lawfulness without the law," in Kant's words.[42] But neither work nor the aesthetic remain static categories, and subjects and purveyors in both realms necessarily transform and expand their scope by appealing to the other. Because they are generatively opposed, these two categories must also appeal to each other for ongoing contrast and redefinition.

This tension continues to pervade art criticism, producing its own local dichotomies. For Adorno, art famously has a "double character as both autonomous and social fact." Adorno's key claim is that although art's autonomy and commodity status are in tension, each requires the other and each may express the other. Jacques Rancière narrates the same tension through the language of art history: "The mixing of art and commodity is not a discovery of the [19]60s . . . as soon as art was constituted as a specific sphere of existence, at the beginning of the 19th century, its producers began to call into question the triviality of reproduction, commerce, and commodity [and] as soon as they did so, commodities themselves began to travel in the opposite directions—to enter the realm of art."[43] Jacques Attali is perhaps the most succinct: "The artist was born at the same time his work went on sale."[44]

Today we know this tension under the endlessly asked, although not endlessly interesting, question: *Is art a commodity?* If it is a commodity, is it of the same kind as a car or a t-shirt? If it is not a commodity, why isn't it? This kind of internally generative tension not only delimits many discussions of art; in Boris Groys's account it has become definitional of what contemporary art *is*. The question has been incorporated into the artwork itself through this rhetorical chain: Is art a commodity? Yes. Should it be? No. Therefore, the artwork will become a commodity that is self-critical of its own commodity being; it is a commodity that wishes it were otherwise. Groys uses this opposition to construct the term "paradox-object": "to be a paradox-object is the normative requirement implicitly applied to any contemporary artwork," he states.[45]

While tensions between art and commodified labor are both philosophically and historically rooted, they take specific forms at discrete historical moments: sometimes the distance is greater; sometimes an intimacy is produced. From the Dadaists to the situationists, from the constructivists to Fluxus, the avant-garde has long refused the distinction between the categories of art and work, arguing that the very categorical separation itself is yet another form of social unfreedom and proprietary regulation. The constructivist instruction for artists to "abandon their inquiry into art as a mode of production and enter the realm of production itself" is perhaps the most direct confrontation with this separation, but there are others.[46] Think of the situationist staging of actions on the way to work, the Duchampian nomination of mass-produced commodities to "readymade" art objects, Fluxus sales or Andy Warhol's adoption of a terminology of production in his studio: it was *The Factory*. To this we can add dancer Yvonne Rainer's "task-based" performances and painter Gerhard Richter's "capitalist realism"—each reminds us of how art incorporates work into art so that art may critique work.

Yet we also see have begun to see business participate in this dialectic and make its own claims. In a fashion similar to that of artists' attempts to overcome this division by challenging the bounds of art, employers too have offered their own ameliorations to work. The activities and durations that constitute work shift constantly even as any given employer will attempt to extract more time from its employees in exchange for less money. An appeal to the aesthetic may provide a route to doing so. For example, an employer may organize an extracurricular excursion for its employees and describe the activity as partaking in the pleasures of the aesthetic away from the demands of the working day. The term "playbor" has recently begun to circulate in the world of "social entrepreneurship" (an equally worrisome term); both denote the miscegenation of labor with its opposite: fun, equality, pleasure.[47]

But surely, such employment strategies that seek to make work fun and pleasurable are only the flipside of a trend in the arts that Julia Bryan-Wilson has called "occupational realism," her term for artists undertaking a work-like task as their artwork. She provides the example of the artist Ben Kinmont running a used bookstore and designating its management as his "art."[48] If artists can call any work-like activity art, then why can't employers label any activity *not-work* and partake in their own avant-garde? And as Marina Vishmidt has so succinctly argued, "any activity that is not work can be art."[49] The closer to work the art dwells, the more radical is its longed-for critique of this divide. Artist Daniel Bozhkov took employment as a Wal-Mart greeter and his actions while working became his piece, *Training in Assertive Hospitality*.

And finally, we see the tension between art's freedom and work's unfreedom in the narration of artists' lives. Cultural critics including Andrew Ross and Sarah Brouillette have argued that the kind of insecurity that pervades today's precarious employment landscape is only the broad reapplication of the working lives that most artists have long lived.[50] So-called new-economy companies took the rebellious, anti-institutional conception of the artist and imported it into their working worlds, not through forms of social critique that such artists espoused but in the form of the social insecurity those artists often endured. As artist Andrea Fraser has argued, "artists have become the poster children for the jobs of insecurity, flexibility, deferred economic rewards, social alienation, cultural uprooting, and geographic displacement."[51] Indeed, Jasper Bernes has noted that the same 1960s moment of "the end of art," in Arthur Danto's famous words, was also declared by sociologists to constitute the end of work.[52] These twin spheres require each other for both expiration and continuation. In each of these categories—themselves staged at different levels of mediation: social sphere and individual response—we see both a *longue durée* of commodification's structural logic and a historical specificity of its contours.

Yet for anything to exist as a commodity, much less for a commodity to become a cultural dominant, certain features must be adhered to: first, a commodity is made by wage labor; second, it is sold on the market. Foremost, that rubric describes the worker herself. Workers are made by their own labor power, a proposition fully expressed by early social contract theorists who claimed that each of us (with the usual race and gender prohibitions) has property in our own body because we work.[53] And the worker made by herself constitutes the basic commodity of labor power that she possesses and will sell on the market. This fact makes labor our most unique commodity, because unlike a car or a sofa, labor daily regenerates itself through the life process of the worker, and usually through women and raced and colonized subjects' care work.

The crux of our problem is not the paradox-object, in Groys's terms, but the paradox-subject, because the basic commodity of capitalism, the rubric of the commodity form, is human labor. As Marx asks, "Whence arises the enigmatic form human labor takes as soon as it assumes the form of the commodity? Clearly it arises from the form itself."[54] To ask whether art, education, medical care, land, and so on, exist as a commodity is a pointed but limiting question. For the commodity is a reflexive form: it presumes its own limits and abilities as able to be surpassed, and this is part of its basic structure. The only way out of this predicament is to leave behind the ontological question, Is said object a commodity or not?, and instead ask, How and when do humans as laborers sell their labor power in the form of a commodity? Crucially for this book, what happens when they are unable or unwilling to sell their labor in arts production?

That question leads us to the decommodification of artistic labor. The ideology of the aesthetic has been to theorize art as outside of the realm of commodification. But historically we know that art very much participates in commodity circuits. Artworks are sold; artistic labor is sold. And yet, as the possibilities to conceive of oneself as one who has artistic labor to sell have multiplied through various schemes of professionalization, labor's share of value has been decimated. This economic fluctuation has transformed art's philosophical claims to nonvalue. The central economic transformation that undergirds this book is located in the mid- to late 1970s, when the U.S. economy was restructured to the advantage of financial operations and to the detriment of labor.[55] While various stock indexes have since 1970 risen three and four times their value—one measure of finance—wages have remained largely stagnant. Labor's share of social wealth has declined. Workers' wages and forms of social welfare have shrunken and in some cases disappeared. Under such conditions, we will work more and more for less and less, and I argue that in some cases we will work for nothing at all. Nowhere is this as true as in the arts. Thus John Roberts proffers that art exists in a "second economy[, a] precarious realm of under-monetized and unwaged artistic activity that the majority of artists now operate within."[56]

Feminist theories of social reproduction, Black Marxism, queer theory— each of these traditions has investigated the necessity of unwaged labor to the perpetuation of capitalism. But those investigations have not extended to art, much less to socially engaged art, an art practice that claims to orient itself differently to the demands and confines of the aesthetic as such by treading on the grounds of material necessity, sociality, and a host of other practical concerns through its explicit engagement with the economy. I find this omission surprising. Nor has the point been made of a radical change in the claims of labor up to and including its decommodification in art generally, even as the problem of representing labor has been fundamental to modern and contemporary art production and critique. In a claim that resonates with the Keynesian moment of the 1940s to the 1970s, and with broad-based artistic commodification, Helen Molesworth notes that "the unifying principle of the extraordinarily heterogeneous field of post wwii avant-garde art was a concern with the problematic of artistic labor."[57]

And certainly the need to address how artists' labor has been transformed was not only a part of art practice but a part of art's expanded field of activism. Think of the Art Workers Coalition, so active in the 1960s and 1970s, which insisted that an artwork is made by the *art worker*; or of the activist group to come out of Occupy Wall Street, "Arts & Labor"; or of the contemporary arts organization W.A.G.E. (Working Artists for a Greater Economy), which attempts to integrate artists into the cooperative economy movement.[58] Arts & Labor perform a certain substitution in their name: they make reference to the 1960s Art & Language group of British conceptual artists. If we accept their substitution, that of labor for language, then we as critics are faced with a problem similar to the one that greeted 1960s critics when they attempted to evaluate conceptual art.[59] Today, however, the shift is not from medium to concept but from concept to social practice, or in the prescient words of Raymond Williams, "from medium to social practice."[60] Economic history, critical theory, art history and criticism, and indeed arts practitioners themselves all suggest that a change in the valuation of labor provides a much-needed site for the contemporary historicization of art's categorical specificity.

I specify, then, that my focus will be trained on changes in both how and why we work, and how and why modes of artwork respond accordingly. The socially engaged art I read herein authors a demand for social reorganization, for economic equality, for education, for space and influence, and indeed for access to the power to transform social relations. And it is precisely in socially engaged art's turn toward social function that it offers a site for engagement with the aesthetic itself. That function, and art's seeming abandonment of its autonomy, I will argue, is itself grounded in labor's decommodification. Engaging with the hermeneutics of the commodity form, and its constitutive obfuscation of labor in particular, Adorno asserts that "the autonomy of art is inconceivable without the covering up of work."[61] It is the commodity form and the wage itself that conceal labor. But in our moment, and with regard to artistic labor in particular, the wage has begun to disappear. We must update our understandings of labor power sold as a commodity.

Thus I follow Stewart Martin, who argues that to truly appreciate the relation between art and commodification, "new forms of commodification need to be examined as the heteronomous scene of new formations of autonomous art; [and] new forms of art need to be examined as the contradictions of new formations of commodification."[62] Throughout this book I argue that the decommodification of artistic labor offers a site to examine how a "new formation of commodification" responds to and reconfigures artistic practice and its critique.[63] Decommodified labor as it appears in socially engaged art allows us to approach anew art's use and uselessness and work's obsolescence and instrumentality.[64] My interest in the "uselessness" or "purposelessness" of the aesthetic is located within its schematic difference from the world of labor and value found within the commodity, and I will use this distinction to elaborate my idea of decommodified labor as both a political economic and aesthetic category.

Yet some socially engaged artists themselves have militated against this precise tradition of "the aesthetic." Think of artist and *arte util* founder Tania Bruguera, whose work I consider in chapter 3. In 2012 Bruguera issued a great polemic that was also a performance: "It's time to restore [Marcel Duchamp's] urinal to the restroom," she claimed. Bruguera indeed accomplished this restoration in the men's restroom of New York City's Queens Museum, with her own signature replacing that of R. Mutt. This action became a site for Bruguera to elaborate her concept of "Useful Art." She states that "Useful Art is a way of working with aesthetic experiences that focuses on the implementation of art in society where art's function is no longer to be a space for 'signaling' problems, but the place from which to create the proposal and implementation of possible solutions."[65] How do we square such an assertion with a legacy of aesthetics, and more importantly, why should we try to do so? What economic conditions make such a useful aesthetics possible? Have we been down this path before? Perhaps. Remember Adorno's claim: "All efforts to restore art by giving it a social function . . . are doomed."[66]

The site to elaborate this discussion is located in labor itself. My labor, as an object, cannot be separated from me as subject. If I cannot exchange my labor, that impossibility does not render it useless, particularly in a post-artisanal society where independent production is as outdated as homemade cutlery. Rather, I now have a form of labor power that should be commodified, or sold to someone else, but that I cannot sell. My labor has been decommodified. Such labor, then, may be seen as a kind of doubling and undoing both of the wage form and of the ideology of the aesthetic that developed in ongoing contradistinction to that form. At the risk of being overly schematic, let us say this: With the decommodification of labor, we no longer critique from useless to exchangeable. Rather, we look at that which cannot be exchanged, labor, and how that labor might urge us to reconceive of the aesthetic. Decommodified labor holds together two antinomies in a reorganized fashion: unlike labor, which has been understood as ceaselessly exchangeable for a wage, art has conversely been understood as powerfully useless. Now, with a new generation of artists, their artistic labor is not exchangeable, and their work is newly purposeful.

Theorizing Decommodified Labor:
Neoliberalism, Real Subsumption, and the Claims of Labor

In 1972 the *Wall Street Journal* ran an article entitled "The Quality of Work," which took note of current labor trends and introduced to its readers a new style of management that had begun to be referred to as "job enlargement." Employees would be encouraged to participate broadly in aspects of work beyond their immediate, assigned responsibilities, thereby ensuring that "there's never a dull moment," in the laconic phrasing of one interviewee. In his classic 1974 study of twentieth-century labor processes, *Labor and Monopoly Capital: The Degradation of Work in the Twentieth Century*, Harry Braverman makes reference to that article and notes that it is one instance of work being degraded through its opposite, what he calls the seeming "humanization of work."[67]

In 2017 the *Journal* ran a similar article surveying work trends, this one entitled "The End of Employees."[68] While the first article contains, as Braverman notes, some equivocation, there can be no mistaking the message of the contemporary one: continual employment has been retired. Economic historian Bethany Moreton's recent article has a similar title with an added historical arc: "The Rise and Fall of the Job."[69] Capital will still extract surplus value through the absorption of workers' time—that constant cannot and will not change. Workers may work more or less; they may be unionized or not; they may capture a greater or lesser percentage of the total surplus; they may have expanded or contracted add-ons such as health insurance and retirement. But the social organization of the basic appropriation—more time for capital than for oneself—will be historically specific, and there is no reason to think it will take the form of a "job" or a "career."

To approach the emergence of these changes is to return to the 1970s. It is there we find that the Keynesian compact—in the United States, the understanding that labor would get more of a share of social wealth in exchange for a less radical labor politics; that the U.S. dollar would set a global benchmark and be fixed to gold—began to falter. The reasons for its demise are many and for us, less important: as Keynes himself famously said of economic durability, "in the long run, we are all dead."[70] In the short run, however, the 1970s would produce shifts in how work was represented, critiqued, and experienced. Union membership began its long decline. Wages began their long stagnation. Faced with the fallout from Keynesianism's demise, the Federal Reserve chairman Paul Volcker foresaw a new path: The federal government would "break unions and empty factories."[71] The United States would embrace a new, finance-led regime, one whose radical initiation became known as the "Volcker Shock."

Indeed, since the 1970s "something very fundamental seems to have changed in the way capitalism works."[72] Thus begins Giovanni Arrighi's beguiling investigation into the *longue durée* of capital's financialization. Arrighi's text periodizes those financial changes but it does not explore how such changes have reorganized critical theories of labor since the 1970s. Braverman's text remains the last real Marxist treatment of capitalist labor processes delivered in a language of labor itself. Written in the early 1970s, the text indeed indexes not only the "degradation of work" but also a transformation in the language for analyzing it.

While the problem of labor has slowly worked itself into art discourses, labor as a site for investigation of the economy has receded from critical theory.[73] Perhaps this trend began to change with the 2011 publication of Fredric Jameson's *Representing Capital* and of *Marxism and the Critique of Value* in 2014; if so, I hope to contribute to such a shift.[74] As Geoff Mann notes, twentieth-century economic thought itself contains a "discursive shift" in the analysis of labor as it transitions from a focus on "poverty to unemployment to inequality." Keynesianism responded to the scare of widespread "poverty"; it sought as its object the management of "unemployment." In its wake, particularly after the 2007–8 credit crisis, "the object of political economy became inequality."[75] Even in this trajectory we see the conceptual diminishment of labor. "Why do we work so long and hard?" Kathi Weeks very plainly, if not plaintively, asks.[76] A question so basic often lacks an answer. Instead Weeks notes how "surprising" it is that the questions themselves are so rarely asked. But is it surprising? Surely it cannot be a coincidence that institutionalized labor and critical theories of labor began to wane at the same time. In recent critical theory, labor as a concept has been diminished in Foucault-based biopolitical discourse, in the rise of neoliberal thought, and indeed, in certain stands of Marxism too, as finance has assumed a more structuring role.

In this section, I derive a theory of decommodified labor, and I proffer that such labor offers a way to think labor after financialization, a way to think the present in both its aesthetic and economic valences. I show how the appearance and form of decommodified labor may be located within, and may interrupt, what I take to be the two dominant theorizations of our economic present: the rise of neoliberalism as an antilabor discourse and the Marxist claim of the real subsumption of labor to capital as a way to maintain labor's importance. Throughout the book I will continually return to these two broad approaches. Both theories mark a change in the understanding of labor: neoliberalism obviates labor; real subsumption argues for its continued relevance and possible intensification. I am using both terms generically in this introduction, although I have written about them specifically elsewhere, and indeed, in each chapter I return to certain aspects of them. Neoliberalism and Marxism might seem to be an odd juxtaposition: socially engaged art and neoliberalism? In fact, all sorts of left-inflected discourses, from union campaigns to the *Nation*, to art criticism, to artists themselves, regularly borrow from neoliberal discourse—whether in reference to "stakeholders" or with claims of "leveraging," whether extolling "human capital" or citing other forms of "self-investment." That should strike the reader as a bit odd. Arrighi is right: something has changed.

The first analytic I will return to throughout—that of neoliberalism—has been made popular not by economic neoliberals such as Friedrich Hayek and Gary Becker but rather by Foucault's readings of them. Within economically oriented critical and cultural theory, we have seen the transformation of Foucault's attack on a Marxist-derived critical theory of labor under the rubric of "neoliberalism" transform into perhaps the most widely accepted cross-disciplinary account of our economic present.[77] Because part of the impetus of Foucault's original challenge to a Marxist account of the economy was to undercut the conceptual leverage of labor as a historical and subjective force, we should be unsurprised that one of the effects of the broad acceptance of his account of neoliberalism has been a move away from labor as a conceptual orientation. Foucault writes: "I don't think we can simply accept the traditional Marxist analysis, which assumes that, labor being man's concrete essence, the capitalist system is what transforms labor into profit, into hyperprofit or surplus value." And then, crucially, he continues: "The fact is [that] capitalism penetrates much more deeply into our existence."[78] In the neoliberal account, subjects cease to be "laborers" and become investors in their own capabilities, now understood as a form of "human capital." Yet Foucault's interpretation, so often hailed as prescient, was also descriptive: the role of organized labor in capitalist democracies, its ability to shape public conversations and to participate in developing a social infrastructure, was, at the time of Foucault's writing, beginning its decline. Coinciding with the end of Keynesianism and traceable to the 1970s, in this scheme, labor becomes an obsolete concept.

The second analytic for understanding of our economic present is found in Marxist critical theory's understanding of the changing referent of labor in terms of an analysis which it called "the real subsumption of labor to capital." This construction likewise captures a transformation of labor and is likewise traceable to theoretical flourishing in the 1970s, as questions about the potential for class struggle and the limits of "the factory" emerged.[79] Originally a concept Marx himself used to describe large-scale industrialization and mechanization, "real subsumption" has become somewhat of a metaphor for the ability of capitalism to progress, to intensify, to extract more, and to encompass all. There is no "outside" here; capital has no other. Marx himself distinguishes formal and real subsumption as based on a move from relative to absolute surplus value. In a regime with a goal of extracting absolute surplus value, the working day can be extended to increase profit. But that increase has an end, obviously, and after its limit has been reached, a regime to extract relative surplus value takes over. There, labor may be intensified through processes internal to capitalism. As Moishe Postone explains, in the "latter stage, the determinations of the valorization process are materialized in the labor process: direct human labor materially becomes the object of production."[80]

For some, real subsumption is a historical category: first formal, then real. For others, it is a logical category: these two models of capitalist appropriation are always available and shift back and forth. Perhaps the theorists who have done the most to turn real subsumption into an optic for contemporary analysis are the Italian workerists (those associated with *operaismo*). For Antonio Negri, Silvia Federici, and Mario Tronti, value extraction is hardly limited to waged work or financial schemes, and the subjects who might transform our social structures far exceed those found in unions, syndicates, and so on. Labor, the value-generating result of the sale of human labor power, is understood, through their interpretation of real subsumption, to have expanded and to refer to a whole host of human activities outside formal places of work. The conceptual specificity of "labor" loses some of its critical purchase in this tradition, too. But it does not diminish; it expands. As Jason Read explains in his wonderful reading of Negri, "capital no longer simply exploits labor, understood as the physical capacity to transform objects, but puts to work the capacities to create and communicate that traverse social relations . . . with real subsumption . . . there is no relationship that cannot be transformed into a commodity."[81] Tronti goes further: "The social character of production has been extended to the point that the entire society now functions as a mode of production."[82]

The direction in which some strands of Negri's thought have progressed— outside of the law of value—is not one that I will follow. Indeed, Negri and Hardt ultimately end up borrowing from Foucault what I would argue are certain neoliberal tendencies. But we need not track those down now. Rather, what we must note is that throughout the 1970s, as the Keynesian moment drew to a close, multiple theorists from various and conflicting traditions argued for a new understanding of the relation between capital and labor. The emerging neoliberal Foucauldian tradition and competing Marxist traditions, then, isolate a crucial shift in the category of labor: what constitutes it, what it refers to, and what it may be used to motivate.

These changes are indexed at different levels of abstraction. For Foucault, the change is categorical, prescient, and normative: labor will cease to be an operative epistemological category for the self-understanding of social reproduction. When Foucault writes that labor is dissolved "into capital and income," his incipient anti-Marxism has led him to make a remarkable statement.[83] Namely, the self-narration of a subject as one who is compelled to sell his or her labor under less than free conditions has expired. Now the subject will understand herself as a possessor of "human capital" who seeks a return on her investment. Through the problem of real subsumption, theorists investigated how accumulation could transpire through and after the Keynesian wage with its unionized, stable employment and currency. These theorists used real subsumption to make crucial addenda to conceptions of who works and how.[84] Silvia Federici's work on the constitutive relation between the unwaged and waged has been foundational to this discussion.[85] Paolo Virno's discussion of general intellect follows from this moment, as does Hardt and Negri's discussion of immaterial labor, "social labor," and ultimately "immeasurable value."

Yet some correlation may be located between the conceptual staging of real subsumption and neoliberalism. For Read, neoliberalism "is a discourse and practice that is aimed to curtail the powers of labor that are distributed across all of society—at the exact moment in which all of social existence becomes labor, or potential labor, neoliberalism constructs the image of a society of capitalists, of entrepreneurs." Reading a similar history, George Caffentzis rejects "immeasurable value" but does cite Hardt and Negri to note that, "in the same moment when theory no longer sees labor, labor has everywhere become the common substance. The theoretical emptying of the problem of labor corresponds to its maximum pregnancy as the substance of human action across the globe."[86] As many of us come to work longer, harder, and for less money, the neoliberal theory of the economy arrives on the scene to declare an end to labor.

Furthermore, both constructs challenge the wage as the rhetorical and material centerpiece of capitalist organization and subjectivity. Indeed, they both respond to the end of the Keynesian compact.[87] When human potentiality is renarrated as human capital, all actions may be reconfigured as both an investment opportunity and hence, as a choice and as a site of "freedom." When laboring life is reconceived as real subsumption, one is never "off the clock," because all activities have the ability to produce surplus value; that is, all activities might be labor. In Foucault's scheme, there is no labor; after real subsumption, all is labor. In Foucault's scheme, the investor of human capital might turn anything (a crime, an illness, a marriage) into a site of risk-based profit; in real subsumption, capital might turn anything (an email, a fantasy, a nap) into a site where surplus value is generated.

Within the conceptual space between these two traditions and the historical realities they index, I want to suggest a configuration of value in which the wage is diminished but the formal organization of work—its rhythms, commitments, and narratives—remain. This I call *decommodified labor*. Already in its terminology, "decommodified labor" may appear paradoxical. "Labor," as opposed to work, already *is* a commodity; labor implies the incorporation of work into capitalism. Why wouldn't "decommodified labor" simply be labor power—that with which humans are endowed—before it is sold? Why route labor power through a commodity chain only to then claim an exception to that chain? The answer to such questions is that with decommodified labor the commodity chain is still in place, as are the presumptions of wage labor and the infrastructure of associated benefits and losses, but the wage itself is either refused, rejected, or deemed incommensurate with the work. Decommodified labor may be understood as one experience of real subsumption. On the one hand, we can't stop working; everything seems to be able to produce a profit. On the other hand, labor that is waged has been in retreat. We can't stop working and we can't seem to get paid for the work that we do. Enter neoliberalism, under whose logic wagelessness may be narrated as a failure of self-investment: it's not that one didn't get paid, it's that one's investment did not produce the desired return.

Decommodification comes to us from the social sciences, particularly political science, international development, and economic sociology, where it has a flat and often uncomplicated theoretical history. If commodification denotes the sale of an object or process on the market, then decommodification implies the circumscription of that sale. And because commodification often, though not always—and certainly not always deservedly—has pejorative connotations attached to it, decommodification is understood to constitute a better state of affairs. Gøsta Esping-Andersen, whose book *The Three Worlds of Welfare Capitalism* inaugurated the term in its current critical capacity, claims that "the concept [of decommodification] refers to the degree to which individuals, or families, can uphold a socially acceptable living independent of market participation."[88]

The "three worlds" of welfare capitalism outline the actual degree to which this independence is possible in capitalist democracies. Scandinavian countries circumscribe market forces most forcefully in the provision of healthcare, education, and housing; thus, their version of decommodification offers the most protection to their citizens from the caprices and deprivations of the market. The Anglosphere of England, Canada, Australia, and New Zealand somewhat circumscribe the commodification of these provisions but offer a lesser degree of protection. And the United States permits the highest degree of commodification of basic services, and thus its social sphere ensures the highest degree of precarity for its denizens. At its most immediate and concrete articulation, as the scholar John Vail argues, "decommodification is conceived as any political, social, or cultural process that reduces the scope and influence of the market in everyday life."[89]

While introducing the basic concept of decommodification, these theorizations have the additional force of underscoring that commodification is the most fundamental physical, social, and imaginative infrastructure of our present. Decommodification presumes commodification; it does not presage it. And for me, decommodification carries more modest ambitions than communization or than "commoning" precisely because it recognizes the intransigence of commodification. In this sense, any homology between decommodified labor and the commons seems misguided. Once in a commons, uncompensated labor would no longer be decommodifed because the scene of commodification itself would not exist; there would be no labor but rather, as Marx says, "really free working."[90] We would not say that Zuccotti Park was decommodified during Occupy Wall Street; we would say it was commoned. Conversely, Bruce Carruthers suggests that in the wake of the 2007–8 credit crisis, the federal government "decommodified" many securities. This decommodification preserved their value but halted their circulation until the market could bear their exchange at stable prices.[91]

In the specific case of decommodified labor, the status of the commodity is preserved, but its circulation is halted and its possibility for exchange is foreclosed. The duration of that foreclosure varies. Child labor, for example, has been decommodified in most capitalist democracies for some time. It was for centuries an important source of both waged and unwaged labor. In the United States it has been illegal since 1938, and now very few children in the United States are workers.[92] Yet children still possess the ability to be laborers; were restrictions on child labor lifted tomorrow, we would again have child-workers.

If decommodified labor is labor that fails to return a wage even through it requires expending energies and affects in a scene indistinguishable from formal employment, then we can locate some analogue of it in both neoliberal and real subsumption–based understandings of the economy. Perhaps one cannot "invest" one's human capital because the market for investment is overcapitalized. What, then, when one is forced to hold onto one's human capital for longer than one would like? Or because one is always working, perhaps the wage derives from other, indistinguishable work than that for which one is supposedly being paid. In each scenario, we might speak of some equivalent to decommodified labor.

As I move through the chapters, I examine how the appearance of decommodified labor in art both borrows from and critiques the expanded labor theorized in real subsumption and the forms of investment and pricing theorized in neoliberalism. In chapter 1 I look at the tension between student-artists not being able to sell their labor and being encouraged to invest their human capital in their education. In chapter 2 I examine how artists create alternative economic institutions in order to correct a decline in, or a simple lack of, artists' wages. In chapter 3 I explore how animals have been positioned as artists as a way to represent the devaluation of artistic labor. Finally, in chapter 4 I analyze how artists who work with children sometimes allow children to be "investments in the future" because they cannot work, and other times put children to work in a similar manner to how artists work—namely, for free.

Although many artists and critics are invested in the idioms of neoliberalism—whether knowingly or not—it is within the analysis of real subsumption in which decommodifed labor in art seems most germane. Even as Negri himself has moved beyond the construct of real subsumption, indeed of labor, I remain interested in some of Negri's explications of what happens to the temporal and spatial coordinates of work after real subsumption: How do we mark the sale of time to and from the worker, that which is the basis of the wage? The worker sells a quality (her labor power) to the capitalist for a quantity (the time for which she will work). But with real subsumption, capital loses one of its key metrics: "the working day"—or perhaps "the hour," "the clock," or any other of the metaphors through which exists the ability of capital to mark the relation between time and value—no longer possesses indexical meaning. Negri introduces a theory of tautological time and explains that "the tautology takes an intensive form, exemplified by the inability to distinguish measure from substance ... [and] the inability to [distinguish] the totality of life from the totality from which this life is woven."[93]

When all life is work, when should we get paid and for what? For showing up at work? For the time it takes to travel there? For making it back home? For (not) sleeping through the night? Artist-led campaigns such as "Wages for Facebook" contend that if value is extracted everywhere, then people should be compensated for everything.[94] That demand might seem utopian, but it does hint at some of the affective registers that real subsumption engenders: a feeling of both entitlement (Facebook should be ours) and dispossession (no time is my own). "When the entire time of life has become the time of production, who measures whom?" asks Negri. Not only Negri's tautology should be remembered here but Federici's, too, which is expressed as a contradiction: "wages for housework" are at the same time "wages against housework."

In art, decommodified labor reveals that the tautological time of real subsumption has been captured and transformed within the space of the aesthetic. Decommodified labor appears as a strange pause in accumulative temporality. It was always the possibility of nonwork that conceptually sustained not only the autonomy of art but also the category of the aesthetic itself. Now that time of work and nonwork must be relocated. With decommodified labor, some of the contingencies of commodification disappear; a new time is found and a new art created.

Economies of Art Criticism

The past ten years have seen the beginnings of the canonization of socially engaged art through figures including Theaster Gates and a renewed critical interest in the ontology of the art object itself. From Mark Bradford's representation of the United States at the 2017 Venice Biennale to *October*'s roundtable on "The Social Artwork," across disciplines the various historical contingencies of art's autonomy have come to the fore.[95] *FIELD*, a new journal founded by art historian Grant Kester, emerged in 2014 to foster conversations about "the remarkable proliferation of artistic practices devoted to political, social and cultural transformation."[96] As art historians including Claire Bishop, Shannon Jackson, Kester, Gregory Sholette, Julia Bryan-Wilson, and Yates McKee have sought to distinguish socially engaged art, they have largely turned to a political register to do so, appealing to Jacques Rancière and Alain Badiou, among others. Conversely, critical theorists including Dave Beech, John Roberts, Nicholas Brown, Jasper Bernes, and Marina Vishmidt have produced, using the works of Marx, Keynes, the Frankfurt school, and Bourdieu, a corpus that positions economics, not politics, as the ultimate horizon of artistic legibility. Their critical concern is not necessarily the emergence of socially engaged art per se, but rather how the aesthetic as distinct from the economy may be theorized in different regimes of accumulation. For these critics, politics is understood as an always already economic expression.

This divergence between the political and the economic has produced a critical body of work that is organized through a certain displacement. Those critics who do offer sustained attention to socially engaged art—work that I believe makes a fundamentally economic claim—largely do so through a political register. Critics oriented toward the economic have not tended to engage this work as fully, preferring more formally inventive and formally legible traditions including photography and conceptual art. Critics whose orientation is political (Bishop, Jackson, Kester, Sholette) often use "neoliberalism" as a kind of shorthand for an socioeconomic present in which capitalism is understood as more pernicious and omnipresent. Those who engage art economically (Brown, Roberts, Beech, Vishmidt) might use neoliberalism to periodize capitalism as contemporary, but they use real subsumption as their analytic in order to insist on the economic specificity of capital and labor. Meanwhile, many artists have as one of their own guiding narratives that their work is somehow "anticommodity." Cumulatively, when we try to think art and the economy together, what do we have? "A morass, to be sure," in the wise words of Jasper Bernes.[97]

In this section, then, I offer a methodological argument for the economically oriented interpretation of socially engaged art. We must ask: When should the economic be thematized? How should it be periodized? When should we rely on static or formalized economic norms? When should the economy be rendered as empirical and when should it be rendered in more broadly metaphorical strokes? It matters on what level of abstraction these questions are staged. For example, whether socially engaged art best represents decommodified labor because performing art will always be less commodifiable than fine art, or whether decommodifed labor in socially engaged art appears legible as art only because the aesthetic has been transformed by the inflation of finance and the deflation of labor are very different questions. In attempting to maintain a categorical specificity throughout, I endorse, and try to remedy, Stewart Martin's contention that "institutional theories of art and the 'artworld' . . . have so far been developed at a level of generality that fails to register the specificity of capitalist forms."[98]

My concern in this book is organized around a transformation within waged labor. Wages, one metric of the sale of human labor power for a period of time, have seen a steady decline if not slow evacuation over the past forty years.[99] My specific concern, then, traces the resulting effects when that allotment of time does not generate money, a transaction that subtends decommodifed labor. Methodologically, this construction needs to be located at multiple levels of abstraction as it moves between art and economy: it should be thematized, it should redound with an empirical specificity, but that empiricism should resonate with the infrastructure of the commodity form, itself generative of the aesthetic. That level of specificity might then undergird a periodization.

As I will use the term, "decommodifed labor" indexes an empirical reality but it cannot be reduced to one. From cultural work in museums and galleries to reality television, to professional sports, to the leagues of "volunteers" who manage schools and hospitals, to firefighters, to prisoners—millions of Americans freely and through force work without pay. *Fortune* magazine explored the situation in a 2014 article, wondering, "Unpaid Jobs: The New Normal?"[100] Using the feudal language of "serfs" to describe workers, that article detailed the pros and cons of unpaid jobs from management's perspective while noting how "normal" their presence had become. This avenue of investigation follows a series of books published in the 1990s that predicted work would be rendered obsolete through technology—a prognostication that has not come to pass. Work will never be rendered obsolete. Being paid for it might.

Because it is so pervasive in arts and culture, decommodifed labor has routinely been figured by artists themselves, both in their performance documentation and in the work they produce. The socially engaged artist Ernesto Pujol has commented very plainly that "the theatrics of cheap even free orchestrated local labor often try to pass for [collaborative art]."[101] Artists have responded to this reality in a variety of ways: they have attempted to form unions, institutions, and departments and programs in universities in order to agitate for paid labor.[102] Sometimes this agitation remains adjunct to their art; other times, such agitation becomes their art. Thus some of these practitioners conceive of themselves as "artivists," or artist-activists.

Critics have widely noted this reality of artists integrating labor activism into their work. Using terms such as "collaborative labor," "dialogic labor," "delegated performance," and "dark matter," art critics and historians have produced concepts that resonate with decommodifed labor. Grant Kester's wonderful book *The One and the Many*, for example, locates "a series of elisions in recent critical theory that have led to a privileging of the un-worked and simultaneous over the labored and durational." To amend this, Kester "outlines a new framework for the analysis of collaborative art practice rooted in the reinterpretation of labor."[103] Shannon Jackson, with her theorization of what she calls a "de-autonomized aesthetic," asks that we understand that the autonomy of art has always been a social fiction, requiring labor from many groups, however invisible such labor may be.[104] Perhaps most well known is Claire Bishop's isolation of what she calls "delegated performance," which accounts for how outsourcing various labors within the artwork changes what that artwork is.[105] For Gregory Sholette, the art world comprises "dark matter," a mass of uncompensated, undifferentiated energies, desires, and ambitions that render visible, and profitable, a miniscule number of "famous" artists. Lane Relyea's 2013 *Your Everyday Art World* offers a slightly different approach as he investigates "how today's network paradigm lends itself to a neo-entrepreneurial mythology about volunteerism and 'do it yourself' (DIY) agency."[106]

But some critics do use the term "decommodify" even if they do not connect it to labor. Julia Bryan-Wilson quite plainly states that "[al]though artists conventionally make highly valued objects, many art workers . . . of the early 1970s vigilantly attempted to decommodify their work via conceptual and performance art."[107] If we pair this comment with her wonderful book *Art Workers*, in which she suggests that "the late 1960s and early 1970s were marked by an international mobilization of artists seeking to validate their efforts as work; that is, as effortful, productive, and managed by economic constraints imposed by subjugating ruling-class interests," we begin to see the emergence of a critique of artistic labor.[108] Instead of investigating such "work" alongside the commodity form, however, Bryan-Wilson has introduced the term "occupational realism" to designate art in which "the realm of waged labor (undertaken to sustain oneself economically) and the realm of art (pursued, presumably, for reasons that might include financial gain, but that also exceed financialization and have aesthetic, personal, and/or political motivations) collapse, becoming indistinct or intentionally inverted." Here, she continues, "the job becomes the art and the art becomes the job."[109]

Bryan-Wilson's "occupational realism" offers an almost perfect conceptual inversion of "decommodified labor" as it appears in the arts. In her scheme, most work can be artwork because so little art-based work can be labor (that is, sold as a commodity). In my scheme, because the space of art as labor maintains its integrity, because the work keeps happening in a shadow of wage labor, because it could have been commodified, I suggest that we understand it as decommodified. Indeed, one can see here a recapitulation of the discussion between Marxist "real subsumption" and Foucauldian "neoliberalism" I offered in the previous section: Bryan-Wilson offers the neoliberal version in that labor itself disappears; I offer the version in which labor maintains some categorical integrity.

That conceptual disappearance of labor reflects more than anything a neoliberal view of the world, one likely unintended. In insisting on the importance of labor as a continuing analytic, I follow John Roberts, who rightly argues in *The Intangibilities of Form* that "we need . . . a rereading of capital that captures labour for aesthetic theory."[110] Roberts then tracks how "artists labour, and how these forms of labour [are] indexed to art's relationship to the development of general social technique (the advanced level of technology and science as it is expressed in the technical conditions of social reproducibility)."[111] His more recent *Revolutionary Time and the Avant-Garde* continues this critique by redefining the avant-garde as "the recurring name we give to the conflict between free artistic labour and capital."[112]

In this book, my name for that conflict is decommodified labor, but other names exist. And indeed, there are other stagings of the conflict in which either capital or "free artistic labour" assumes from the outset a stronger role. In his "The Work of Art in the Age of its Real Subsumption under Capital," Nicholas Brown states that today we have entered a moment in which "whatever is genuinely inassimilable in artistic labor [ceases] to make any difference."[113] Under such conditions, of course, the category of art itself might vanish, but—and Brown is absolutely correct to note it—there is no historical reason that art must remain an operable category. Yet still it does. Brown appeals to Pierre Bourdieu's "field of restricted production," a nonmarket site where art might still flourish and in fact will gravitate toward more formal concerns. Noting the dialectical nature of "real subsumption," Brown notes that its seeming totality will wax and wane. Steven Shaviro takes yet another route to arrive at a similarly foreshortened moment, but he designates aesthetic judgment, not art, as the possible casualty. Appealing to a moment of generalized capitalist production, Shaviro explains: "It's not just that sensations and feelings are trivialized when they are packaged for sale . . . it's also that the two most crucial qualities of the aesthetic according to Kant—that it is disinterested, and that it is non-cognitive—are made to vanish."[114]

While I claim that decommodified labor is the necessary category for analyzing and periodizing socially engaged art, I am not the first to consider decommodification itself as a paradigm of arts production. Dave Beech, in his recent and sweeping *Art and Value*, indeed turns to the work of Esping-Andersen to consider, if to ultimately reject, whether art should be considered a form of decommodification. To the commodities of housing, medical care, education as potentially decommodifiable, Beech suggests that in a Keynesian welfare state, art too could be understood through such a lens. Art too needs a public subsidy. But Beech ultimately decides that art never was a commodity. And if it were not one, how could it be decommodified? He argues that art may "be more accurately understood as preservation, conservation and expansion of a precommodified sphere of culture."[115] Beech suggests that "art has been commodified without being commodified."

In moving through modern economic thought's consideration of art, Beech spans a history from Adam Smith to neoclassical theories to the neoliberals themselves and concludes that art is "exceptional." No real economic home for it exists. I would add that any single commodity studied closely would probably be found to be exceptional (although not in the manner that art is) because much economic thought relies on normative categories that are not applicable to particular commodities. Think of "oil" as it plays the role of exceptional commodity in Timothy Mitchell's book *Carbon Democracy*.[116] "Cotton" does something similar in Sven Beckert's *Empire of Cotton*. But I would also suggest that, in a study with as much breadth as Beech's, there should be some consideration of how the economic categories themselves might be seen differently as a result of being criticized through an artistic lens. Indeed, this reconsideration of economic categories as a result of artistic analysis is something few studies attempt, preferring instead to let the economy be a benchmark against which art is measured.

Each of these theorists seeks to locate in art what Roberts labels "a dissensual space within the heart of wage labor," to which Roberts himself assigns the term "second economy." I expand on their work by specifying the kind contemporary artistic production that allows such a space to be realized both in and as socially engaged art. I seek to include a multiplicity of economic theories that may be understood as both symptoms and diagnoses of what this art's capture of our economic present reveals by being attentive to how neoliberalism's claim of the end of labor and real subsumption's claim of the expansion of labor appear in and may be mediated by art itself. Doing so not only allows for a better understanding of the limits and possibilities of economically oriented arts criticism; it allows for the possibility of art itself to contribute to the economic specificity of those conversations. It will not do to read only from economics *to* art. We must be able to read from art *to* economics as well.

1

Art Student, Art Worker

The Decommodified Labor of Studentdom

"What does it mean to form human capital . . . which will be remunerated by income? It means, of course, making what are called educational investments."
—MICHEL FOUCAULT, *The Birth of Biopolitics*

"Dear Allan," began artist Robert Filliou's 1967 letter to Fluxus member and Rutgers professor Allan Kaprow, "you've asked me to give you my thoughts . . . regarding the type of creative programs that could be carried out in universities [under] the auspices of artists."[1] Kaprow's entreaty was itself the result of his potential involvement in a new, planned experimental college to be opened through the State University of New York. Filliou's response came in a series of epistles reprinted in his 1970 book, *Teaching and Learning as Performing Arts*, in which Filliou went on to suggest an "Institute of Permanent Creation" as one way to bring art into the university. Guided by principles of "poetical economy" and grounded in the "common creative work of students and artists," the institute would not have grades, majors, or courses even. Filliou thought John Cage, La Monte Young, and Dick Higgins, among others, might collaborate on it.

Filliou's suggestion was only one of many moments in which universities and artists approached and responded to each other throughout the 1960s and 1970s, a time when, according to Howard Singerman, the university played a "crucial role as both patron and scene for the art[s]."[2] It's not only that the period's various avant-gardes, such as Fluxus and Experimental Music, "originated in the college classroom," but rather that the expansion of arts education in universities would change what art was and who could be an artist.[3] As part of Keynesian economic management, which centrally included rising wages and expanding opportunities for the commodification of labor throughout the 1942–73 period, the federal and state governments bolstered universities to levels never seen before or since. Sharon Zukin notes that these investments undergirded the "state's contribution to artistic careers . . . [and] encouraged many more young people than before to go to college. In the sixties, more artists were college-educated than in any previous generation."[4] She further claims that such fiscal support had a "democratizing" and "professionalizing" effect on art. Placing artistic education within an expanding university "opened art as a second career for people who had not yet been integrated into the labor market in a significant way. . . . By the late sixties and early seventies more than a million adults in America identified their occupation as in some way connected with the creative arts."[5] In Singerman's words, by the time this expansion was over, the master of fine arts (MFA) would emerge "unchallenged [in its] administrative success."

Literary critic Mark McGurl has called the period of 1945 through our present "the program era" to note the expansive formal and pedagogical transformation of creative writing under the rubric of an MFA program.[6] Singerman has provided a parallel history of the fine arts that focuses on the infrastructures, accreditations, and professional societies that have given rise to the university-formed career artist.[7] Both of these wonderful studies trace the emergence of the university-based "art student" from the mid- to late twentieth century. And both studies note the deep irony that out of avant-garde anti-institutionalism and modernist individuality, the path to becoming an artist was transformed into a university-based, professionally credentialed degree. What these crucial studies do not do, however, is understand that art students, like all students, "are already workers."[8] Nor do they explore the political economy of the university that enabled the infrastructural expansions on which those studies are predicated. I begin with artistic labor's commodification within the university in order to track the dramatic reversal that underpins this chapter: artistic labor's decommodification through the figure of the art student. In this chapter I examine the work of Cassie Thornton and Thomas Gokey, two socially engaged artists who have inherited the mantle of the MFA's radical potential and institutional authority, but also the debt that now often accompanies the degree. Thornton and Gokey became artists by going into debt to obtain their MFAs, and now, as artists, they work on their debt. In the fact and critique of these artists' art school debt, I locate the decommodified labor of the art student.

I thus chart a different history of art's university-based institutionalization from the 1970s to our own day. As universities expanded by subjects taught, degrees granted, and populations served, they became ever more radical places.[9] While many studies have considered the politics that emerged from this moment, I keep my own focus on the economics. I am particularly interested in the forms of economic critique, both emancipatory and neoliberal, that this moment fostered and how the genealogies of those critiques are still present in art today. In the 1970s, as MFA programs began to assume their career mantle, as universities became cheaper and more accessible, students and Marxist political economists, for their part, saw possibilities for expanding free education and for reconceiving education as a form of labor.[10]

In one of the few issues published of *Zerowork* magazine, a 1970s periodical whose title was both firmly rooted in the language of labor and a hope for moving beyond its grasp, the university was a central topic of consideration.[11] A 1975 piece of this sort was simply titled "Wages for Students" (figure 1.1).[12] Based in New York and Massachusetts, the group that issued this communiqué argued that the work of the student was nothing less than the work of reproducing capital by reproducing a new generation of skilled workers. As such, it was not sufficient to provide free tuition, which, for example, the City University of New York did from 1969 to 1975 and the University of California had done since its founding in 1868. Rather, they argued, students should be waged. "We are fed up with working for free; we demand real money now for the schoolwork we do. We must force capital, which profits from our work, to pay for our schoolwork."[13] As its name indicates, "Wages for Students" was deeply influenced by the international Wages for Housework movement.[14] Just as feminist scholars in the 1960s and 1970s demanded that the political economy of the home be repositioned as integral to social reproduction, so indeed, students suggested, should be the political economy of the university.

Political economist George Caffentzis's *Zerowork* essay, "Throwing Away the Ladder," offered perhaps a more nuanced critique of the changing landscape of university education. "What goes on at the university is work, namely schoolwork.... [It is] unwaged work [whose] unwaged character gives it the appearance of personal choice."[15] Caffentzis offers a crucial interruption of the presumed relation between economic choice and necessity, between the wage and the gift, between the wage and happenstance. We often assume that if one does something not for pay, then the coercive logics of capital did not motivate them. Caffentzis reminds us that the reverse scenario more often prevails: marginalization and disempowerment lead people to engage in unwaged labor whose further stigmatization—precisely because of its lack of wage—makes it seem to have been a choice. After all, who in their right mind would work for free?

Viewing the same historical moment of educational expansion and wage increases, neoliberal economists, including Milton Friedman and James M. Buchanan, for their own part, "suspected some kind of causal connection between free public education and the rising militantism of the student movement."[16] Students should not be waged, these economists argued. On the contrary, they should be indebted. As Melinda Cooper has argued, the neoliberals sought to "replace public [spending on education] with private deficit spending." Grants would be converted to loans. Tuition would be made more expensive. Federal and state subsidies would be curtailed. Today, of course, we know which vision became dominant. At the same time, we realize that the height of that radicalism politically also marked the beginning of a certain contraction economically. In her wonderful study, Cooper notes that even the original American neoliberals themselves could not have "anticipate[d] how closely [today's] student loan market would approximate their policy prescriptions."[17]

If there is an equivalent radical organization of Wages for Students in our contemporary moment, one that takes the political economy of the university as its object of critique, it is "Strike Debt," one of the many groups to emerge after Occupy Wall Street. While Wages for Students claimed in the 1970s that "students are unpaid workers," Strike Debt now claims, "You Are Not a Loan."

Note how the language of labor from the 1970s cedes to a language of belonging and affect today. Wages for Students made a demand to receive money for their schoolwork; Strike Debt demands not to return money its members borrowed to attend school; "We Owe You Nothing" is another of their slogans. Again, note how an affront to "capital" has morphed into a personal affront to "you."

We do not know the specific disciplines out of which Wages for Students participants emerged, but we do know that "in the history of Occupy Wall Street and its offshoots such as Strike Debt, artists have been essential to the development of the movement."[18] Indeed, both Thornton and Gokey were participants; Gokey himself was a crucial founder and organizer of Strike Debt. Why these artists would found Strike Debt, and why more artists would turn up en masse to the group's meetings and actions, surely bears some relation to the *Wall Street Journal*'s 2013 findings that "Graduates of Art-Focused Schools . . . Rack Up the Most Student Debt."[19] And some of these indebted artist-activists received their professional training in Social Practice art. Dur-

EXAMINATION BOOK

Name_____

Subject_____

Class_____Section_____

Instructor_____Date

1.1 Wages for Students, 1975.

ing that training, they likely were exposed to the new paradigm that Yates McKee, following in the footsteps of Walter Benjamin's notion of the "artist as producer," calls the "artist as organizer."[20] According to McKee, in its post-Occupy instantiation, the socially engaged "artist has moved from merely 'expressing the correct political tendency' to an engagement with the 'living social context' of direct action, education, and media infrastructures [necessary to build] a social movement."[21]

It is between these two historical moments of student-based economic critique, from Wages for Students to Strike Debt, themselves so demonstrative of a changed political economy of the university, that we may locate the expansion of credentialed art practices and arts education within the university. Tuition has increased, but so have the number of MFA programs.[22] As universities incubate the fine arts, as students fund their fine arts education through what will become for many a lifetime of student loan repayments, art students use the freedom of what Rosalind Krauss called the "post-medium condition," but what is now more accurately referred to by John Roberts as "art after art in the expanded field" to confront the political economy of the university itself. Artists then make works that conform to Roberts's expansive definition of a contemporary avant-garde as "an evental process . . . a theoretically driven set of socially transformative practices."[23]

Joseph Beuys, founder of the Free International University in 1973, may have argued that "everyone is an artist," but Claire Bishop's amendment of that famous phrase—"everyone is an art student"—seems more appropriate today.[24] As the MFA transformed into a teaching degree throughout the 1970s and 1980s, a credential to remain in the university system that itself provided the degree, universities curtailed their expansion of long-term employment through tenure and substituted majority short-term contracts through adjunct positions—one nascent moment of artists' transformation into decommodified laborers. Nonetheless, and with full knowledge of the economic scene, the number of arts graduates has increased 31 percent since 2002.[25] Adjusted for inflation, university tuition has risen 259 percent since 1971. The increase relative to wages and accounting for gender disparity in wage rates means that in 1971 men could have expected to pay 6.2 percent of their income on tuition and women, 17.8 percent. By 2012, men would pay on average 26 percent of their income; women would pay 41 percent of theirs. From then until now, the gradual availability of credit for students via loans would both ameliorate the difficulty of increasing tuition for individuals and exacerbate the problem collectively, as the availability of loans leads to an inflationary increase in tuition.[26]

Thornton and Gokey are part of a generation of artists who have ceased to demand wages; rather, they refuse their student loans on both political and artistic grounds, and in doing so, they show the extractive exchange they have been offered in place of wages for their work as art students—what they call their "debt." A loan denotes a present exchange of money for future repayment, usually with interest; a debt, in Marx's ever-apt description of value, is "a social relation."[27]

As a result of the 2007–8 subprime mortgage crisis and the subsequent expansion of that crisis into a global credit contraction and "Great Recession," the language of debt has entered the public imaginary through reportage, fiction, and of course, individual experience. Debt has likewise entered academic discourse in the work of a new generation of social theorists, including David Graeber, Miranda Joseph, Richard Dienst, Annie McClanahan, and Maurizio Lazzarato.[28] In many of these theorists' works, "debt" itself becomes unmoored from the familiar Marxist vocabulary of commodity, money, capital, and value so often used in cultural critique in order to be rearticulated as a disciplinary apparatus of temporal and spatial organization, an omnipresent site of ongoing psychic desire (mutuality, futurity, access) and dread (anxiety, alienation, shame). Debt, according to Joseph, always is "the product of knowledge production."[29] And while I stay with the idiom of "debt"—that is, after all, the language the artists use—I understand debt in this context as a nodal point where the decommodified labor of studentdom is engaged artistically and prolonged into the future. Holding together the connection between the lack of wage and the student loan enables me to locate an aesthetic reflexivity that traverses the other side of the commodity form—the place where labor cannot be sold.

Scholars and art critics alike have increasingly critiqued the MFA itself as a site of debt production. While I appreciate the admonishments of Coco Fusco and Jerry Saltz about the financial infrastructure of the MFA, and of the ties between a "post-studio" practice and the price of studio space in cities like New York, these critics take it as axiomatic that an art practice travels the path of what Michael Denning has called a "wageless life"—what artists Coco Fusco and Noah Fischer call the "artist as debtor."[30] These admonishments contain certain truths, of course. Saltz has called the MFA "straight up highway robbery."[31] But such admonishments do not lead us to a point of aesthetic reflexivity from which we can connect the political economy of the university with socially engaged art practices that have emerged from it.

Thornton and Gokey are two socially engaged artists who work on their own student "debt." They became artists by going into debt and now, as artists, they critique their debt, refashioning it, exploring it, attempting to discharge it through what Gokey calls "creative" means and what Thornton calls "debt as medium." It is between this space of work and not-work, of the artwork that emerges from unpaid student work, that I locate the decommodified labor of studentdom, a labor that, as we saw in this book's introduction, is routed through commodity exchange and yet nonetheless remains unwaged. Students are, crucially, decommodified laborers, and art students are a particular subset of that category. If we return to Caffentzis's claim, it is not simply that by doing work students are training to do more work. Rather, we can specify that by engaging in decommodified labor, students are training to be decommodified laborers. Nowhere is this as true as in the arts.

Cassie Thornton's Debt to Art

"As I get closer to it [the debt], the wind picks up. There are dead dry leaves in the air. It seems so far away, it looks like a huge pointy skyscraper, pointy, sharp at the top. It's gray, no clouds. Farm fields surround it; the ground here is dewy, bare, with short dead grass. I'm completely alone."[32] So begins the text of one the artist Cassie Thornton's "debt visualizations," an artistic practice in which Thornton uses "debt as a medium" in order that it might become "materialized," "collectivized," and might "change forms." Working in and on her own debt and that of her family and art school colleagues, Thornton uses a combination of photography, performance art, sculpture, nonfiction narrative, text, and hypertext to explore the cost and consequence of the accumulation of private and government-subsidized student loans. In the case of Thornton herself, the better part of her loans were subsidized by the government and were obtained while she was studying for an MFA degree at California College of the Arts (CCA). In 2012 she received her MFA in Social Practice, the newest concentration on offer at one of the oldest art schools in the United States.[33]

For this transposition from student loan to "debt as medium" to be legible in contemporary arts discourse, socially engaged art must first be situated in the context of an emergent mode of arts-production, one whose practitioners, theorists, and nascent degree-granting programs are entangled with universities at multiple levels. Such artwork emphasizes a work of art's ability to intercede into a delimited social world of economic exploitation, including those relations that adhere to the unequal distribution and accumulation of material resources such as wealth, as well as to immaterial resources such as feelings of belonging, respect, and possibility as they are distributed through the social logics of race, gender, and nationality.[34] Such an orientation changes what constitutes the work of art itself, and socially engaged art has ties to community art practices and to more canonized modes such as performance art and institutional critique. Nicolas Bourriaud has theorized a mode of "relational aesthetics" that has some overlap with the works I study here. He notes that what have come to be called relational artworks have as their substrate intersubjectivity.

In contrast to traditional modes of artistic practice in which one speaks of the visual, musical, or plastic form of artworks, or of the ready-made or performance art, Bourriaud urges that we concern ourselves with "formations" and argues that "present-day art shows that form only resists in the encounter and in the dynamic relationship enjoyed by an artistic proposition with other formations, artistic or otherwise."[35] While it is no doubt correct to claim that "all good artists are socially engaged," as we saw in the introduction, what differentiates socially engaged art is that scenes of economic and affective inequality are represented with specific attention toward some sense of restitution or recognition.[36] The social formation achieved through the work, then, marks a possible configuration of the world and of affects and experiences therein, one that, though itself transient, models and stimulates iteration and variation of the same.

Thornton uses both traditional and nontraditional artistic materials and practices to explore the substrate of the sociality of debt in art school. As she does so, she returns to the modernist question of medium. In reading her work, we are reminded of W. J. T. Mitchell's expansion of the definition of medium to include "not just the canvas and the paint but the stretcher and the studio, the gallery, the museum, the collector, the dealer-critic system."[37] And yet we also see how that definition omits a crucial condition of possibility for the creation and circulation of artworks—namely, the cost of training as an artist. By calling the socioeconomic conditions of artistic production and exhibition into service as the substrate of the art itself, Thornton follows in a long tradition of modern and contemporary art practice, particularly that of institutional critique. From Hans Haacke's detailing of the alleged real estate holdings of one of Manhattan's most notorious landlords in his *Shapolsky et al. Manhattan Real Estate Holdings, a Real-Time Social System, as of May 1, 1971* (1971) to Michael Asher's placement of the sales office of the Claire S. Copley Gallery directly within the gallery's exhibition space in 1974, artists have long turned a critical gaze on the infrastructure of the economic world that supports them. These institutions, in turn, have learned to assimilate such critique and eventually to welcome it in the form of artists' residencies and public art commissions.[38] But Thornton's precociousness leads her to critique not the assets of the board of directors for the museum that invites her, but rather the economic organization of the art school that accepted her. Indeed, her precociousness leads her to critique her student loans while she is still a student living off them. That is, while her loans are still functioning in place of her "wage" and while they enable her social reproduction.

Thornton locates her critical practice within an ambivalent site of artistic infrastructure: the financial scene of an MFA program, that odd, leveraged gateway to artistic professionalization. The Social Practice program at CCA is a place where, Thornton insists, students learn to "make art *and* debt." That contention could be rephrased: because students make art, they make debt.

Thornton estimates her graduating MFA class will produce and absorb about $3.2 million of student debt. (figure 1.2) Thornton's work demonstrates that art students are being trained to work in various traditions and to circulate their work through an art world whose conceptual and economic structures rely more and more on the unwaged worker, whether that unwaged worker is a student, an intern, or (as we will see in later chapters) a child or an animal. Thornton's first exposure to this scene of decommodified labor, to the inability to sell her artistic labor while she continues to act as a professional, is through being trained in making debt and in living, working, and creating art in a condition of indebtedness on the way to becoming a credentialed artist.[39]

One cannot sell one's labor in school because one's time is devoted to "schoolwork." Undergraduates may qualify for "work-study," and graduate students may act as "apprentices" (to use the feudal language that universities and courts often do when denying students labor protections) in the form of teaching and research assistantships. Yet school is not the place for a student to collect a wage; the wage comes later as a result of the schooling. Instead, loans fund the majority of an art student's social reproduction. Those loans will need to be repaid, with varying degrees of interest depending on whether they are subsidized by the federal government or given by private lenders. The interest on government-subsidized loans does not start until the student graduates, an insistence that "school" constitutes an exception to working life. Students, then, cannot be workers because they are students. Yet students engage in schoolwork, which entitles them to money. They are compensated for their work but they are not waged. There is no market for their student "labor." There is no hourly rate for being a student, and one person's loans do not render another person loan-less. Loan accumulation is noncompetitive; indeed, according to some it is a site of surplus distribution—the opposite of market competition.[40]

Unlike commodities, students as students are not made by waged labor, nor are they sold on a market. Indeed, it is telling that the organization W.A.G.E. (Working Artists for a Greater Economy), which publishes a respected, if not followed, guide of wages that should be paid to artists on the basis of various institutions' budgets, does not include in its "wage calculator" a wage for the art student. This is a quite striking omission when compared to the demands of Wages for Students.[41] My distinction between art-student wage and art-student loan does not imply that a wage is necessarily a better state of affairs—Marxist political economy has long criticized the wage as a veil whose function is to obfuscate the inequality of the labor-for-money exchange. But it does imply that a wage is a different state of affairs. A wage provides a less free present, because one is constrained by the schedules of a working life, but perhaps a freer future; a student loan provides a freer present but insists that the future will need to follow certain contours of repayment. In Thornton's case, debt can be read as a normative introduction to decommodified labor.

Indeed, in one of her early debt-focused works found in the performance-based compendium she labels the "Fedora Archive," Thornton explicitly links the seeming fecundity of loan-generated money to the lack of a student wage.[42] While still a student at CCA, Thornton hired a performance artist to stage scenes of financial distress at important, quasi-professional campus events such as the Open Studios, an event where gallery representatives and collectors view students' work. Created by Thornton and played by Lara Gold, Fedora is a "fictional student in the MFA Fine Arts Program at California College of the Arts." Thornton describes her work as "performing dramatic and precise breakdowns about the financial and emotional precarity of pursuing an MFA."[43] In one unnamed performance, Fedora collected discarded scraps and materials from various CCA students' studios and arranged them in her own studio, proclaiming a link between the by-products of art and the fact that their art itself was a "by-product of debt." More dramatic still, Fedora was awarded the school's prize for this work by a panel of outside, visiting judges who were unaware that "Fedora" was a performance by Thornton.

In another performance during the school's MFA Thesis Show in May 2012, Fedora "proudly exhibited her work: a biography, curriculum vitae and press kit, all displayed on an elegantly lit shelf hung on an all-black wall." She presented herself in a "smart new outfit" and proclaimed her "availability for commission work and her interest in gallery representation." She simultaneously told of her need to service her art school loans of $100,000. Thornton describes that "the most common exchange [Fedora] had with people attending the show was the inquiry of whether she had any work to show *besides* the collateral documents neatly arranged on the shelf:

> VIEWER: 'What else do you do?'
> FEDORA: 'This is what I do. Am I not enough?'"[44]

Fedora reduces her cumulative creative work in school to its professional representation: the CV, the press clips, the biography, and so on. One often hears the cynical dismissal of university credentials as "just a piece of paper." "Why should I pay x amount of money for a diploma that is 'just a piece of paper'?" is a common rhetorical if reductionist question. But Fedora embraces this reduction. Her art derives from what the transaction of tuition for credential can represent. Only now, that transaction is imbued with an affect of anger and instability. Thornton's use of the word "collateral" to describe Fedora's paper accoutrements reminds us that what distinguishes student loans from other loans is precisely that they do not have collateral. With a secured loan, an object serves to guarantee the loan's repayment: a car loan is indexed to a car, a mortgage to a house, and so on. But a student loan is indexed to an experience rather than an object. It is unsecured to anything other than the physical person of the debtor.

In the performance documentation of the Fedora installation, Thornton stresses the link between her own debt and the wage paid to Gold for her role as "Fedora": "The $250 per performance I paid her was funded through my own government-issued student loans," she explains. That is, we must see the Fedora Archive as an attempt by Thornton to expose with the artwork the decommodifed labor of art-studentdom and the loans necessary to compensate for this state of affairs. Thornton is unwaged in that she has no salary. But she does receive money for being a student; she receives government loans. In her Fedora project, she then turns those loans into a salary—a wage—something she cannot garner for herself but can provide to someone else. The loans become a wage paid to someone else that represents the lack of wage that Thornton receives. Fedora demonstrates concisely and directly what it might be to conceive of "debt as [the] medium" of this work.

Yet "debt as medium" seems to be in stark tension with modernist aspirations of medial fidelity, specificity, and reflexivity. Rather, one might be tempted to read such a claim as an embrace of a "post-medium condition" in which any constellation of materials, technologies, affects, institutions, and social dynamics may be formed into a work of art.[45] Nonetheless, what is so interesting about Thornton's practice is that in choosing "debt" for her radical departure from traditional media through the specific construction of the "student loan," Thornton locates an instrument that has a similar reflexive potential as the modernist medium itself.

The medium's reflexivity comes from its hermetic ability to explore its own limits and possibilities. This definition has a Greenbergian valence, of course, and it also has a distinctive idealist genealogy. As Diarmuid Costello notes: "Greenberg appealed to Kant on several fronts, the most famous being his invocation of Kant as the 'first real modernist' . . . because he used reason to immanently criticize reason, and thereby entrench it more firmly, if more narrowly, in its area of competence."[46] Any given material's endlessly self-referential loop as conceived through its medium specificity maintains a space to consider aesthetic value as separate from economic value—one differentiation that subtends the "autonomy" of art. Art's autonomy *from* commodity society means it can be judged only by its own criteria, as determined by its medium. But as Adorno would have it, that autonomy is only granted *by* commodity society. Yet we must specify which commodity exchange is required for which notion of autonomy.

We know that the basic commodity exchange of capitalism transpires when the worker sells her labor power and receives a wage in return. We also know that aesthetic theory of the Adornian variety has used this exchange to undergird its notions of autonomy. It is true, as many have claimed, that autonomous art is a commodity. However, it is also true that autonomous art is made possible by another commodity—namely, wage labor. This need not be a one-to-one exchange—that bourgeois dream of evenness and equality—but is a conceptual exchange, one whose axis turns on the wage. Thus Adorno states, "The autonomy is inconceivable without a covering up of work."[47] Here the wage has central importance. It both acknowledges the formal sale of labor power and obfuscates the value of that labor.

On the one hand, the development of autonomy through the commodity sale of wage labor may be seen in the history of aesthetic discourse as it moves from Kant's idealism to Marx's materialism. As Stewart Martin narrates, a "(post-)Kantian philosophy of subjectivity has been transformed into a (post-) Marxist philosophy of capital, the pivot of which is the subjective character of self-valorizing capital."[48] That process is both destructive and emancipatory; art seemingly becomes a commodity and in its seemingly commodified state it makes a claim on exchange value, the very root of the commodity's ability to circulate freely. Thus John Roberts notes that "it is precisely the autonomous artwork's adoption of the illusion of independence from exchange-value (through the rejection of the customary forms of production and reception of art) that actually provides a real space for a reflection on the gap between art and the heteronomy of the commodity form."[49]

On the other hand, we may suggest, even if at a radically different level of mediation, that economic change might also renegotiate the coordinates of the relationship. Decommodified labor produces a different relation to autonomy and thus to medium. Thornton does not have a wage. She has a loan. And that loan is not collateralized through an object independent of her experience. Indeed, her experience *is* the collateral. As painting or reason reflects only itself, so the loan reflects only the life-world of Thornton. Here the loan may be seen to represent the historical moment that Martin alludes to when "self-valorizing" capital becomes subject. Creating a certain sense of space and possibility, but never offering collateral beyond the person, the student loan maintains the space of "medium." At the same time, in the specific case of Thornton, the student loan stands in for, and indeed eclipses, the wage itself, thus pressuring any possible space of autonomy.

Today, of course, we have many theoretical options for renegotiating how art makes claims on autonomy or whether art still dwells as a site to be reflected on through aesthetic judgment. Did Greenberg misread Kant, as Costello maintains? Has art become postmedium, and therefore unmoored from such philosophical considerations, as both Krauss and Peter Osborne claim, albeit in radically different idioms?[50] Does autonomy now function as a political assertion, as Nicholas Brown asserts?[51] In Thornton's work one can see that only by abandoning traditional mediums does the emergence of a new medium— debt—with its own material, conceptual, and social specificity, become possible. When "debt" does work as medium, art's autonomy is foreshortened.[52] To follow this claim, we can and must localize it to the early twentieth-first-century art classroom.

Coincident to art's expansion into universities, to the initial commodification and ultimately decommodification of artistic labor, the artist herself has become the center of art school. She is, in Singerman's precise language, both "who and what is taught" through performance lectures and visiting artist gigs, through her persona as artist, through the artist as teacher.[53] The classroom emerges as critically important. It simultaneously produces the space for the "post-medium condition" and the instrument, the student loan, that allows for artists like Thornton to access a "post-medium" pedagogy that becomes the object of their postmedial reflection, that is, debt as medium.

The art classroom also makes a somewhat surprising appearance in Yve-Alain Bois and Hal Foster's "Recessional Aesthetics: An Exchange." They consider a similar problem of the relation between debt, aesthetics, and pedagogy, and they worry that "if artists become indebted to their situation they become finite, impotential . . . ."[54] Foster and Bois attend to a state of indebtedness as a constraint on critical and artistic flourishing. The trajectory of their concern, too, ultimately ends in the art classroom. They continue:

> Debt to the situation translates into a sense of "responsibility," like the artist who today finds him/herself in the midst of a capitalism in crisis— nothing new there!—and is compelled to make art out of a sense of pathos

and guilt rather than affirmation. Aesthetic production becomes hopelessly derivative and mimetic in the worst sense of the operation. It becomes positivist rather than appropriative. And it is against this general weakness that we have thought of a fundamental question for artistic pedagogy—naturally, many others remain buried beneath the surface. The question is: how to change the classroom so that it will produce subjects (artistic, political, scientific)?[55]

Some irony exists in the fact that Foster and Bois deploy the language of debt and capitalist crisis to highlight a lack of aesthetic autonomy without acknowledging that such an economic scene is also a requirement for autonomy. Indeed, they go so far as to venture into the practice and structure of artistic education without noting that for most students, "debt to the situation" first and foremost takes the form of a responsibility to repay student loans.

But if "indebtedness" leads to lack of autonomy and generates "derivative" aesthetic production for Foster and Bois, we see the flipside of the relation between medium specificity and autonomy in the work of Shannon Jackson. Her *Social Works: Performing Art, Supporting Publics* repositions the problem to arrive at an affirmative answer. For Jackson, socially engaged art flourishes through its formulation of what she calls "medium-unspecificity," what for her, as for Claire Bishop, finds its genealogy in a legacy of theatre and performance. If art's autonomy from commodity society demands a consideration of art's medium specificity, then for Jackson, medium unspecificity produces what she calls a "de-autonomizing" aesthetic, which she claims constitutes one of socially engaged art's "artful gestures."[56]

These multiple accounts of the status of autonomy and medium in our current moment stand in some opposition to each other. Yet what is missing from each is the transformed status of artistic labor. Art beyond autonomy must also be conceived of as art after the wage. Bois and Foster do not use this language, of course. Their notion of "recessional aesthetics" does not extend to the wage form. Nor, in fact, do "medium unspecificity" and a "de-autonomizing" aesthetic make the wage central. Yet the commodity form and its transpositions undergird this discussion, as Martin, Osborne, and Brown make clear. Bois and Foster *worry* that something like decommodified labor will transform art; Jackson realizes that it already has, although she does not theorize *how* that transformation occurred.

I want to follow Thornton and consider how the very form of unsecured student loans that Thornton works with invites a return to and a reconsidera-

Name		Amount	Graduation Year	Department
	1	98,000	2012	Video
	2	80,000	2012	Fibre
	3	8,500	2013	SOPR
	4	55,000	2012	Painting
	5	68,250	2012	Sculpture
	6	61,000	2013	SOPR
	7	51,400	2013	SOPR
	8	25,000	2012	Photo
	9	76,719	2012	Sculpture
	10	?	2012	Sculpture
	11	61,000	2013	SOPR
	12	108,000	2013	Photo
	13	220,000	2013	Photo
	14		2013	Photo
	15	72,000	2012	Drawing
	16		2013	SOPR
	17		2013	SOPR
	18	92,000	2013	SOPR
	19	86,000	2012	SOPR
	20		2012	Drawing
	21		2012	Painting
	22		2012	SOPR
	23	62,000	2012	SOPR

Presently at CCA, 94% of the school's $73 million dollar budget is funded by tuition. As a student, one purchases equity in the school, owning a share of the school for the duration of their time in attendance. The current value of a US Dollar buys .0000014% of the school. At CCA the average graduate student owns about .115% of the school and I currently hold .06%.

1.2 *Application to London School of Economics.* Courtesy of Cassie Thornton.

tion of the seemingly conservative impulses of aesthetic Modernism, only now from a position of decommodified labor in which the loan has replaced the wage. Thornton's work might be understood less as a critique of traditional concepts of media and more as an attack on them. For Thornton, economic specificity and medium specificity ultimately compose a singular problem. At the site of their enjoining, we may locate in Thornton's work an aesthetic reflexivity, a "serious art," and indeed an "appropriative" logic. Not only theorists of the canon (Krauss, Bois, Foster) but the canon itself—in this case Richard Serra—come to be seen as part of Thornton's "medium of debt."[57]

Application to London School of Economics

During her final year of study for her MFA at the CCA, Thornton tried to obtain an artist's residency in the college's financial aid office. The letters she wrote recommending herself for this position and her proposals for artistic intervention, though ultimately unsuccessful, came to be part of her master's thesis, a project eponymously titled *Application to London School of Economics*. Although the unsolicited application was also unsuccessful in its manifest aim of obtaining an artist's residency at the London School of Economics, Thornton's application testifies to her multifaceted approach to rendering unsecured debt accessible and malleable as a medium of art. *Application* includes documentation of Thornton's social and multimedia practices, including personal narratives of her own life, institutional correspondence, graphs, charts, photographs, both images and content appropriated from other artists, and the text of what Thornton has come to call "debt visualizations," which she performed with members of her graduating class.[58] The fifty-three-page artist's book extends into digital space, where additional debt visualizations and associated images are collected on Thornton's website.

Perhaps the most immediately striking feature of *Application* is that much of its content is blacked out, as though sensitive information had been redacted. Or perhaps we might see this as an economic repurposing of Marcel Broodthaers's own artist's book, *A Throw of the Dice Will Not Abolish Chance*. The first page of *Application* introduces us to an ambiguous constellation of visual, textual, and structural elements that undergird the debt-based style that *Application* develops. The book performs a persistent and agonizing negotiation of the representability of debt's form and content and of the changing epistemological ability of the debtor to comprehend her debts. How does a student who knows her education will be unlikely to place her in a professional position comprehend repaying $84,000? How is such a debt located in space and time? The refusal or impossibility of representation is continually refigured within *Application*, reflecting the structure of the unsecured loan itself, which, as we have seen, refers to only the debtor; the debtor is the collateral. In this case, however, debtor and artist are a singular category. Thus the unsecured student loan refers to the artist. Most crucially, however, *Application* investigates whether the affect that the indebted situation engenders can be discharged even if the debt itself cannot be.

Application begins by explaining itself: "I have declined the opportunity to use the formal application as my current research, which I hope to continue during the residency. . . . [My work] adheres to strategies that require that I interact with all institutional communities using alternative logic and methods representative of my experimental practices, including this application process." Thornton goes on to explain both the generic character of Social Practice artwork and her own creative endeavor to "reveal a hidden logic central to the economic relationship in educational institutions of all types."[59] The play between disclosing and performing hidden logics continues as the artist thanks her collaborators and supporters in this project.

Thornton then moves jarringly from official, if nonetheless imploring, prose to first-person narration, positioning herself in a network of debtors along familiar lines of twenty-first-century economic precarity. No one in Thornton's orbit, it seems, has access to a secure wage. She describes how one parent's job loss resulted in the termination of health insurance, which ultimately produced medical debt, while another parent's stagnant wages and periods of unemployment generated credit card debt. She recounts her own passage through the global credit contraction caused by the American housing bubble and subprime mortgage crisis, in which low interest rates and predatory lending created an opportunity for her family to accumulate a home and an outsized mortgage, only to be followed quickly by foreclosure and bankruptcy. And finally, there are Thornton's own debts: small debts incurred to pay for emergency flights home to attend to family members in crisis, and the looming debt for an arts education that inflects her writing style with a lilting, associative quality and her dreams with images of rocks and sculptures by the minimalist and possibly murderous Carl Andre. Every facet of social reproduction in Thornton's orbit, it seems, transpires through a matrix in which the lack of a wage cedes to the necessity of a loan. Some of these debts begin as sites of genuine hope, even utopian potential—a hope that still flickers in the form of her MFA and gives the thesis project a kind of urgency, even desperation.

SPECIAL THANKS TO

1.3 *Application to London School of Economics.* Courtesy of Cassie Thornton.

In her evocative personal history, found in a section dryly but not ironically titled "Financial History," one gets the sense that Thornton is making a profound effort to convey her experience in a manner that, if not factually complete, invites the reader into her interpersonal world. Her disclosures contrast to the black-block redactions that appear on most of the book's pages and visually limit the reader-viewer's access to information, and they stand in tension with the provocations and evasions in which Thornton is clearly engaged in her correspondence with the institutional authorities at CCA. The shifts between openness and opacity and between visual and textual modes of communication create a readerly text whose protonarrative structure the viewer is entrained to complete. And yet, one does not know whether to fill in the gaps with images, texts, economic data, or psychological speculation. The uneven and mixed media expand an imaginary of debt into multiple registers, and one begins to comprehend how all-consuming it is to support oneself through this extractive wage we call a student loan, a kind of ghostly compensation for the decommodified labor of studentdom.

To understand the implications of her own debt, Thornton consults a certified financial planner, and the viewer is privy to the planner's analysis. From the planner we get the sense that she is close to Thornton, but the text does not explain their intimacy. As "someone who loves you [Thornton]," the anonymous financial planner writes in a correspondence that has been reproduced, "I think it's great that you're creating images/visual experience around debt. I wish more people would do this." The planner continues: "Many people's 'ships' are dangerously close to icebergs and they don't have a clue!" The planner's own visualization, what the planner herself refers to as "scribbles," shows a series of leveraged triangles balancing on each other and is designed to help the debtor decide what ratio of productive to unproductive debt exists in the debtor's portfolio. Using drawings and texts, the planner wants Thornton to understand where her education should be considered on the spectrum.

> So, from a purely analytical standpoint, we need to consider what your capitalized lifetime earnings are anticipated to be both WITH and WITHOUT your Master's Degree from CCA. Based on our discussion and your estimates, it looks like over a 33 year career (allowing an initial two years to get your bearings or "foot in the door") that you may conservatively earn about $600,000 more than if you did not complete your Master's. Using a discount rate equivalent to the inflation assumption I used of 3.5%, on a present value basis, this equals $180,000. Because your Graduate School component of your debt, and in fact, all remaining student loans, total about $100,000, we can legitimately categorize this debt as "productive." YEAH![60]

With the financial planner's help, we are led to understand that Thornton's net worth might be about $80,000 more over the course of her career than it would have been had she not obtained an MFA. By the time a photograph of an iceberg appears in the final pages of Thornton's book, the reader is likely to have forgotten the financial planner's explicit analogy of the frozen mass with financial danger. And instead the reader will have more likely come to associate its shape and texture with the rocks, imaginary objects, and sculptures with which Thornton compounds our associations with debt.

Moving between a language of love and lifetime earnings, and encouraging Thornton to see her present debt as a nascent manifestation of future profit, the financial planner introduces into Thornton's project the problem of what neoliberal economist Gary Becker, following George Schultz, has explored as "human capital," that set of human attributes capable of allowing us to transform and sustain ourselves.[61] In looking forward to her "capitalized lifetime earnings," Thornton can retroactively be sure that the investment she made in herself through her MFA, and the concomitant transformation of her sense of self into a human with capital, was the right one. That the work of Thornton's studentdom does not provide a wage becomes relatively unimportant in such a scheme. The financial planner, then, encourages Thornton to adopt a "neoliberal" position, a philosophical accompaniment to the history of neoliberal policy prescriptions we saw in this chapter's introduction.

Indeed, for Becker, and subsequently for his most famous interpreter, Foucault, the "wage" has become an obsolete construct. Foucault arrives at this conclusion through a reading of the neoliberal economists who claim that their economic theory "puts [us, the theorists] in the position of the person who works [and turns] the worker into an active economic subject." Foucault's exposition of the ground on which a "wage" ceases to have categorical importance should be quoted at length:

> Why, in the end, do people work? They work, of course, to earn a wage. What is a wage? A wage is quite simply an income. From the point of view of the worker, the wage is an income, not the price at which he sells his labor power . . .[;] if we accept . . . that the wage is an income, then the wage is therefore the income of a capital. Now what is the capital of which the wage is the income? Well, it is the set of all those physical and psychological factors which make someone able to earn this or that wage, so that, seen from the side of the worker, labor is not a commodity reduced by abstraction to labor power and the time [during] which it is used. Broken down in economic terms, from the worker's point of view labor comprises a capital, that is to say, it as an ability, a skill . . . .[62]

One can puzzle over the logic of the transposition from wage to income to capital. Note, for example, the repetition of the verb "to be." Its usage by Foucault denotes multiple theoretical reductions and abstractions. The effect of the repetition is that of rendering commensurate processes that are anything but. In the move from wage to income we see less a process of induction than one of casuistry. Nonetheless, as a discourse of self-narration, the language of self-investment and self-entrepreneurship has become hegemonic in the world of commerce no less than in those of art and education. Foucault was especially attentive to education, asking, "What does it mean to form human capital . . . which will produce income? It means making educational investments."[63] So we can and should follow this language. Indeed, the essentially descriptive nature of much neoliberal economic thought is one of its aspects that is brought into sharp relief when neoliberalism is put into conversation with decommodified labor.

After having invested in herself through letting out her human capital and receiving a loan whose collateral is her own person, Thornton now needs to reinvest those skills; she needs to transform that person whom she has become, a credentialed artist, into someone who has income and thus can garner a return on her improved human capital. But without a market for her own kind of self, where should Thornton invest her human capital? The market for human capital is a limited one, and as Becker points out, student loans are one of the few places where the market actually functions as such. Becker writes, "If I invest in my human capital, I cannot in modern societies use my capital as collateral to borrow loans. That's why we have such a poorly developed commercial market for loans and investments. You look at student loans: they've developed extensively in the United States because of the government guarantee and subsidy to student loans . . . if I buy a house, I can give my house as mortgage. If don't make my payments, they take my house away from me, as we're seeing all these foreclosures going on now."

Yet Becker quickly presents the limitation that I noted has become an artistic possibility for Thornton, one specifically concerned with the wage. The fact is that in school, with government support, Thornton can invest in herself. But after school, opportunities for further self-investment of her human capital are difficult to locate. Becker continues: "I can't give myself as collateral. Now, in the past with slavery and other forms of indentured servitude you could do that. In modern society we've ruled that out, for good reasons I think . . . [but] it makes it very difficult for poor people who don't have other forms of capital to invest in themselves."[64]

Notwithstanding Becker's odd understanding of slavery as a form of "giving [one]self as collateral," he notes a paradox: human capital as student loan allows one to get into debt, but possibly not out of it. The site that holds the contradiction is the person of the debtor. This is not a new condition; one is reminded of the etymology of the word "finance," derived from the French verb *finir*, "to end," which makes reference to the end of one's life, a relation also seen in "mortgage," which breaks down into "death" (*mort*) and "pledge" (*gage*). The idioms of neoliberalism have updated this language to our age.

In this book's introduction I contrasted two forms of contemporary economic critique, both of which argue for a changed status of labor. I introduced the Marxist problem of real subsumption, in which all activity is reduced to labor in that it produces surplus value, and the Foucauldian paradigm of neoliberalism, in which all activity forms a site of potential investment. I wondered which understanding of our economic present better supports an attempt to link decommodified labor to the aesthetic—which better obtains in a situation in which one either cannot sell one's labor or cannot garner a return on one's investment? This is a problem we will return to in each of this book's chapters and with each of the book's artists, and I ultimately argue that neoliberalism's discounting of labor limits its ability to make claims within the realm of the aesthetic.

In Thornton's work, however, we note elements of both approaches as possible frames through which to understand her artistic and economic present. The MFA in Social Practice is represented by the financial planner as a wise investment for Thornton to have made—except that an investment is only wise if liquidity exists in the market in which one made the investment. An investment, no matter how sterling, must be considered limited if it cannot be resold. In Thornton's case, for her investment in herself to be considered wise, she must locate a market in which someone desires to purchase her artistic labor. But there is none. That fact then calls into question whether her experience at CCA should continue to be understood as an investment or whether it is something else entirely. (It also calls into question the financial planner's interpretation, too.) Here we see most discretely and directly how the "loan" takes the place of the "wage." We also see the different levels of mediation that must be held together in order to comprehend the transformation: self-narration and institutional narration; the discourse of political economy and the space of actual economic dealings. At times these two frames may be located simultaneously; at other points, one seems to supersede the other. Thornton may have been an investor when she took out the loans, but by the time she comprehends her need to repay them, she has become a decommodified laborer. The point is not to resolve this theoretical tension but to show how it exists and is managed in the field of the aesthetic. Likewise, the point is to explore what the aesthetic can contribute to this discussion, and to capacitate the aesthetic to make, not simply to reflect, economic claims.

A series of conceptual and visual tropes emerge alongside Thornton's narrative to fracture *Application*'s sense of plot and direction. The viewer feels both energy and enervation as Thornton attempts to "transform the material of debt" yet seems gradually unable to locate a social space in which such a transformation would be possible. An association emerges from Thornton's artist's book of debt as an imposition, an omnipresence whose impenetrability is both psychic and physical. Yet Thornton simultaneously struggles with this idea and wonders whether debt may still become constitutive of a shared reality in which it might be intercepted and reorganized. "Once its material form is identified, there is hope that the debt may be harvested and used as a pedagogical, social, and fiscal resource," she writes.

Application's affect conjoins openness and intimacy—sometimes friendly, sometimes militant—with a willingness to share in her aspirations for debt as well as a determined pursuit of those who are reluctant to become involved in her project. With a mixture of sincerity and aggression, Thornton takes her appeal to restructure both her own and all forms of student debt to the director of her Social Practice MFA program. In a series of reprinted letters, much like those found in Filliou's text, *Teaching and Learning as Performing Arts*, Thornton writes, "I'm anxious to hear your perspective on Social Practice and its many forms of social exchange in relation to the capitalist mechanism. As always, I appreciate your enthusiasm for unorthodox thought when everything seems doomed to utilitarianism. I'll swing by your office. Best! Cassie."[65] The contraction of "I will" and the exclamation point renders her anxiousness friendly and intimate; at the same time, if the director has repeatedly told her "no"—and he has (we have read the correspondence)—then why does she insist on casually swinging by his office? One might almost say that Thornton repurposes the affect of a debt collector's telephonic presence: friendly and persistent, seeking all information and any form of contact because contact and positive identification of the debtor holds open a space for continued contact. While the time period differs by state, all that is required for a debt to remain active is for the collector to maintain contact within that period, ranging from three to seven years. Debt collectors hounding those who owe is not simply their approach to collecting the debt, but to keeping the debt alive and extending its futurity.

Ultimately, *Application* and Thornton's practice itself cohere around the debt visualizations that she conducts with her cohort of MFA students. She explains the process using a vocabulary appropriate to the plastic arts: "I am in the process of interviewing every MFA student about the financial liabilities they've accrued while attending CCA. Each is asked to describe the essence of [his or her] debt as an expression of texture, aura, scale, material composition, etc, from within a meditative state."[66] Conducted in a private space ritually purified by the burning of sage, Thornton invites her fellow debtors to free associate to the word "debt" and to imagine approaching their own debt from a distance. What results from these dialogues is a new verbal, visual, style-oriented—and specifically art historical—discourse through which MFA students trace their own path to artistic professionalization and indebtedness. As the possibility of individual debt enabled each of them to pursue an MFA, so the possibility of collectivizing debt in a shared imaginary enables Thornton to mold and sculpt, indeed we might say to begin to "restructure" the subjective—if not the objective—conditions of their cumulative debt burden.

Despite *Application*'s attempts to literalize and concretize, a new metaphor does emerge prominently from its collection of debt visualizations. Certain images and tropes appear so often they come to seem generic. Debt is heavy, vast, terrifying; it looms but is not necessarily present. But what is perhaps most surprising is that during their debt-visualization sessions, indebted MFA students produce recurring references to and images resembling the work of the postminimalist sculptor Richard Serra. In one sense, it is rather unremarkable that the debt visualizations of MFA students would generate images and anxieties tied to successful, practicing artists. But the force of the association is nonetheless striking.

"There is an imponderable vastness to weight," Serra once commented, in reference to his own work.[67] As Thornton suggests in her own analysis of this trend of debt-induced Serra associations, students' unsecured loans, which have become their debt, like Serra's sculptures, always seem on the verge of collapsing, and yet these terrifying, precarious objects somehow endure through space and time. Indeed, Serra's emerging presence in *Application* may lead the viewer may consider the financial planner's use of a metaphor of fulcrums with new attention. They could be reread as a study for a work such as Serra's *Trip Hammer* (1988), in which one steel slab balances atop another, stabilized only by the precise angle and distribution of the weight of each component. The financial planner writes: "The size of the fulcrum is important. While a properly-sized fulcrum can provide the added lift or leverage to catapult you to the next level, if it is too large, you may just slide back down. In other words, if your debt is too large for the projected return, it could act as a weight instead of a level and pull you down (below where you would have been had you not taken on the debt in the first place)."[68] In light of such associations, we might even be tempted to retroactively read Serra's works as debt visualizations. We may also start to see Thornton's own use of black squares and rect-

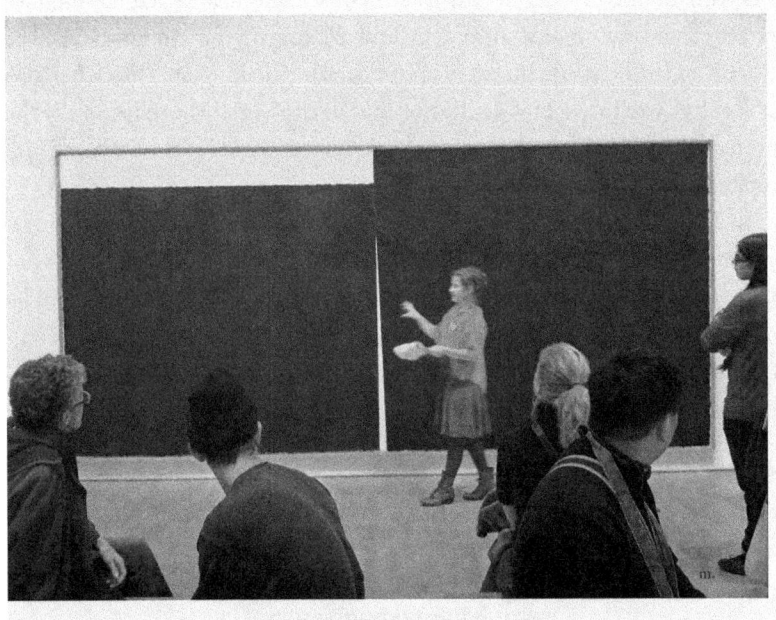

1.4 *Application to London School of Economics.* Courtesy of Cassie Thornton.

angles throughout her text in a different light, as an appropriation not only of Broodthaers, but of Serra himself.

Thornton is particularly drawn to Serra's oil-stick drawings, which she incorporates into her ever-capacious debt imaginary by offering gallery tours of Serra's work and appropriating images of Serra's *The United States Government Destroys Art* (1989) to serve as an economic graph comparing credit card and student loan debt. When asked why he worked at one end of the color spectrum, Serra explained "from chartreuse to pink inevitably leads to metaphors that deflect attention elsewhere and take you away from the graphicness of drawing . . . [but black's] main association is to writing and printing, and to drawing. If it represents anything, [black] represents graphicness."[69] In the new context of Thornton's work, however, black acquires other associations: both of anonymity and to the financial vernacular phrase "in the black." When a ledger is "in the black," there is profit; when it is "in the red," there is loss. In an early iteration of this project, Thornton played with these colors and their financial inflections on her artist website, where her collection of debt visualizations was displayed. She presented a series of multicolored numbers which linked to specific experiences of student debt: Each red number indicated an amount of student debt, and clicking on that number linked to the text of the debt visualization of said debtor. Clicking on a black bar also took the viewer to a debt visualization, but in these cases the redaction of the numerical "amount" owed doubled as a visual metaphor for the obtrusive and impenetrable burden of the debt itself.

In an exercise reminiscent of the concrete poetry of Carl Andre and Robert Smithson, Thornton presents one particular debt visualization as a kind of poetic form in which the line breaks of the text "sculpt" its content. The halting, interrupted, repetitive language suggests the inability of this MFA student to speak or think linearly about their unsecured debt, whereas the poem's form evokes debt as a workable three-dimensional substance:

debt is

future self is paying

"future" dad is paying

her son, will he pay to play ex post facto?

what is the motivation to pay

after the value is used up?

the value of the mfa is my life

hard to imagine not doing it,

doesn't want to imagine regretting it

it's weird that it has a monetary value

the life has a trail of debt

heart races when

she passes the debt on the street

there is a murky cloudiness,

a wall coming out of it

over her head

NO!

Richard Serra steel and leaning
instead of a sky,
it's a steel plate sloping down[70]

For this debtor, too, encountering their debt through visualization is like encountering a Serra sculpture: one must walk around it, and in doing so, one's perspective continues to change as every new angle and vantage point offers the opportunity to begin again. But the content, the sculpture itself, remains massive and unmoving.

Thornton's social practice of sculpting affective and intersubjective relationships through the medium of debt, by contrast, intervenes in the material substrate of our contemporary economy in which the value of financial instruments far outweighs the value of material commodities, including the labor commodity.[71] Indeed, Thornton's work organizes the "by-products" of our finance-heavy economy much as postminimalist practice—Serra's work in particular—presciently memorialized and rendered artful the by-products of a deindustrializing economy. Throughout the late 1960s and early 1970s, postminimalist artists repurposed materials of steel, oil, blighted urban space, privatized and empty corporate spaces, and asphalt and concrete to mark artistically what they understood as an economic transition.[72] In Serra's case, his own life and labor followed this trajectory: he moved from working in steel mills in order to fund his education to transforming the labor processes he found in steel mills into his art. Serra speaks of his own education in a retired idiom and uses the Fordist language of the wage. He reminisces: "When I worked in the steel mills there were a lot of people who had just come through the Second World War, wanting to find money by joining the labor force. I was working my way through school; and there did seem to be an ethos of putting in a day's work for a day's pay."[73]

In this sense, Thornton's process is similar to Serra's: they both work out of the labor processes of an older economy, and they both anticipate the economic processes of an emergent one. But for Thornton, there is no pay for a day's work. There is a loan for a day's work, and then managing the loan becomes the day's work, a labor that is decommodified. For her, managing the loan becomes the artwork, too. That constitutes one part of her work's aesthetic reflexivity; the second part of that reflexivity is that the loan refers to the person herself; there is no collateral. Thus the reflexivity of the object (the loan) also constitutes the reflexivity of the subject (the "lendee"). By introducing Serra into *Application*, Thornton introduces some crucial, if necessarily speculative, questions: What constitutes, or what will constitute, the detritus of a financialized and increasingly wageless economy whose pivots of value veer between the management of financial transactions in the upper echelons and low—or no—wage work in its lower echelons? We often hear this called "a service economy," or an economy that relies on "affective labor" or "immaterial labor."[74] Thornton's work encourages us to focus not on the service itself, or on the affect itself or its immateriality, but rather on the wageless consequences of labor configurations regardless of their genesis.

Thornton hints at a relational triangle between an older economic formation and its avant-garde, and a new economic formation still waiting for its own style. Thornton engages in an unexpected move of debt bricolage as Serra, too, becomes interpolated into Thornton's community of debtors. Not only do her debt visualizations disclose his work and general style as a trope for debt that resonates widely among her fellow students, but Thornton attempts to entrain Serra in her project. She composes a letter to Serra that she mails to him and also has surreptitiously left on Serra's kitchen table in his New York City townhouse by anonymous, an art handler she knows.[75] She writes to him, "Dear Mr. Serra, . . . your forms represent an omnipresent debt to us, or vice versa . . . [and] there is a sense that on the way to becoming an artist of your stature we are encouraged to acquire debt." Thornton goes on to suggest that Serra collaborate with her cohort of indebted students in her MFA program by auctioning off one of his sculptures: "but now referring to it as representation of debt—donating some proceeds to the class. (I was thinking of one of the pieces that have been removed or have gone unused, like a part of Tilted Arc.)" Much as debt collectors call family members or anyone who might have psychic or financial access to a debtor, Thornton renders Serra guilty by art-practical association. The suggestion that a part of *Tilted Arc* (1981), a public sculpture commissioned and then removed from Federal Plaza in New York City after eight long years of rancorous debate, be donated to MFA students also provides a path for that work's return to the public. While Serra and his supporters claimed that the sculpture was successful in heightening viewers' attention to their own movement through the space, the work's critics decried it as a rusty eyesore, a magnet for rats and bombs, and most pertinent to our discussion, a gross obstacle to public use of the plaza. Thornton's appropriation of the sculpture as a means of heightening awareness of debt in the public consciousness might offer Serra a kind of redemption.

As with her entreaties to her own college's financial aid office, Thornton's invitation to Serra is duly rebuffed. Like a debtor avoiding a collection agency,

Serra knows that the best response is no response. Indefatigable, Thornton appropriates another of Serra's works. As part of the performance-based aspect of *Application*, Thornton becomes licensed as a docent and leads tours of the 2012 Richard Serra Drawings retrospective that serendipitously happened to be on exhibition at the San Francisco Museum of Modern Art while Thornton was finishing her MFA. Thornton titles this part of her project "Urgent Richard Serra Debt Tour." As Michelle White explains in her catalogue essay of the show, Serra's drawings are "about the intangibility of conceptual thought and the visceral immediacy of direct physicality."[76] This understanding of Serra's work could be transposed onto Thornton's conception of debt. Indeed, figure 1.4 invites the reader to do just that. Thus we are introduced to yet another site of debt as a medium and another presentation of the sensuousness of indebtedness. Thornton's work leaves us with the sense that such bricolage and entraining of the figures of the art world into art students' debt could continue ad infinitum. Such a limitless extension results from the relation between art as value and art as expression, a relation that is simultaneously cemented and jettisoned by the institutional world of art, which includes both the places where Serra's work is seen and sold as well as the art schools where students are trained and impoverished.

The riffs on Serra lead not only to canonical art but also to the critics who sustain it. It was Rosalind Krauss herself who argued that "Serra's sculpture is about sculpture."[77] With this modernist claim of medium specificity we may assert fully one of the central concerns of this chapter: namely, that the unsecured loan as a radically new and seemingly postmedium medium returns us to some of the traditional problems of medium specificity after the wage form. How, ultimately, do unsecured loans develop a modernist, aesthetic reflexivity? They follow a logic Marx already laid out in his discussion of nineteenth-century public debt: "As with the stroke of an enchanter's wand, [the state] endows barren money with the power of breeding and thus turns it into capital."[78] Financial instruments carry with them a similar reflexive possibility—although Marx cautions that to see only the reflexiveness is to experience the "height of misrepresentation." However ethereal a financial operation seems, finance presumes and requires a material word. Thornton seizes the reflexiveness of the student loan, and as it becomes capital, it also becomes critique.

One of the criticisms of so much debt activism is that debt, particularly debt accumulated during the course of postgraduate liberal or fine arts education, is the result of a sense of entitlement in the debtor. As scholars including Joseph and McClanahan have noted, debt always seems to be assumed freely, much as unwaged work presents as a choice freely made as well, as we saw in the introduction. If Thornton did not want a lifetime's worth of debt, after all, why did she pursue an arts degree, of all things? That question needs to be answered on both a structural and an individual level. Structurally, of course, like Serra's *One Ton Prop (House of Cards)* (1969), capitalism itself falls apart without a system of mass indebtedness. One only gets paid *after* one works, and the time before payment is always possibly a time of debt, whether from the company store in older days or from a credit card company in our own time. Individually, however, Thornton did feel "entitled" not only to go into debt, but to transform that debt into something else through the site specificity of the scene of its accumulation. And it is the site specificity of the debt itself—accrued in an MFA-granting institution that specializes in Social Practice—through which we arrive at the ultimate reflexivity of debt as a medium. It was only by going into *more* unsecured debt for her MFA that her own undergraduate student debt could be endowed with the reflexivity required of a modernist medium. In other words, her MFA debt is both cause and object of her ability to formalize indebtedness as a medium. In Krauss's language: Thornton's debt is about debt.

Rolling Jubilee

I have been working for free for the last three years.
—THOMAS GOKEY, *A Soft Spot in a Hard Place*

When Bois and Foster worry that artists "indebted to [their] situations" will produce work that is "hopelessly mimetic and derivative," perhaps they have this in mind: *Total Amount of Money Rendered in Exchange for a Masters of Fine Arts Degree to the School of the Art Institute of Chicago, Pulped into Four Sheets of Paper* by artist Thomas Gokey (figure 1.5). Gokey explains that he "acquired the exact amount of cash ($49,983) that my tuition cost in shredded form from the Federal Reserve Bank of Chicago." He then "pulped [the money] into four large sheets of paper" so that the "artwork [becomes] the act of selling this paper piecemeal for the amount of money it is made out of. For example, 1 sq in costs $4.22, 1 sq ft cost $607.70, etc." For the full duration of his residency at ArtPrize, Gokey planned to "sit next to my art and sell it off in any dimension to viewers. Once I sell the last piece I will have paid for school."[79]

Too easy in its literalism and too ambitious in its demands, *Total Amount of Money* might be understood as a kind of ransom note: I will not make art

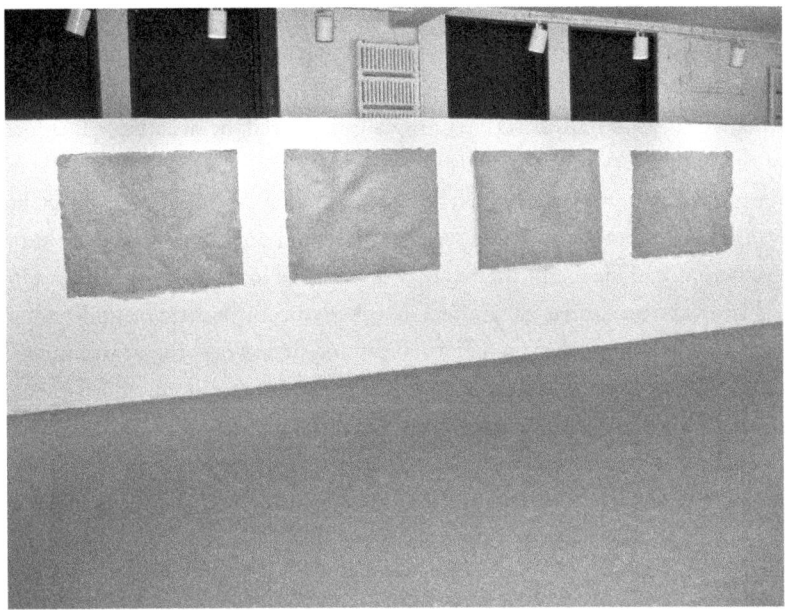

1.5 *Total Amount of Money Rendered in Exchange for a Masters of Fine Arts Degree to the School of the Art Institute of Chicago, Pulped into Four Sheets of Paper.* Courtesy of Thomas Gokey.

beyond the claustrophobic horizons of my own art school loans until I am out of debt. Made for a white cube gallery, the four works shown here might be said to evoke an Ad Reinhardt color series, one block of monochrome after another, with a focus on serial repetition amidst minimal variation in shade and dimension. Like the diploma it seeks to critique, this work might be dismissed as "just a sheet of paper."

Gokey's stated goal, both artistic and fiscal, was similar to Thornton's: to discharge debt by means other than the impossible tactics of repayment or bankruptcy. Thornton does not indicate in the presentation of her work whether her *Application to London School of Economics* or later projects such as her *Debt Scream* or *Debt 2 Space* installation were successful in discharging her debt. But Gokey has explained this work of his—individual, formal, gallery- and market-ready—as a failure. No one purchased the work and he was left not only with the debt, but with its artistic derivative.

That sense of impossibility underlies the reason that Gokey's professional website has not been updated since 2008, and that this work is memorialized, Havisham-like, online.[80] From being a student in the Art Institute of Chicago's MFA program to an adjunct professor at Syracuse's MFA program, when Gokey narrates his professional history, his portfolio stops when he stops being able to support himself as an artist. It is almost impossible to make art when one is, as John Roberts has caustically described the situation, a member of the "vast reserve army of artists."[81] Adjunct life kept Gokey nominally in the university system from which he had just graduated and through which he was indebted, but with limited resources he could not flourish as an artist or teacher; indeed, he felt himself as now responsible for entraining other aspiring artists into a similar quagmire. Gokey's predicament must be understood as a rather routine one. Too many degrees, too little work; the degree constitutes another node of a loan-based value chain, mediated, as we have seen, through the body of the artist-debtor. Like Thornton, Gokey too alludes to embodiment-as-collateral through the person of the artist. But unlike Thornton's projection of an interior, affective space into her work, Gokey ultimately designed a more collective, infrastructural, and spectacular outlet for his affective if not literal refusal to repay: namely, the much-lauded, highly visible, and of course criticized Rolling Jubilee.

Launched to great fanfare in 2012, Rolling Jubilee emerged as the signal project of the collective Strike Debt. With an original plan to raise $50,000 and use it to purchase $2 million of discounted outstanding debt on the secondary debt market, Rolling Jubilee was a phenomenal success if measured by its stated goals. The project has raised around $700,000, which was used to purchase some $32 million of medical and student debt. That is, the collective purchased outstanding debt for "pennies on the dollar." [82] That purchased debt was then absolved. Along with art critics including Yates McKee and Chris Kraus, I understand Rolling Jubilee as a kind of socially engaged artwork. McKee notes that the project "could have been at home in the subgenre of microeconomic experimentation that had gained traction in the contemporary art system in the late 2000s, including time banks, barter networks, gift exchanges . . . and more."[83] I will explore these precise systems of barter and exchange in my next chapter, as their infrastructure relies almost exclusively on decommodified labor. But unlike McKee, I do not understand Rolling Jubilee itself as one of those systems. Rather, I think Kraus offers a more perspicacious reading: "[Rolling Jubilee] goes straight to the conceptual heart of semio-capital, in ways that material-based, old-fashioned 'political art' can only contemplate. Instead of producing objects that fetishize past revolutions, projects like the Rolling Jubilee abstract the concept of debt with wit and elegance, and, in the same gesture, attack and ameliorate it."[84]

While I agree with Kraus's generic assessment, my reasons for considering Rolling Jubilee an artwork differ from hers. I focus on the labor, thus following Gokey, who notes that "a lot of us who were working on Strike Debt or the Rolling Jubilee or the debt collective came from cultural work of one variety or another."[85] According to Gokey, then, many people working on Strike Debt could claim the experience of being trained as decommodified cultural workers, those without access to a wage. Furthermore, they understood that to execute Rolling Jubilee would require an expensive and elaborate infrastructure. During discussions there emerged a common consensus that "if [we] call it art, people will fund it."[86] That is, a proportionally large number of Strike Debt participants were artists who concluded that labeling their activities "art" would generate a certain political and organizational freedom that calling them "politics" would obviate. Peter Osborne calls this particular invocation of the aesthetic the "functionalization of [art's] autonomy." He notes that "this integration is by no means an outright negation of autonomy by commodification and political rationality, so much as a new systemic functionalization of autonomy itself—a new kind of 'affirmative culture.'"[87] That term has pejorative connotations, of course. Indeed, this work might seem to be closer to Nicholas Brown's already cited comment that, in our current economic moment, autonomy may be used as a political claim.

But even if we do conclude that Rolling Jubilee may be discussed as a kind of socially engaged artwork—that which both demands and attempts to affect material redistribution—we also must contend with the question of whether Gokey himself should be discussed individually in an authorial position to it.[88] He explains that it would be a "jackass move" to claim that "Rolling Jubilee is this work that I made." One can see his point—many people made it. But many people make most artworks, and according to Gokey, he and several others, including David Graeber and Micah White, had the idea to purchase debt/abolish debt almost simultaneously. Few interesting ideas have a single source, and this one is no exception. Yet it was Gokey who encouraged Strike Debt to explore the project, who did the research in secondary debt markets, who laid out a plan of infrastructural feasibility, and who, by giving interviews (like this one with Gough and another in *Utne Reader*), has enabled himself to be read as one of its artist-authors, even while reminding various interviewers that he would rather not be in that position—indeed, even while reminding them that "maybe the only reason I call myself an artist is because I went to art school," a logical consequence of Singerman's contention that in art school, "the artist is who and what is taught."[89]

Gokey's and his interlocutors' series of claims as to who may be considered an artist and what kind of organizations artists can capacitate generate a rich series of contradictions. One is an artist if one goes to art school, but the student loans that art school generates circumscribe one's professional life as a practicing artist. Out of school, one can band together with other artists and cultural workers to make political economic demands, but not from a place of politics or economics. Rather, those demands must be issued from a place of art, because art has a freedom and latitude, an ability to circulate through different media and social spheres, that politics and economics lack. Art can generate funding for groups but not waged labor for individuals. Indeed, it generates the opposite of waged labor—namely, decommodified labor, as the artist will be asked, will be expected, and will volunteer to work without pay. Yet out of that scene of decommodified labor one can, paradoxically, produce art that itself makes the demand for economic redistribution.

The art that will be produced in a project like Rolling Jubilee might be seen to reappropriate what Benjamin Buchloh worried would become a dominant "aesthetics of administration," after the medium's expiration and along with it the disappearance of formal properties for judging a work of art. Buchloh writes that "the result of [a post-medium condition] is that the definition of the aesthetic becomes on the one hand a matter of linguistic convention and on the other the function of both a legal contract and an institutional discourse (a discourse of power rather than taste)."[90] This sort of discrete sense of the aesthetic is, of course, exactly why the concept curries such limited favor in socially engaged art. Conversely, it is why someone like Thornton stresses the need to see "debt as a medium" so that the valences of medium, what is considered possible as formal variation and consistency, do not need to be ceded to administrators, whether of museums or of student loans.

Rolling Jubilee produced an "aesthetics of administration" of a different sort. The project required logistical research on small-scale debt buyers, involved negotiations with lawyers, and ultimately the incorporation of the group as a legal entity. To accomplish its Rolling Jubilee, Strike Debt would transform itself into a small-scale debt buyer, and from that standing they would interact with other small-scale debt shops (not large institutions like Wells Fargo or Sallie Mae). They had to set up bank accounts, process payments online, and research the integrity of various debt portfolios. Without the expertise to navigate debt markets, the group worried that they themselves would be scammed. For example, one debt seller offered a portfolio that seemed too good to be true: it comprised federally backed student loans that would have enabled Strike Debt to cancel the loans while collecting the amounts owed from the federal government. Thus consultants had to be hired. As the project developed, these artists and cultural workers began to undertake white-collar administrative work.

Gokey describes this transformation from artist to financial white-collar worker in an autochthonous vocabulary. The group engaged in what it understood as "cold calling" debt buyers—the term used by stockbrokers and other sales people to describe a phone call to someone unknown who has expressed no interest in a purchase. The group's actions, too, became oddly similar to those of the same financial industry their project sought to critique. They incorporated in Delaware—the so-called Panama of the United States—because of its ease of conduct, low-fee structure, and lack of transparency. Gokey estimated it would take six months to put in place the infrastructure needed to purchase a debt portfolio. It took two years.

What kind of "art" is Rolling Jubilee, then? While it could obviously be called socially engaged art, it seems as though it could also be categorized as a form of "Occupational Realism," Julia Bryan-Wilson's suggestive term for the blending together of performance with work-based duties.[91] Bryan-Wilson explains that such art comprises "performances in which artists enact the normal, obligatory tasks of work under the highly elastic rubric of 'art.'"[92] Here, the "job becomes the art and the art becomes the job." She provides the example of artist Ben Kinmont, whose installation *Sometimes a nicer sculpture is to be able to provide a living for your family* is ongoing and consists of him running a used bookstore. Bryan-Wilson continues: "It is important that his business function as a business; it is not enough for him to gesture symbolically towards the world of commerce by, say, printing up ironic letterhead or opening a fake storefront."[93] While a used bookstore might not seem the obvious choice for financial security, no doubt its dividends, unreliable as they may be, are more reliable than the average sale price of a socially engaged artwork.

The "occupational realist" steps out from art's existence in the shadows of capital and makes a claim on the wage in the name of art—he inverts the traditional role of the aesthetic. But the decommodified laborers of Rolling Jubilee double down on the inversion: they work as professionals on their art, the first inversion, but they do so without making a claim on the wage form, the second inversion. For their efforts, Gokey specifically underscores that "we worked very hard for several years [and] none of us got paid a penny."[94] I am less concerned to evaluate this difference in terms of categorical consistency than I am to note that Bryan-Wilson's "occupation realism" is an almost perfect conceptual reversal of "decommodified labor" in the arts. In her scheme, most work can be artwork because so little art-based work can be labor (that is, sold as a commodity). In my scheme, most art will be work because most work that artists do no longer commands a wage. Indeed, one can see a recapitulation here of the discussion between real subsumption and neoliberalism as two understandings of our economic present: Bryan-Wilson offers a neoliberal version in that artistic labor disappears; there is no artist's wage. I offer a version in which labor maintains some categorical integrity, as decommodified labor is still labor although it does not generate a wage. Here we might also think about the notion of tautology I included in the introduction, borrowed from Antonio Negri's concept of tautological time. Occupational realism is mimetic; decommodified labor is tautological.

The argument I want to make, then, is that like Thornton's work, Rolling Jubilee is governed by decommodified labor realized as art, and that realization contains its own medial potential. As we have seen, Gokey notes that those involved in Strike Debt were likely to be what he calls "creative workers." By that Gokey means that those who were motivated to strike their debt had been trained in artistic or cultural production. Yet during their training, instead of being waged as students they were indebted. As a result, they were transformed into a certain kind of worker who cannot find waged work. Thus—and this is itself a moment in which socially engaged art may be located in Rolling Jubilee—they began to work as skilled professionals, for free.

Their unwaged labor may seem expected, but the context in which it is found is different from most do-it-yourself institutions of community-based art practices. Rolling Jubilee produced something few other such projects will ever claim: a surplus of money. The goal had been to raise $50,000 to use to purchase debt; in fact, the project raised over $700,000. Gokey relays that some members of the collective wanted to use the surplus funds to put in place an organizational infrastructure to build a debtors' union—which one assumes would have included paying people to work. If the project had purchased the planned $50,000 instead of $700,000 worth of debt, its symbolic impact would have remained unchanged. Yet that diverted $650,000 could have changed the working lives of certain artist-organizers. Ultimately, however, the group decided that to do so would have been to violate the spirit of their call for donations, which was to purchase debt and thereby liberate individual debtors, not to compensate people for the liberation. One can see their point here. The surplus was generated because of the broad social resonance of the idea of using some money to abolish a debt worth even more money. The power of this seemingly counterfactual possibility should not be understated. David Graeber notes that during the 2007–8 credit crisis, when the U.S. federal government was willing to buy banks' compendium of junk mortgages at par but was unwilling to rescue individual homeowners, people got to understand who "really makes money out of nothing: the financiers or the ordinary citizens."[95] Now, Rolling Jubilee offered a chance for non–financial institutions, nonfinanciers, to make nothing out of money.

One can also hear in Strike Debt's decision not to produce more of a robust infrastructure that could have moved beyond the live-streamed, highly publicized spectacle of Rolling Jubilee a fear of the critique often lodged at so many nonprofit organizations. During a disaster, various nonprofits ask for and usually receive increased donations. Then, after said disaster has passed, it is revealed that the donations went in large part to sustain the organization, not "directly" to victims of the disaster. My point is not to agree with such criticism, but to show why Strike Debt organizers would have used their excess Rolling Jubilee funds in the manner they did.

But, then, what exactly is that criticism? It is one that counterposes the ethical to the wage. One can see here how deeply entrenched a model of nonpayment in such arts has become and the deep ironies this generates. In debt because they were never paid, these artists-as-organizers now refuse payment, as accepting it would interrupt the ethics of their art, which aims to free people from debt. A comparison to Gokey's discussion of lawyers reveals the depth of the division. As Rolling Jubilee developed, the group needed legal counsel, and in particular it sought to "find creative ways to use escrow accounts." Yet it could not secure the participation of lawyers like it could artists. Gokey explains: "You have to go $200,000 in debt to become a lawyer. That means you work in corporate law [when you graduate]. Not with artists and activists." Note the difference of thinking through the problem of decommodified labor in the legal profession. Unlike artists, lawyers don't work free, even as they go into as much, if not more, debt.

An understanding of the manifestation of decommodified labor in Rolling Jubilee finally allows us to address some of the criticism of the project. Joshua Clover has made the quite appropriate claim that to purchase discounted debt on the secondary market, as Rolling Jubilee did, is to legitimize not only particular debts but more crucially, the structural apparatus of all debt. Clover describes Rolling Jubilee's approach as one of "work as best as possible within the very legal framework that maintains and enforces debt." More to the point, Clover correctly claims that "we must also note immediately that the outcome here—a paper claim on future income put to the fire—is business as usual for capitalist crises. Generally, capital handles this itself."[96] This is true: capital regularly writes down its own value; it likewise regularly inflates its own value as well. Why join the process? Clover mounts his criticism at the level of efficaciousness. In doing so, his language matches that of Gokey as well as the language both artists and critics use to discuss the uniqueness of socially engaged art.

Gokey is a heavily indebted artist with a background in critical theory from the European Graduate School who underwent what he called an experience of "being born again" through the event Occupy Wall Street. After the "wild creativity" of Occupy, Gokey notes, much artwork "seemed bloodless and boring. Why go back to it? These works felt like playacting our desires. But in [Zuccotti] park we could actually realize and live them."[97] Gokey introduces here the question of efficaciousness that I too have used to contextualize contemporary socially engaged art. Such art not only makes a demand but moves toward its realization. Gokey asks, "Can [artists] move away from the representational realm?"[98] For him, Rolling Jubilee moved from representation to action: debt was represented, but it also was transformed and ultimately abolished.

Gokey's art-oriented desire to leave the world of representation and enter that of realization and living is not new. Rather, such an aim has been the calling card of the avant-garde for one hundred years. But it is here that we may also refine that categorical impulse by turning again to the work of John Roberts, who redefines the avant-garde through the relation between capital and labor. He suggests that "the avant-garde is the recurring name we give to the conflict between free artistic labour and capital."[99] I would then specify and refine Roberts's claim: the avant-garde of Rolling Jubilee is the conflict between the lack of student wage and the fact that to counter that lack requires intensifying decommodified labor. Whether that intensification is interpreted as a critique of capital or as a mimicking of capital becomes the site of contest. Clover calls their actions a form of mimicry—Rolling Jubilee did what capital always does. Gokey understands these same actions as "leaving the realm of representation" to enact a difference.

To consider Gokey's celebration and Clover's dismissal of Rolling Jubilee, one has to delimit what constitutes efficaciousness—When does one actually leave the field of representation and enter the field of causality? This question goes to the very heart of the category of the aesthetic. Today's socially engaged art defines itself through its interventionist aims; it asks to be adjudicated in the realm of the practical, not the formal. Thus Clover contends that in the realm of the practical, the radical devaluation of debt is not so radical. To this, several Strike Debt organizers, including Andrew Ross, have countered that the event in itself is not radical, but the symbolic import of the event might produce a sense of radical possibility. Yes, capital regularly inflates and devalues itself, but few members of a nonfinancial class have any sense of that possibility, or of the truly plastic nature of value.[100] Another way of saying this: value already contains a series of representations, and those representations can and must be challenged.

This art, then, might be better said to represent a sense of efficaciousness and to represent the possibility of social causality. In his repositioning of Kant as perfectly compatible with conceptual art, Costello explains that for Kant, "art allows the experience of an idea with a completeness" that could never be encountered in "everyday life."[101] Thus art presents what Kant calls an "aesthetic idea." In Rolling Jubilee that aesthetic idea is the plasticity of value, because value has no internal, only social, coordinates. And Rolling Jubilee did accomplish the communication of that, even if this language was not present in Gokey's or others' explanations of the project. I cited in the introduction Kant's famous claim that an aesthetic experience produces a sense of "purposefulness without purpose." That is a retired idea, but it still designates something unique to art. In socially engaged art, the sense still overdetermines the purpose, but the purpose also transforms the sense.

Conclusion

Like many collectives, whether artist or activist, Strike Debt disbanded after several years. Before it did so, however, it produced—in addition to Rolling Jubilee—the collectively written and freely available *Debt Resistors' Operations Manual*.[102] Some of its former members, Gokey included, continue to work on the idea of a "debtors' union" in which resistance to loan repayment would take a collective form. A debtors' union brings us full circle, as it were, to the earliest concerns of this chapter: the transformation of student demands for a wage into student refusals to repay what they were offered in exchange for that wage, a loan. In forming a "debtors' union," Gokey and his collaborators make an argument for a structural relation between debt and labor, an argument that perhaps sees debt as a kind of labor, one that not only does not offer payment but also extracts payment. Thus I have understood these particular debts as a form of decommodified labor.

As both Thornton's and Gokey's work exemplifies, without access to a student wage, art school becomes in part an experience of being trained as a de-commodified laborer, and once so trained, one then uses that training in the service of critique, what used to be called "institutional critique." Yet now the object of critique has itself been transformed; the institutional target is not the museum but various sites in which education and finance seamlessly support each other. "Debt as medium" offers a critique of both. But "debt as medium" also insists that medium has heretofore been a theorization lacking, no matter how expanded its field of possibility has become. More interesting still is the claim to emerge from both Gokey's and Thornton's work: the postmedium condition is the postwage condition. With the emergence of both, critics must reconsider some of the basic categories associated with the aesthetic that have emerged alongside of wage labor. The conceptual difficulty is that those terms—"purpose," "medium," "autonomy"—have not always been associated with wage labor. It is to the credit of Thornton and Gokey that those connections become visible.

Institutions as Art

The Collective Forms of Decommodified Labor

"If artists want to survive in a corporate capitalist society,
they must organize themselves externally."
—THEODOR ADORNO, *Aesthetic Theory*

In 2014, the artist-run institution BFAMFAPhD, founded by Caroline Woolard, released the publication *Artists Report Back*. The report concerned with
how artists function as professionals, including how they pay rent, how they
pay back loans, how they obtain supplies—in short, how their professional
lives as artists are sustainable and how they make do when such a life becomes
circumscribed. Perhaps the most relevant of the group's findings for my own
study is their claim that while there are over 2 million arts graduates in the
United States (there are more artists, the group claims, than there are doc-
tors and lawyers combined), only 8 percent of those artists—some 180,000
people—make a living from their art (figure 2.1). How, the group wondered,
can one sustain a career as a professional artist if one cannot make a living
through the remuneration of one's artistic labor, particularly if one has paid to
train as an artist? If the increasing number of conferences, calls, and directed
residencies is any indication, one answer seems to lay in the collectivization
of artistic labor through artist-run institutions.[1] In this chapter I read the
works of Woolard and Renzo Martens, both of whom have created their own
institutions for other artists as their art in an attempt to redress the decommodification of artistic labor.

Artists Report Back located what are essentially two categories of art graduates. The first group, the majority, functions professionally as artists through
a network of nonwaged concessions: artist residencies, museum sponsorships,
access to university-based facilities, self-created artistic communities, commu-

nity centers, and so on. The second group, which is much smaller, comprises those who do in fact make a living through the sale of their artistic labor. This group predominately includes musicians, photographers, and filmmakers, all of whom probably sell their labor through vocational channels. The striking irony to emerge from *Artists Report Back* is found in the fact that artists trained in art school, artists professionalized qua artists, are probably unable to live off their artistic labor, whereas artists not trained as such were better able to support themselves via their craft. That irony is amplified by the likely art school debt that, as we saw in the previous chapter, often comes as a consequence of arts professionalization.[2] Furthermore, the report included demographic analyses of race, class, and gender: more women and people of color attend art school than are represented in the general population, but fewer of those groups than represented in the general population will make a living from their art.[3]

BFAMFA PhD's results in *Artists Report Back* empirically amplify the theory undergirding my book: that artists often function outside of the wage system in their specific work as artists. The accuracy of this claim increases in the fine arts, and indeed in socially engaged art in particular, which itself has a higher percentage of women artists. Many scholars have made the claim about the wagelessness of art as a generic category, if without the data to support it. John Roberts plainly says: "Artists are not wage laborers." Dave Beech contends that "it is clear that artists are exceptional to the wage structure." Artist and theorist Anton Vidokle's argument in "Art without Market" is rather eponymous. He argues in a slightly different idiom that "art is not a profession."[4] No less an observer than Karl Marx claims that artworks are not included in his study of capitalism for they are "of a special nature." My book both assumes that "special nature" of art to the wage and asks how and why the relation between the two has been transformed and represented in our economic present. And while critics have long made such claims about art's exceptional status to the wage structure, two features of this contemporary discourse have been updated and deserve attention. First, artists themselves are now making such claims and incorporating those claims into their art. This fact is something that critics, including some of our best on the topic of art and economy—John Roberts and Dave Beech in particular—have not addressed. John Roberts suggests art should be understood to participate in "second economy"; Beech suggests that art is structured by a process he calls "commodification without commodification," in which art is not made as a commodity but sometimes is sold as such.[5] What neither Beech nor Roberts attends to, however, is the manner in which

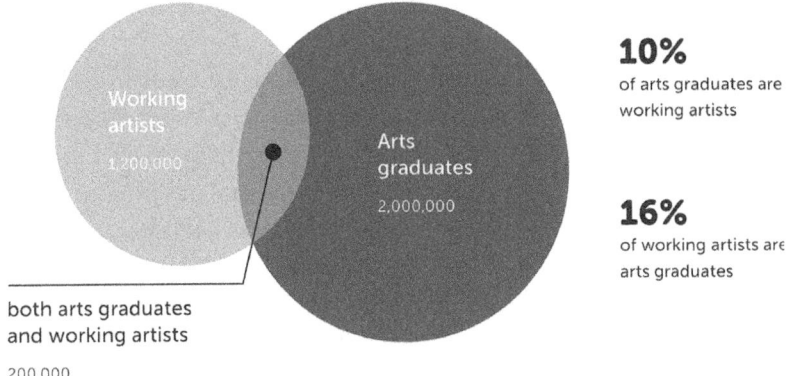

10%
of arts graduates are
working artists

16%
of working artists are
arts graduates

2.1 *Artists Report Back.* Courtesy of Caroline Woolard.

such economic processes are not only the social conditions under which art is often produced; rather, these economic limits become both productive possibilities and heuristic devices in their own right. Art produced without wages must be read, in part, through its wagelessness.

Art has long been positioned as independent of the world of goods and labors, of the world of commodification—a separation that, as we saw in this book's introduction, constitutes "the aesthetic." This separation undergirds art's "autonomy."[6] Yet, as we saw in the previous chapter, oppositional independence often belies a connection, and the institution of art history has been entangled with the wage form.

Capitalism hides the value of labor through the wage, which comes to assume the seeming totality of labor's value. Marx's own understanding of how and when labor is perceptible suggests that the wage may be a heuristic form. He writes, "In respect to the phenomenal form [of] 'value and price of labour,' or 'wages,' as contrasted with the essential relation manifested therein, viz., the value and price of labour-power, the same difference holds that holds in respect to all phenomena and their hidden substratum. The former appear directly and spontaneously as current modes of thought; the latter must first be discovered by science."[7] One must begin, not end, with the wage.

Once we move past the phenomenal form to the essential relations of wage labor—with all of its compromises, dependencies, and exploitations—the independence of the institution of art is threatened. Conversely, the structures of our capitalist economy make labor power in its commodified form difficult to see and, according to Peter Bürger, provide art as a compensation for that loss of sight. One can't see the economy, but one can see art. Thus the institution of art, oppositional to but entangled with the wage form, is endowed with the possibility of critique.

Decommodified labor in art designates a similar if more local struggle over art's potential emancipatory possibilities, the realization of which requires a confrontation with labor's unfreedom. Without a wage to which it is counterposed, it becomes difficult to say what, precisely, art is independent of. Yet those changed coordinates of aesthetic disinterestedness do free art to occupy a place that is not only "interested" but insistent, demanding, organized. Indeed, this is the precise tone of the work with which I ended the previous chapter. When, for example, Thomas Gokey explained that funding for Strike Debt's Rolling Jubilee would be easier to solicit if the event were understood as "art" as opposed to "politics," he was drawing precisely on an understanding of art as a separate sphere of social activity. At the same time, he was claiming that the separate sphere of art would no longer be "autonomous," or "critical," but would move toward institutionalizing new economic possibilities; Gokey envisioned a debtors' union emerging from the Rolling Jubilee.

It is by now a common enough historical narrative to place socially engaged art after institutional critique, a dating that relies on the assumption that, in David Joselit's words, "Institutional Critique, as we know it, is obsolete."[8] Joselit's is a claim that is both true and incomplete, and what I want to do in this chapter is examine how certain artists' historicization of their own and other artists' decommodified artistic labor has organized a particular aspect of the movement from institutional critique to socially engaged art.[9] While the art produced through institutional critique offered critical assessments of the museum, the gallery, their financing, their ties to American imperialism, and the race, gender, and class politics that subtend the foregoing, institutional critique largely did not critique *the wage*.[10] That is, it did not critique the fact that many artists are not paid for their labor and that we live in a system in which social reproduction is only possible through labor's remuneration.

That omission has begun to change. At the height of the 2008 global credit crisis, the artist group Temporary Services staged a national conversation called "Art Work," devoted to art and labor. The organization W.A.G.E. (Working Artists for a Greater Economy) now makes demands for wage rates and work standards for arts. But neither of these groups articulates demands for wages *as* art. Indeed, W.A.G.E. states, "W.A.G.E. is made up of practicing artists, but we are not an art collective and our work is not art. We are an activist and advocacy group. Our participation is never in the capacity of being artists."[11]

Woolard and Martens have inherited the mantle of institutional critique and enjoined it to their own understandings of the decommodification of artistic labor. And they have done so through the construction of new *institutions*, a crucial term that, in this chapter, will mediate the aesthetic, the historical, and the practical. Caroline Woolard uses the term "institution" to describe many of her collaborative, long-term practices and installations, whereas Renzo Martens uses the term "institute" to name his ongoing agitation for artists' wages in Congo. Tarrying with when and how to move beyond institutional critique, these artists quite consciously engage in forms of institutional elaboration. They construct what we might call "institutions as art." And as different as these artists and their projects are, their respective institutions have as their foundation the question of how artists might continue to make work outside of the wage form or whether they must organize themselves and fight for inclusion in the wage, as this chapter's epigraph from Adorno suggests that they must do: "If artists want to survive in a corporate capitalist society, they must organize themselves externally."[12] The previous chapter addressed how artists respond to decommodification at the level of the individual work. This chapter examines artists who quite consciously construct durational institutions. Without secure access to a wage, these artists have developed their own institutions to address their own and other artists' precarity. Why, I ask, have artists turned from institutional critique to institutional elaboration and how, as a result, have we come to understand certain institutions as art?

"Something has to come after Institutional Critique," artist Caroline Woolard has said. "And something has to be possible other than ironic institutions," she insists.[13] Such an "afterness" and otherness of artist-run institutions in the wake of institutional critique has been given a variety of names by critics. There is the "counter-institution," so named by Yates McKee; there is "institutional detournement," a term proposed by T. J. Demos; the "anti-institution" is Tom Finkelpearl's term for a similar insistence[14]; David Joselit speaks of a turn toward "institutional responsibility" in his discussion of the artist-run Orchard Gallery; Chris Gilbert notes that Anglo-American collectivism often takes what he calls an "institutional form."[15] In each term we may locate a remainder of the power of both institutional critique and something retrievable from the institution itself. The institution persists, it outlasts any individual, it embodies a historical memory. Perhaps curator Maria Lind best captures the spirit of this kind of work with her term, "constructive institutional critique," itself similar to Claire Doherty's claim of a "new institutionalism" now present in contemporary art.[16]

Indeed, the past ten years have seen a flourishing of actual artistic institutions as well as considerations of them. What both distinguishes Woolard's and Martens's work and places them on a continuum with institutional critique is that their institutions are centered on the problem of arts production—that's the continuity—but specifically, they isolate the problem of decommodified artistic labor, which is the distinction. The works I read in this chapter are durational in that they are ongoing and that they have transpired over a matter of years and continue to do so; Renzo Martens jokes about a series of Soviet-style "five-year plans" for his Institute for Human Activities. These works attempt to reclaim duration as it has been embodied in labor; "what the worker sells is time," reminds Harry Braverman.[17] But these decommodifed workers do not sell their time; rather, they possess time, and it is that resource that will mold and contour the shape of the institutions they construct. The relation of these works to duration echoes Peter Frase's description of the benefits of decommodification. Highlighting the emancipatory sense of the word as Gøsta Esping-Andersen originally used it, Frase writes, "we can think of the de-commodifying welfare state as giving people a *choice* about whether or not to commodify their labor . . . . The choice that is involved here is not merely about income. It ultimately comes down to how we want to organize our time, and how we want to structure our relations with other people."[18]

If socially engaged art is that which seeks to ameliorate restrictive social conditions, then perhaps the aesthetic reflexivity to be found in the institution-building work of Woolard and Martens is best located in how these artists seek to change their own working lives and those of other artists. In Woolard's work there is no negation, no irony, no moment of "institutional detournment"; rather there is a commitment to endurance. Her work asks us to question whether art that remains decommodified may remain recognized as art. In Martens's work there is an irony, a negation, and that happens through the explicit discourses of price, entrepreneurship, and creativity as they circulate through art's various institutions unevenly across global space. His work asks us to follow him from a place of wagelessness to wage*ful*ness. In this chapter, then, I want to suggest that we instead think about "institutional reflexivity," the manner in which the institution as a kind of art returns the ability to understand how decommodifed artistic labor frames the work of the art institution itself.

Caroline Woolard's Institutions as Art

Artists Report Back

An international network of schools in which anyone may take classes by bartering with teachers, in which any collective may start a branch in their own town or city; a barter network for artists to offer and receive skills, materials, and labor; a café installed at the Museum of Modern Art where visitors are invited to invent the value of their own currency on notes provided and to use this currency to purchase tea; a real estate investment cooperative that aims to remove land from market-based circulation and place it in a community land trust thus precluding its future sale. Each of these works is a project of the artist Caroline Woolard and a rotating cast of interdisciplinary collaborators, and in each we notice a particular orientation toward the construction of value: how we value, why we value, and for whom. The first, Trade School, conflates the act of trading with the language of craft but also with the commodification of education; the second, OurGoods, makes a public claim to utility in the face of the more common assignation of value to the individual possession of talent; and the third, Exchange Café, asks its visitors to reimagine the act of using money within the defining experience of a museum-based café, itself so often the place to find respite from whatever artwork-viewing opportunities the museum has on offer; and, finally the Real Estate Investment Cooperative aims to suspend the commodification of a piece of urban land.[19]

These collaborative creations have different members over the course of their institutional lives, but what they each have in common is Woolard herself. Beginning with the 2007–8 credit crisis, which coincided with Woolard's graduation from the once–tuition-free art school Cooper Union, Woolard began constructing what she now understands specifically as "institutions," what I will call throughout this chapter "institutions as art." Woolard's institutions comprise shifting coalitions of artists who devote themselves both to making art and to making it possible for other artists to make art. For Woolard, the institution concretizes and navigates a space more capacious than the individual—thus institutions as art mitigate against being reduced to the artist's ego, to the artist's oeuvre, or to some potential canonical assignment; rather, the institution remains open to change but also simply remains as a form of duration. Yet the institution as art must avoid the well-known temptation of focusing on its own duration over the ends it supposedly serves. According to Woolard, if an institution can maintain that nuanced space, it may exist as both an art form and as a social form for artists.

Each of the above "institutions as art" might be seen as an answer to a question about how artists can sustain their practice in an age of decommodified labor. Where do artists go after school, if they want to continue their education? They go to Trade School, that is, they learn to continue their own schooling through nonmonetary exchange. How do artists make artwork after being displaced from their studios, and if they don't have the resources that art school had afforded them? They use OurGoods to find a network of like-minded practitioners with whom to exchange skills and materials, time and space. Where should artists work and where should they practice? They might join the Real Estate Investment Cooperative in an attempt to create permanently affordable space or to find others with whom to share a space. What do they do when they realize that their art education has seemingly no better prepared them to be a working artist than had they not gone to art school, particularly if they are a woman or a person of color? They might join BFAMFA PhD, a group that investigates the political economy of arts education and arts professionalization.

Taken together, these questions continue an investigation into the transformation of artwork and artists' work under conditions of the decommodification of their artistic labor. If decommodification allows for the removal of land, labor, or money from market-based circulation, then many artists, socially engaged or not, are already working within its historical ambit. Like deindustrialization, decommodification moves in a cyclical fashion, and for labor to be decommodified it must first have been commodified. Our current moment of the decommodification of artistic labor follows, as both Sharon Zukin and Donna M. Binkiewicz have detailed, a 1950–60s expansion of "artists' ability to claim their art as a career" through the proliferation artist's agencies, granting bodies, foundations, universities' arts programs, and so on. This was an economic moment when, as Binkiewicz recounts, New York Senator Jacob Javits could suggest that "since the principle of government subsidy . . . [is] well established with many industries . . . why could this same principle not be applied to the arts?"[20] And yet, simultaneously with this flourishing of an artistic life as a possible professional life, a foreshortened labor market for artists appeared on the horizon. Zukin notes that by 1963 the U.S. Labor Department was already producing "gloomy projections" about art-based employment. Furthermore, she qualifies the kind of workers sociologists and government officials believed artistic work would engender: "Expanding jobs in the arts could be expected to produce a fairly amorphous and relatively quiescent labor force."[21]

Woolard's practice, including her work on *Artists Report Back*, might be understood as a contemporary, artistic response to the kind of social history of the professionalizing and commodifying art world that Zukin and Binkiewicz provide. In their respective histories, the Kennedy administration inaugurates the National Endowment for the Arts; in Woolard's public presentations of the barter network OurGoods, she notes the fiscal decimation of that agency. In Zukin's history, the federal government expands arts funding through universities in the form of student grants; in *Artists Report Back*, funding sources are understood to have been converted from grants to loans. After school, artistic careers are still possible in universities, but those careers will be restricted to a few, while the majority who attempt them will become part of the contingent academic labor force. Such facts must be read as a reminder that much as commodification famously delivers what Marx calls the "double freedom" of a waged life—you're *free* to sell your labor to whomever you choose; you *have* to sell your labor—so does decommodification: you're free *not* to sell your labor; you *can't* sell it. The works I examined in the previous chapter were highly critical of such a situation; the works I examine in this chapter are more nuanced and pragmatic, and the tenor of their responses derives in part from their institutional forms. Indeed, they insist that artists will keep working, even without a wage; that artists refuse not to work; that even as they are deprofessionalized, they will remain professionals.

I began this chapter with the Woolard-founded institution BFAMFAPhD's publication *Artists Report Back*. And while I used the group's data, I did not consider its presentation and formal instantiation, which is *institutional* in more ways than one. Nor did I consider its artistic forerunners, among whom Art & Language figure prominently.[22] As a colloquial expression, the adjective "institutional" denotes a kind of unspecific blandness, a soporific consistency of shape, color, tone, and texture. The airport lounge, the dentist's office, the bank lobby, all places of impersonal yet communal waiting that might be called "institutional." Of course, in arts discourse, "institution/al" resonates with the art movement of the 1960s to the 1990s, institutional critique. BFAMFAPhD's report may easily be conceived of within both traditions: it critiques the institution of arts education and does so institutionally. Yet it also exemplifies why Maria Lind differentiates a new genre that she calls "constructive institutional critique," in which the critique suggests realizable amendments. *Artists Report Back*, for example, includes recommendations to render artists' funding and wages more equitable between races and genders; it includes resources for artists to use as they attempt their own forms of social reproduction. It invites its readers to join the group, itself an institution.

Artists have long built institutions, of course. Some have been real entities (Black Mountain College); others fictive, part of an artwork (Department of Eagles); some serious (Printed Matter and UBU Web); others an ironic combination of the foregoing (the Bruce High Quality Foundation). But these institutions have largely been understood as adjuncts to their proper business of facilitating the artwork that might derive from them or circulate through them—what Gilbert differentiates between the collective, those who make work together, and the institution, in which artists pursue their own projects but advocate for each other. What is so timely and distinctive about Woolard's practice is that, for her, the institution *is* the artwork. She forms, recruits, establishes, and then lets circulate and develop different institutions as art. I want to argue that such an understanding both results from and is made possible by the decommodification of artistic labor. I explore how such institutions develop, how they look, how they sound, how they exist in time and space, as well as what these institutions attempt to do and what they represent themselves as doing.

BFAMFA PhD's *Artists Report Back* may be downloaded from their website. It has been cited by popular art publications, including *Hyperallergic*, and by government entities and funding bodies: author and cultural policy director of New York City, Tom Finkelpearl, has given Woolard a platform to speak from about the report and so has the National Endowment of the Arts, inviting Woolard to deliver a keynote address on the occasion of the agency's fiftieth anniversary.[23] But *Artists Report Back* has additionally been shown as an installation. On view in 2014 at the Brooklyn Museum's *Crossing Brooklyn*, the installation was presented as a series of wall-mounted plaques alongside a six-minute video.[24] Both the video and etched plexiglass plaques contain numerical and text-based information derived from the report's finding.

"What is a work of art in the age of $120,000 art degrees?" one plaque asks. This question, a recognizable translation of the Benjaminian problem of the status of a work of art into a new idiom, suggests an answer in its very mode of presentation. The work of art in the age of the six-figure art degree will present as semicorporate, office-oriented, more at place in a white-collar workplace lobby than a museum. A plexiglass plaque affixed to the museum wall, its presentation is institutional to an exaggerated degree. The series of plaques that adorn the long wall mimic the many plaques any museum itself uses to indicate donations, provide histories, or even organize the viewer in museum space. Other of the *Artists Report Back* plaques offer statements on the basis of census research: "There are more artists than lawyers, doctors and police officers in this country." Still others suggest a course of activist transformation: "What might we, 1,827,087 [art] graduates since 1987, do together?" That final question doubles as an invitation: spectators may become participants by joining the group.

If popular appraisals provide any indication, the installation form of *Artists Report Back* found few takers. The *New Yorker*'s Peter Schjeldahl began his review by offering his own genealogy of how socially engaged art arrived on the historical scene: "[*Crossing Brooklyn*'s] . . . curators shun the abstract painting and portable sculpture that pervade [Brooklyn's] gallery scene [and instead] promote institution-dependent installation, performance, and conceptual work, including the 'community practice' that tends to occur when artists live within walking distance of poor people."[25] Of course, this type of sentiment, that working artists may be influenced through their proximity to "poor people" but do not themselves constitute "poor people," evidences exactly the kind of perceived common sense that BFAMFA PhD's report attempts to interrupt. What is the difference, precisely, between an artist and a "poor" person? Schjeldahl does not explicate what grounds his distinction, but we may surmise that he believes it is something akin to what Pierre Bourdieu famously called "cultural capital."[26] "Poor people" never choose their poverty nor do they receive social dividends from it. But anyone who chooses to be an artist could have chosen otherwise, and even if her wages are poverty level, the artist is not seen by social structures as spiritually "poor" (unwilling or unable to work, intellectually depressed, socially disorganized, etc.). Rather, she is feted at such places as the Brooklyn Museum, and if she is lucky, she will receive "wage-like" recognition in the pages of the *New Yorker*. Thus she comes to possess "cultural capital," something of cultural value that may be parlayed into other forms of cultural value.

Several problematic assumptions exist here on the part of both Schjeldahl and Bourdieu. For the moment, it will be sufficient to use Schjeldahl's language of "poor people" to engage the common retort to my theory of decommodified labor in the arts: Don't artists receive cultural capital, even if not a wage? And thus: How can their labor be understood as decommodified if they receive wage-like payment in the form of cultural capital? Although Bourdieu's notion of "cultural capital" is often cited in discussions of "cultural industries" and "cultural economies," we must realize that it is not a theory of capital in the classically political economic use of the term around which my book is structured. It's not simply that one can't pay rent or buy food with cultural capital (although one can't), but rather that what is so unique and powerful about Marx's theory of capital—that capital is a social relationship of exploitation that often appears as one of equal exchange—is omitted from Bourdieu's notion.[27] Capital for Bourdieu functions as something similar to recognition and affirmation: there is no way to explain within his theory why certain people accrue cultural capital and others do not, aside from the fact that those who have real capital also have cultural capital. And once one possesses any kind of capital, we know the path to accruing more capital is that much easier.

Such claims are no doubt true, but they have very little to offer by way of a theory of how labor circulates as a commodity or why it fails to do so. Perhaps more to the point, *Artists Report Back* does not track cultural capital. Schjeldahl's review concludes by asserting that "the collective BFAMFAPhD spreads a homeopathic wet blanket on the show's high spirits with statistical documentation of the hard lots of current graduates—the staggering number of artists, debt burdens, iffy prospects." The *New York Times* hinted at the installation's "didacticism," whereas the *Wall Street Journal*'s Peter Plagens commented: "A row of elegant plaques floating off the wall, casts in shadow bullet points complaint[s] about how much it costs to become an artist, is the contribution of a group calling itself BFAMFAPhD . . . .The complaint is justified economically, but visually it goes right to the mental circular file."[28]

Artists Report Back's jarring division between the economic and the visual is certainly deserving of criticism. This work, especially in the context of the show's other work, does appear flat, didactic, and overly pedagogical, as the group's name, BFAMFAPhD, would seem to foretell. Its duration, its inability to expand in size and shape as a result of viewer response, a kind of refusal to distinguish the collective's art work from the collective itself—each of these components fits awkwardly into a museum or gallery space. At the same time, the traditions of closely reading an individual piece, of aesthetics as a discourse, are themselves challenged by socially engaged work such as Woolard's. John Roberts's understanding of how such work moves in and out of a museum setting is apt. He contends that "if [this type of] work ends up in a museum . . . this is primarily as a means of 'reporting' back to the art world on what has been going on beyond its remit."[29] Roberts's sentiment certainly rings true for *Artists Report Back*.

These are the precise reasons that Shannon Jackson has encouraged critics of socially engaged art to reorganize the boundaries of the art object well beyond the "expanded field." The terminology on which her discussion pivots, as we saw briefly in the last chapter, is that of "autonomy." Social practice works such as Woolard's should be understood, Jackson suggests, as a "de-autonomizing of the artistic event." Jackson then notes, however, that "de-autonomizing" is not the equivalent of "de-aestheticizing."[30] "Rather," she explains, "the de-autonomizing of the artistic event is itself an artful structure, more or less self-consciously creating an inter-medial form that would subtly challenge the lines where the art object ends and the world begins. It is to make art from not despite contingency."[31] Jackson's reading of socially engaged art insists that "questions of aesthetic autonomy gain an acute urgency when we consider what it means to sustain not only the life of art, but also the lives of artists."[32]

Her line of argument moves us in the right direction by attempting to introduce a new language for interpreting socially engaged art, one that insists that such art is categorically different from community service or social work, the terms some critics have used to dismiss it. Thus her book's title: *Social Works*. But Jackson doesn't quite substantiate the train of thought because she stops short of a consideration of labor as a concept, preferring instead metaphors of mutuality and interdependence in the production and maintenance of contemporary art. Her terminology of "support," "contingency," and "artists' lives" introduces a certain materiality that hints at the claim, not of autonomy's opposite, heteronomy, but rather of a bypassing of this vocabulary in favor of one which reveals a material co-constitution between the art practice and the social practice.

We see a different conceptual reorganization of art's autonomy from Brown and Roberts, both of whom see a political and indeed categorical virtue in asserting some autonomous space for producing and circulating art, for generating and conveying meaning. For Brown, it is the possibility of a claim of autonomy that distinguishes art from a commodity. In an age of the real subsumption of labor to capital, he argues, that distinction has political and social importance. Yet it is necessary to note the type of art that Brown focuses on: photography, sculpture, popular music, and film. People might confuse the difference between art and commodity for a hit song or a commercial photo, but they probably won't do so for much socially engaged art. Rather, the ontological confusion in that case would probably be between art and "community practice," art and "social work." Woolard's works, particularly the two we turn to next, are a case in point. The constitution of autonomy has changed as the economy has changed; both Brown and Roberts agree on that point.

For Brown it becomes a political assertion. For Roberts, "autonomy is a social relation" that must "be won anew from the diffuse, digitalized, temporalized character of contemporary art." And it must be won, for autonomy "allows for a defence of art against reductively heteronomous notions of art as social practice, but from within the space of art as social practice."[33] Roberts here introduces reasonable worries of a possible horizontal art-oriented Deleuzianism in which all practices might be art practices and should be interpreted through their own local logics (something we will return to in the next chapter).

Yet another way to carve out some space between the autonomous and heteronomous, in Roberts's Adornian language—between market and nonmarket, in Brown's neoliberal language—is to examine the role of decommodified labor, that labor which cannot circulate as a commodity. This concept provides a different articulation of the liminal space between the polarities in question while keeping the focus on a historically variable commodity, the labor commodity. Socially engaged artworks may be read through decommodified labor, and when socially engaged artworks bring in other practices, those practices too become subject to decommodification. Consider the use of statistics and numerical data, of the social-scientific presentation of *Artists Report Back* as a form of both data and labor. Whereas early examples of institutional critique, such as Hans Haacke's *MoMA Poll 1970*, played with similar forms of data, none of the attendant irony is present in *Artists Report Back*. In Haacke's poll, for example, whoever appears at the museum constitutes the sample population of his study. In contrast, *Artists Report Back* carefully notes that it has made use of the "US Census Bureau 2012 American Community Survey—Public Use Microdata Sample." Of course, BFAMFAPhD is not the first collective to make or to solicit data-specific claims in a museum space. Not only Haacke's *MoMA Poll 1970* but the more recent and ongoing (1995 to the present) collective, the Guerrilla Girls, has made data-based art. Think of some of their museum-directed billboards, one of which, for example, asks, "Do Women Have to be Naked to Get into the Met Museum?" only to answer that "less than 5% of artists in the Modern section are women but 85% of the nudes are female." The Guerrilla Girls are certainly concerned with how institutions (museums, arts funding agencies, and so on) affect artists, but with their gorilla masks, their global anonymity, their theatrical presentation of both themselves and their data, we would hardly characterize their aesthetic as institutional or unplayful.

Artists Report Back's empiricism eludes easy categorization. We realize that Hal Foster's early and prescient worry about the socially engaged "artist as ethnographer" could also be construed as a worry about the artist as social scientist generally. The ethnographer and the social scientist present their findings with a positivist bent.[34] In an incisive critique of some of the problems that would become generic to socially engaged art, Foster writes that in "new site-specific [community] work . . . values like authenticity, originality, and singularity, banished under critical taboo from postmodernist art, return as properties of the site, neighborhood, or community engaged by the artist."[35] As an installation, *Artists Report Back* exemplifies Foster's worries. Yet the "community" engaged and criticized from a social-scientific perspective is the community of would-be arts professionals, the very community out of which BFAMFAPhD emerges. The ethnographic lens is turned on itself, as it were.

Perhaps more to the point is Claire Bishop's contention that, "from a disciplinary perspective, any art engaging with society and the people in it demands a methodological reading that is, at least in part, sociological . . . an analysis of this art must necessarily engage with concepts that have traditionally had more currency within the social sciences than in the humanities: community, society, empowerment, agency."[36] Bishop rightly notes how we should approach such art but does not indicate what the specific parameters of such criticism should be. Are art critics now expected to develop statistical, demographic, and epidemiological forms of literacy? How expanded has the expanded field become? How did the artist's manifesto come to resemble a peer-reviewed social-scientific study?

In the statistics on view in *Artists Report Back*, working artists are divided into the usual demographic categories of income, race, age, and gender, as well as a category we seldom see in such data: medium specificity, including sculpture, photography, video, painting, and so on. *Artists Report Back* does indeed contain a "methodology" section and intimates that it might be read as an academic text. In providing a methodology section, the installation seems to rise to that challenge set out by Bishop.

The data's categorical constraints do not invite questioning, which renders such data rather positivistic. After enumerating the number of arts graduates (almost 2 million since the mid-1980s), the text asks, "What might we do together?" but the conservatism of the presentation seems to constrain what the range of answers might be. One is tempted to say, "We might produce more data." This boundedness presents itself in other parts of the report, too. The "methodology" section, for example, reproduces one of the chief failings of social science: it does not answer the most basic, analytic question of *why* this method was selected, but only the descriptive question of *what* constitutes this method.

Mostly oriented toward artists' wages, or lack thereof, the empirical data contained in the installation is certainly germane to our discussion. But what is more germane, perhaps, is the question of why an artist group would claim the mantle of information and why it would turn to such data production and collection. First, a certain irony is found in the data, which of course is time- and resource-intensive to produce. What we are led to understand, then, is that to produce this report, these artists had to work both as and with statisticians and demographers. This is the same organization of decommodified artistic labor we encountered in the last chapter in our reading of Strike Debt's Rolling Jubilee. Working without compensation as artists-cum-statisticians, these artists produce data about their own inability to work as artists. This social-scientific approach might be seen as a response to the incorporation of arts within the university; also it may be seen as the artist taking on the job of the statistician or demographer, but *as art* and *unpaid*. How different, though, this artwork appears from Bryan-Wilson's "occupational realism" in which labor itself is in need of further definition as a category.

Such work necessarily includes a labor component: these artists have become statisticians, social scientists, demographers, and all the while they are unpaid. Thus decommodified artistic labor both represents and in turn decommodifies other forms of labor. This claim should be seen as the logical conclusion of Bishop's argument: if art uses other academic fields, it must be measured by other academic fields. Through the lens of decommodified labor we now understand: if artists labor in other fields, other fields become sites of decommodified artistic labor.

OurGoods and Trade School

What I claim is the need for artists to secure their own forms of labor exchange outside of the strictures of the art institutions of the waged world, Woolard sees as "a need to make both artistic objects and an institutional context in which those objects can meaningfully circulate," because artists' lack of a wage will limit their ability to circulate in formal art spaces.[37] When Woolard graduated from the Cooper Union with her own Bachelor of Fine Arts degree, she emerged into the 2007–8 credit crisis and subsequent "Great Recession." She supported herself by continuing to work at Cooper Union and then by collecting unemployment, an allowance she lists on her CV under "grants and funding sources." It is fitting that being compensated by the government for not working provided the time, space, and the decommodified freedom to develop two institutions that both respond to and allow for a (partially) decommodified artistic practice. And it is more fitting still that Woolard conceives of her own decision not to pursue an Master of Fine Arts but rather to develop her own artist-run institutions of education and resource sharing as themselves crucial parts of her practice.

OurGoods and Trade School are two barter-based networks that Woolard organized with collaborators who included grant writers, computer programmers, graphic designers, and a range of visual and performing artists. OurGoods is a web-based network for individual barter, whereas Trade School provides a similar web-based network for group barter; groups of students barter for classes with instructors. We might understand the second as an expanded application of the first. Founded in 2009, OurGoods had at its peak nine thousand members, most of whom were based in New York City. Members create a profile detailing what skills and materials they have to offer and what skills and materials they need for their own artistic projects. They communicate how any barter will be incorporated into their project or practice. "I need translation services for an art poster," one profile might say, for example, or "space for an event." The benefit of a single barter is that one agrees to trade what one has (figure 2.2). The disadvantage is that forms of socially accepted measures of equivalence, time for money, still obtain here as members decide how or whether to trade a higher income-generating and often masculine skill, say web development, for a lower, often feminized one, say childcare. Yet unlike the similar, short run artist-run institution *Time Bank* by Anton Vidokle, OurGoods does not enforce such a form of equivalence, that is, you put in an hour, you get back an hour. Rather, members negotiate these exchanges on their own.

The site does not track the actual barter exchanges to which members agree. Rather, members engage in these exchanges in real time and space, trading messages through the OurGoods portal. This individual correspondence doubles as a limit on how barter is represented in a manner reminiscent of the challenges of performance art and its documentation. Much like a performance never happens the same way twice, barter has an improvisational quality. Unlike performance, however, there are no spectacles here: one doesn't get to watch others barter. To watch, you have to do. Woolard has compared barter acts to storytelling and oral traditions in which the same story produces different effects when told or enacted by different tellers and listeners. I want to follow the project's own literary language and think about how, when read as art, the barter-based transactions facilitated by OurGoods may be seen as a kind of metaphor in that word's historical sense of being a vehicle for conducting meaning.[38] "Metaphor" etymologically breaks down to mean "to carry over"; it denotes a movement in which meaning is transported from one object to another in speech and writing. Barter structures a specific type of metaphor, perhaps akin to what David Halperin calls a practical allegory, in that it is instantiated through activity.[39] The barters performed through OurGoods metaphorize what an other, new economy would look like while simultaneously constituting that other economy. If I barter two hours of my editing skills for one hour of soundtrack-laying ability, our exchange represents a mode of economic transformation. It also constitutes that mode. The representation and its efficaciousness become one.

OurGoods follows the movement that Jackson describes as a transposition from a "discrete notion of the work of art to a process-based notion of the work it takes to make art."[40] Why do artists barter? They barter because they have potential artistic labor but no market in which to sell it. Why else do they barter? Because they need others' potential artistic labor but have no money with which to purchase it. Their labor and consequently their potential to earn a wage have been decommodified, and now each will find another in a scene of decommodification in which the definitional properties of commodification as such—"made by waged labor and sold on the market"—will not be brought to bear. OurGoods instead offers the chance to work for one's self, but not through a conception of the kind of neoliberal self-capitalization that we were introduced to in the last chapter. Rather, one works through a different form of being "a partner in exchange" in which another is required for mutually enhancing but not profit-generating reciprocity.

As a practical metaphor, when read as an artwork, the barters performed through OurGoods avoid the problem Peggy Phelan alerts us to in her trenchant critique of Andrea Fraser's exchange-themed work. Phelan reads Andrea Fraser's video *Untitled*, in which she videotaped herself having sex with a collector, as an all too telling comment on the relation between artistic labor and the potential for its sale. "If I'm going to have to sell it, I might as well sell it," Fraser explained of her artist person.[41] This work, Phelan rightly concludes, disintegrates through an "utter loss of metaphor."[42] The metaphorical space should have been locatable between the two clauses of Fraser's statement: if/then. But there is no "then." Fraser provides only an "if," which is followed by an action: "sell it."

"Selling it" has long been a metaphor of choice for the easy corruptibility

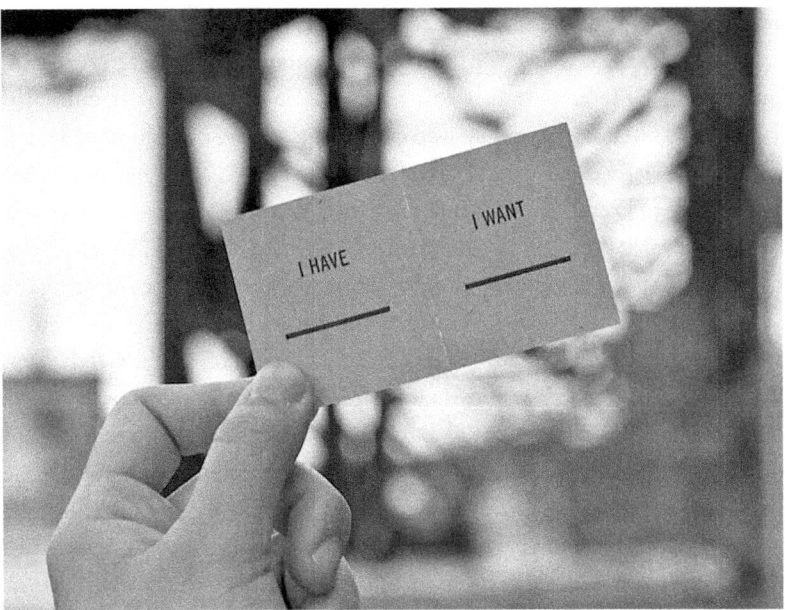

2.2 OurGoods. Courtesy of Caroline Woolard.

and perversity of the artwork in relation to the commodity. Fraser's video was perhaps an overly dramatic attempt to have a final say on the matter, but art's relation to the commodity as a theme in art is not an easily ended topic of discussion. Rather, artists concerned with art's commodity status continue to seek out sites in which to display the proximity between these categories. Think, for example, of Martha Rosler's *Meta-Monumental Garage Sale*, staged at MoMA in 2012. In this installation, spectators purchase others' discarded commodities in a museum setting. Described by MoMA as "a large-scale version of the classic American garage sale," the museum's press notes that "... visitors can browse and buy second-hand goods organized, displayed, and sold by the artist" and that "the installation fills MoMA's Marron Atrium with strange and everyday objects donated by the artist, MoMA staff, and the general public, creating a lively space for exchange between Rosler and her customers as they haggle over prices."[43] The forced intimacy generated out of the contradiction between "priceless" works of art and "worthless," discarded everyday items functions as both the installation's critique and its irony.

Still, other works that are concerned with art's commodity status dramatically refuse the process of "selling it" by connecting money to the anonymizing structure of the global labor obfuscated by the commodity form. Think of a work such as Harrell Fletcher's *Made in India*.[44] Here, Fletcher attempts to trace a particular woven rug back to a particular Indian weaver after a mail order company serendipitously sent him an extra of this $1500 commodity. He ordered one rug and was delivered two, thus setting this durational work in motion. Fletcher's two new rugs, like many textiles, had "made in India" tags affixed to them. Working in conjunction with two galleries, he was able to locate near New Delhi a factory that likely made the rug. Then, venturing to India, partnering with a local arts organization, and documenting the journey as he went, Fletcher "returned" his rug and gave $1500 to an Indian textile worker, Sandeep, with whom he also had lunch. *Made in India* represents artistic labor as well as the division between artistic labor, artisanal labor, and commodified labor globally. A performance full of aesthetic and political compromises, *Made in India* attempts symbolically to undermine these divisions by representing in one time/space a lack of economic hierarchy through the undoing of a global commodity chain. The money, in its form of a developed country's retail price, returns to its ostensibly Indian origin where it takes the form of a wage paid to a worker in that developing country's export-commodity sector, textiles.

These two works, different as they are, offer a sampling of the range of commodity-themed art, its relations to artistic labor and to the sale of both artwork and artist's work. Rosler ironizes the sale—which we know can't happen in the space of a museum—by disavowing the labor. Fletcher, conversely, ironizes the labor—any Indian will do, because they all work for so little— by disavowing the sale. As they become "art," the barters found in OurGoods do not engage this red herring of commodity aesthetics—the sale—because the labors contained in such barters *could not have been sold*. There is no binary or pedagogical reminder of art's troubled but productive commodity status; instead, a set of materialized metaphors works in the trenches of decommodification and doubles as a practice to formalize and describe a new economic space.

The potential trades facilitated by OurGoods may expand ad infinitum, even as each individual trade will never be represented to others and composes a niche economy scaled at two. It was the limitation of the one-to-one scale of OurGoods that laid the foundation for Woolard's next collective, similarly decommodifying institution, Trade School. This web-based platform may be downloaded by any individual or group, can be translated into multiple languages, and has spawned "schools" as local as New York and Indianapolis and as international as Quito and Glasgow. In narrating how the project came to be, Woolard herself makes frequent recourse to the availability of time and space that are one possible result of decommodified labor. Writing in *Social Text*, she explains: "On February 25th to March 1st, 2010, we ran [the first] TradeSchool .... Over the course of 35 days, more than 800 people participated in 76 single session classes .... In exchange for instruction, teachers received everything from running shoes to mixed CDs.... We ran out of time slots for teachers to teach and classes filled up so quickly that we had to turn people away. [Thus we reopened] ... in an empty school, paying rent with the support of charitable donations and running on donated time from 8–20 volunteers."[45]

The converse of "having time" to give, of course, is that such projects "take time" to run—again Negri's "tautological time" seems apt. Barters reclaim the tautological time of real subsumption; Negri asks, "When all life is work, who measures whom?" "We will introduce our own measures," Woolard seems to respond. Both OurGoods and Trade School require time for planning, for engaging, and especially for communicating. Before any given Trade School class, teachers agree with students on what their recompense will be. The institution operates through given time and given space, what we may understand as decommodified time and decommodified space. As of 2015, Woolard estimates that around fifteen thousand students and teachers have participated in the project. Barter remains the currency. Anyone may propose a course (for barter) and anyone may take a course (for barter). Different schools will develop different local cultures; for example, Trade School in Glasgow has a mental health and senior care focus, whereas Trade School in New York is more arts-focused.

For Woolard, the representation and self-constitution of artistic labor should transpire on a plane of some mutually recognized equality. The institution, not reducible to any individual, should enable that equality by providing a platform in which artists can encounter each other through the exchange of their decommodified labor. In that temporal constitution of the barter, there must have been, however brief, a recognition of reciprocity. The point is not to assert that the commodification of labor is bad and its decommodification is good—a fundamentally facile claim—but rather to show the course that labor takes in its various forms in the aesthetic realm. The labors of Woolard's institutions do not assume reified status because they are continually called on to circulate intersubjectively, to be exchanged from one position to the other. Crucially, the focus of the barters remains the relationality of the artistic laborers to each other, not the relationality of the object produced by such labor to the viewer. Here we find ourselves quite close to the claim made by Nicolas Bourriaud in his foundational *Relational Aesthetics*—namely, that what distinguishes socially engaged artwork is that its "substrate is intersubjectivity."[46] Yet that intersubjectivity must itself have both a material and an affective form. We may say that the likely form of that intersubjectivity in socially engaged art derives from the content of its decommodified labor.

In the larger discussion of the divaricated theoretical trajectories of the real subsumption of labor and the neoliberalization of the economy that structures this book, the necessary questions for Woolard's institutions remain: Do they produce value for *others* (real subsumption) and/or do they necessitate that the artist assume the subject position of "entrepreneur of herself" (neoliberalization)? Which is the more appropriate framing of the decommodified labor that structures these artworks? Answering these questions will help us to explore another—namely, the fluid boundary that critics have suggested is the sometimes muddled difference between "socially engaged art" and "socially engaged business," a tension helpfully grouped under the rubric Marina Vishmidt has called "social practice [art] as business model."[47] Vishmidt is concerned that the most successful social practice artists engage in what she memorably calls "shovel-ready" art practices. She quite rightly asks, "Isn't it the case that the [art] practices viewed as most successful [have been] the overtly entrepreneurial ones . . . because they occupied both the community-facing and business-minded ends of the relational [aesthetics] spectrum?" Vishmidt continues on to claim that such art illustrates "how entrepreneurialism and autonomy conjoin in a resolutely post-critical and results-oriented agenda," similar to an NGO or a nonprofit.

To support her claims, Vishmidt provides the example of one of the most well-known, certainly protocanonical, socially engaged artists working today, Theaster Gates. Gates refers to himself as a "hustler" and calls his art practice an "insurgent business"; the *New York Times* has designated him "Chicago's opportunity artist."[48] Consider Gates's *Dorchester Projects* on Chicago's impoverished, mostly black, South Side. Partnering with his employer, the University of Chicago, Gates has built community centers, libraries, a cinema, and the like.[49] Vishmidt writes: "Gates's entrepreneurial outlook—promoting the virtues of labor in social change, preferably the labor of others, while he interfaces with real estate developers, art institutions, and NGOs—is resolutely and unapologetically 'post-political.'"[50]

Some of Vishmidt's criticisms could be applied to OurGoods and Trade School. Indeed, OurGoods and Trade School have not been consistently legible as artworks, but as something more like community partnerships. Woolard herself is more agnostic. During their making she didn't necessarily refer to them as art. Now she understands them as institutions for artists that double as art—what we have called throughout this chapter "institutions as art." One the one hand, Woolard herself explains of OurGoods, "We didn't want to call it a work of art because then people wouldn't use it. They would feel as if we were using them for our own performance."[51] Yet, these works have been presented at canonical institutions of art including the Whitney, MoMA, and the Brooklyn Museum, as well as less canonical but still important venues like Creative Time's summit, *Living as Form*. And many artists who make similar work do call them art, appealing, for example, to Joseph Beuys's notion of "social sculpture" to anchor these kind of works in an art historical trajectory.

Nonetheless, while Woolard herself has been identified as the artist, and the institutions she has helped create have been identified as artworks, Our-Goods and Trade School have—perhaps suspiciously—garnered their most substantial attention from members of the world of so-called social entrepreneurship and the recently anointed "sharing economy." Such a sensibility was on display when OurGoods was awarded a Rockefeller Foundation Cultural Innovation grant, when Levi Strauss and Co. offered to purchase and franchise Trade School, and when the real estate developer Ron Spurga sought to organize a monetization of OurGoods's database of members. The intimacy of an opposition often creates opportunities for radical misidentification, and that was the case when OurGoods's and Trade School's scene of almost totally decommodified labor was interpreted as a site for the possibility of their complete commodification.

So-called sharing economy companies such as Lyft or Airbnb truck in the fantasy of being able to commodify all personal time and space while simultaneously "not working." It's not really "work" to drive someone in your car via Lyft (after all, you're not a taxi driver) or have them sleep in your home via Airbnb (nor are you a hotel proprietor). You're just doing what you would be doing anyway—driving, sleeping, cooking, being in your home, and so on—but now you are "sharing" with others and you are making money while doing so. Here we note one example of how the neoliberal disappearance of the concept of labor takes daily, ideological form: Airbnb and Lyft eagerly suggest that their users' activities, those that make money for the company and the individual through the allotment of time, should not be understood as work.

Woolard's collective projects provide the precise refusal of this logic. While engaged in a barter-based transaction, you're doing what you'd be doing anyway and you're still *not* making money. OurGoods and Trade School insist that such activities are serious, real, professional, even; they become a kind of work but without the wage. With Lyft you set your own schedule, but not your own wage. With Woolard's institutions, you enter into a mutual time/space in which your artistic labor may be recognized and evaluated according to new, if nonwaged, metrics.

These aspects of Woolard's projects finally allow us to make a link to our discussion in the last chapter of the neoliberal claim—articulated most clearly in Foucault's famous reading of the Neoliberals—that our contemporary economy has undergone "a breakdown of labor into capital and income."[52] Yet what we concluded in the previous chapter, and what we can affirm here through a reading of Woolard's institutions-as-art, is that the neoliberal, post-labor declaration is essentially a descriptive claim. The activities remain the same only to be conceived of and narrated differently. Thus we can affirm Jason Read's crucial suggestion that "neoliberalism is the ideology of real subsumption," and we can demonstrate its truth in the field of cultural production.[53] This demonstration should help us to clarify the relation between a change in economic organization and a discourse about that change.

My contention in this chapter—indeed in this book—is that a change in the value composition of capital will necessarily result in a change in how labor is valorized. In our contemporary moment of finance's ascendance and labor's degradation, "precarity" has been suggested as an appropriate descriptor. The problem with this suggestion is that "precarity" does not index a change at the level of the labor commodity; rather, it only indexes a change in the social reception of that labor. By using the term "decommodified labor," I hope to isolate a change in the composition of labor and how that changed labor takes an aesthetic form.

In the work I survey throughout this book, the labor that renders the art is not a commodity, nor is the art object that emerges from it. There is no ethical claim to be made here. Nor do we need to turn to the imposition of finance or regimes of accumulation for our heuristics; here, those become too abstract. Rather, we should return the critical paradox set out in Stewart Martin's perspicacious work on art's commodity status. Martin suggests that "within a society in which commodification is dominant, everything that is external to this commodification becomes marginal, liable to be socially irrelevant or merely yet-to-be-commodified."[54] Art cannot be a commodity because if it were, it would forfeit its critical power. But art cannot not be a commodity because were it external to commodification, it would also forfeit its critical power. This paradox presents the balance of the socially engaged art that derives from decommodified labor: namely, that it may be worthless in more ways than one.

If a socially engaged artist like Theaster Gates avails himself of both gallery-based commodification and non–profit-based infrastructural support, then Woolard's two institutional platforms, OurGoods and Trade School, reached neither of these pivot points precisely. Remainders of OurGoods and Trade School were not sold off in a gallery, nor were the institutions in their entirety given over to a nonprofit, as in the case of Gates's *Dorchester Projects* and its association with the University of Chicago. They did not offer themselves up to corporate "sponsors," as did socially engaged artist Rick Lowe's *Project Row Houses* through its association with the Houston-based oil services company, Chevron. What Woolard was offered included franchising and monetizing to private concerns. In her case, had she accepted these offers, money would have been exchanged for labor already done. The institutions in question would have ceased to be decommodifying and would have relied instead on a familiar organization whereby some labor would be done without wages—namely, the bartering relationships—but out of that lack, surplus value would be generated via the organization itself. Here we must remember Marx's point that "the secret of the self-expansion of capital resolves itself into having the disposal of a definite quantity of other people's unpaid labour."[55]

With both OurGoods and Trade School, the offers out of decommodification were rejected. Woolard and her collaborators concluded that if someone gets paid, then everyone should get paid. And once everyone gets paid, not only do expenses increase exponentially, but increasing time must be devoted to organizing, disbursing, accounting for, and tracking payment. Then the artist really does become an entrepreneur, and not the philosophical type memorialized by Foucault. Rather, she becomes a kind of payroll manager. Money has its own expenses and introduces its own scale. The old adage that it takes money to make money is certainly true, but so is its converse: it takes money to break even or operate at a loss. Money takes money. Woolard and her collaborators decided that no commodification was a better state of affairs than some commodification, because *some* money generated through commodification would have demonstrated that there really was a scarcity of money, that all members really could not be compensated for their labor.

Woolard and her institutions adhered to their decommodification. They believed that such a choice gave their institutions more freedom, more inclusivity, indeed, even an ability to be perceived as art. But then, decommodification cannot be hailed as a "solution" in any way beyond the boundaries of the aesthetic. When commodification is the regime, decommodification may offer a pause, a temporary respite, and it does so only in relation to prevailing social conditions of commodification. After running for six years, OurGoods came to a close; the New York City branch of Trade School shut down and Woolard and her collaborators passed the management and software development on to a new generation of artists and activists. The conclusion of these projects in some sense furthers their status as artworks. As Claire Bishop questions of a different socially engaged art project, also a school, run by the artist Tania Bruguera, "Why do you need to call it a work of art? Can't it just be something you do in Havana? For this to be a work of art, you have to finish it. It can't be ongoing."[56]

Without money or sale, without incorporation of some sort, parts of these institutions ended. And yet, other parts continued. This ending seems a likely consequence of decommodified labor. But it also reasserts a kind of singularity so important to the aesthetic. Woolard's work provides a decommodified aesthetics that is itself a decommodification of some of our most important commodities: labor and education. In Esping-Andersen's original formulation, the welfare state decommodifies certain goods and services so that its citizens may socially reproduce outside of certain market constraints. In the postwelfare state, however, this relationship is inverted, and enterprising citizens, in a Foucauldian gesture, structure their own decommodification to achieve a certain freedom. We are not yet prepared to qualify this freedom as misplaced or genuine; rather, in keeping with Foucault's less often examined language of neoliberalism, we can only say that in this moment it is understood as a freedom by those who practice it. Those momentary freedoms are aesthetic, par excellence.

Commodify the Congo? The Institutions of Renzo Martens

In the previous section I engaged with the long-standing artists' metaphor of the sale or of "selling it." This metaphor results from art's unstable relation to the commodity and from the simultaneous commodity/noncommodity nature of the artwork. We see this extended metaphor from Andy Warhol to Fluxus, from Damien Hirst to Theaster Gates, from performance art to institutional critique. Fraser and Rosler (among others) make such selling literal in their *Untitled* (2003) and *Meta-Monumental Garage Sale*, respectively. Other artists including Mierle Laderman Ukeles, who claimed "my work will be my work," or Ben Kinmont, whose eponymous ongoing work *Sometimes a nicer sculpture is to be able to provide a living for your family* offers its own critique in its very title, make a similar insistence by "selling" the labor process, often connecting it to the feminized work of feeding, cleaning, caring, and so on. I claimed that Woolard's institutions enable decommodified labor to act as the fulcrum of exchange and that in doing so they avoid the compromises of "selling it."

But I have also suggested that a scene of decommodified labor changes the coordinates of "selling it" because in most cases "it" cannot be sold. In this section I look at the "institutions as art" of Renzo Martens, who embarks on a similar process of "selling it" but crucially connects the "selling it" less to the object that organizes the commodity than to the labor that that produces the commodity. If Fraser and Rosler (and many others) attempt to literalize "selling it," then Martens does the same with the labor found in "shovel-ready art" and the manner in which "social practice [becomes a] business model," in the important words of Marina Vishmidt. He takes it for granted that socially engaged art *already is* a business model for some—mostly white, male denizens of the Global North—and asks how it might become a business model for others—namely, Congolese plantation workers.

My interest in including Martens in this chapter is that his realization of socially engaged business-as-art transpires through the collective form of an institution whose demand is for artists' wages. Yet those wages are not demanded for Martens himself or his Euro-American collaborators; rather, those wages are demanded by Martens for Congolese plantation workers, some of whom are also his collaborators, and some of whom became artists through their partnership with him. Martens takes it as axiomatic that artists in the Global North have wages and can socially reproduce themselves through various art economies. Now, through his art practice, he attempts to replicate this process in Congo. Thus he desires that art participate in the *commodification of labor*. And yet, as we have seen, art's wages in the Global North are slowly being evacuated.[57] Therefore, Martens's desire for an expanded artists' wage must also be read as a critique of artistic labor's decommodification and an investigation into the scale at which the commodification of labor may be realized in art economies.

Martens's practice as structured by his involvement with Congolese plantations has taken various medial forms: from docudrama filmic representation, to the founding and running of various Congo-based institutions, to the now-in-process building of a "white cube" gallery in rural Congo, to the point that he now understands himself as an artist who is "a producer of infrastructures in which people other than white male European artists can make critique, live off it, and change reality."[58] In his focus on developing institutional infrastructures for other artists who cannot sell their labor as his art practice, Martens demonstrates certain similarities to Woolard. In his active embrace of a foreign, postcolonial, economic spectacle, and in centrally placing himself in the representation of that spectacle through miens both earnest and ironic, he is, of course, quite different from Woolard. Nor does he issue his appeals to that red herring of much socially engaged art—namely, "community."[59] For Martens, the abstraction of "community" becomes meaningless without wages to support individual community members. In his infrastructural relocation of art from Global North to South, his work bears certain similarities to that of the late German artist Christoph Schlingensief, who erected an *Opera Village* in Burkina Faso, and to that of Jonas Staal, whose work *The Art of Creating the State* is based in Mali.[60] One central difference, however, is that Martens continually serves as a liaison, translator, collaborator, curator, and institutional director as his various projects pivot between Congolese plantations and cities such as Amsterdam, New York, and Berlin.[61] His project can be further distinguished from a group such as the Danish collective Superflex, which develops similar commodity projects-as-art-for-sale but does so in a serial manner.[62] Martens, in contrast, has been working with one community in Congo for years; when asked about his project's duration he answered, "five years in Soviet terms, a series of five year plans."

Martens's own involvement with Congolese plantation workers began with his 2008 satirical documentary film, *Enjoy Poverty: Episode III*.[63] Critics have referred to this film's "gonzo journalistic" style in relation to its hyperbolic approach to its subject matter.[64] The film asks whether a well-intentioned white, European artist—Martens himself—may help Congolese plantation workers out of their long immiseration at the behest of multinational corporations, centrally Unilever, a palm-oil producer in Congo and a chief sponsor of contemporary art at Tate Modern. The film then follows Martens's various attempts to allow these impoverished workers to, in Martens's own language, "benefit" from their "poverty" by treating it as "natural resource" that they can "sell."[65] In place of accredited, Western photojournalists who sell images of Congolese famine and war to international news agencies and wire services, Martens encourages Congolese photographers to produce and sell images of their own. He suggests that they should commodify their artistic labor through the photographic representation of their country's misery: from the starvation to the war crimes to the feeble efforts of the United Nations in attempting to respond to these issues. By the film's end, these indigenous attempts at commodification have failed—no one will purchase the Congolese-authored photos—and the film concludes with Martens and his unemployed photographer-collaborators erecting an imposing diesel-powered neon sign illuminating a Congolese riverbank that states, "Please Enjoy Poverty."

Some scholars of African photography and literature have dismissed Martens's film for the racist, imperial visual tropes that structure it and for the attention to Martens as a filmmaker himself in place of the long-lived and well-developed institutions of sub-Saharan African photography and film, particularly those indebted to communist, socialist, and nonaligned movements in the 1960s through the 1980s.[66] To these critiques one could add that Martens's film is generically satirical, and satire does not work from a position of higher to lower social status. The representation of "advice" via the downward economic movement of life worlds and resources, from Martens to the Congolese through his faux-entrepreneurial encouragement, does not allow his satire to achieve its intended effects politically or aesthetically.[67] Indeed, the moment of the film in which the satire achieves a wonderful efficaciousness comes when Martens himself speaks with the author of *The Creative Class* and a highly sought-after consultant to "creative cities," Richard Florida. In that moment, visually suspended between equals—white, professionally respected men of the Global North in a conversation with each other about Congo—Martens indeed produces a sterling satire of "the creative economy," and of Florida's many fatuous would-be concepts, including "the creative stage of capitalism."

Their conversation begins with Martens, who talks from Congo via Skype to the Toronto-based Florida, projecting their conversation on a large screen for several hundred interested Congolese to observe:

RENZO MARTENS: We're sitting here on a former Unilever plantation [in Congo] with about 200 people. They too have to make a transition from a Fordist economy to something beyond that.

RICHARD FLORIDA: When people talk about economic development, they talk about hardware. They talk about companies . . . they talk about using tax breaks to bring a company to a city or a country . . . . I began to see that wasn't the whole story. I began to look at the rise of the group of people who is [*sic*] principally artists, designers, culturally creative people . . . . I came up with a very simple model and I called it the three T's: technology, talent and tolerance. When you put the three T's together in a community, that [provides] the spark [to] this model of development. . . . What's stunning is that artistic creation comes before roads. Comes before schools. Comes before hospitals.

When Florida makes claims such as these about, say, Toronto or Atlanta, places where the school, the hospital, and the road as material forms are never in doubt, even if access to them remains uneven, the claim is interpreted as stage-based and metaphorical. Toronto does not need *more* roads; Atlanta does not need *more* schools; encourage, instead, an arts and technology district. In Congo, however, where the lack of roads, hospitals, and schools forms a lived reality, one that daily causes devastating misery, the same claim seems absurd if not cruel. When Florida claims that "art is more important than roads" to a community that does not have roads, the vacuity of his language is finally cemented.

Yet we must note that the satire between Martens and Florida is only possible because of the presence of the Congolese plantation workers themselves both in and as mise-en-scène. We have seen their suffering. They appear in the background as adjuncts to Martens's explanation to Florida that he and his group hope to engage in a "gentrification program" and make this Congolese plantation similar to a gentrified neighborhood in any one of the "creative" cities Florida has studied and served as a booster for. Yet, while Martens uses the pronoun "we" when talking to Florida and populates his shots with Congolese workers eager for economic change, it nonetheless is presented as *his* film, and *his* project, through his narcissism, itself necessary for the satire to work in the limited manner that it does. Rendered in broadly ironic strokes, this is *his* satire.

Whether Martens now agrees with this criticism we do not know. His later work in Congo—my primary interest—has moved away from the deployment of the imperial gaze in the name of satire as well as from the logic of representation itself. He now makes institutions that address the commodity status of Congolese labor. He has explained, "I got a lot of harsh criticism [for my film] and maybe it was right." Of course, he also received quite a few accolades. Recognition notwithstanding, he did assert that "I would never make *Enjoy Poverty* again." He then narrates: "I figured I needed to find a solution [to Congolese plantation workers' poverty] and deal with the issue in as structural a way as I could." And this is where I want to intercept his project and consider Martens's continually developing artwork of building "institutions as art" in Congo that are devoted to, above all, the artist's wage. His new representational earnestness and dedication of time and resources to Congolese plantation workers does not mean that Martens's work has ceased to be satirical. Rather his satire now appears in the form of a "performance lecture" whose vocabulary veers between Marxist and neoliberal, while his efforts to help the Congolose achieve better wages have become more institutional and indeed have taken on what Joselit calls "institutional responsibility." This bifurcation of institute and discourse was formally unavailable within his film's narrative.

Several years after the film, Martens founded the Institute for Human Activities. Described on its own website as "a research project initiated by Dutch artist Renzo Martens and developed at the KASK—School of Arts in Ghent," it has a mission "to prove that artistic critique on [*sic*] economic inequality can redress it—not symbolically, but in material terms." This claim, of course, recapitulates the definitional claim of social practice art: to ameliorate, not only represent, social inequality. To this end, the description of the institute explains that "since 2014 the IHA has collaborated with the *Cercle d'Art des Travailleurs de Plantation Congolaise* (CATPC)." Together they set up the Lusanga International Research Centre for Art and Economic Inequality (LIRCAEI). Both by itself and in conjunction with groups such as CATPC and LIRCAEI, Martens's Institute for Human Activities works "through exhibitions, presentations and the instigation of critical reflection [to] facilitate the global dissemination of the artworks created with the CATPC, the profits of which return directly [to] Congo to support the makers and their families, as well as community projects in Lusanga."[68] The text remains unclear—perhaps purposely—whether Martens himself was also a cofounder of the group of plantation worker-artists, but it seems probable. He credits René Ngongo, former head of Green Peace Congo, as "cofounder" of the union. He and his institute certainly were involved in the creation of the Research Centre.

At their current intersection, the many institutions of Martens—the IHA, the CATPC, and the LIRCAEI, in addition to galleries in Berlin and Amsterdam—are working collectively to sell sculptural self-portraits made by plantation workers. Their production process follows a familiar chain of global commodity circulation, if with some crucial and dramatic inversions. At their art center, at an undisclosed location in Congo (the first disclosed location was destroyed by Unilever), plantation workers engage in "critical curriculum" with Kinshasa-based artists and visiting international critics. Out of this ongoing collaboration, the plantation workers have begun to make sculptural self-portraits in river clay in the style of Pende sculpture, whose style was first appropriated by the likes of Picasso and Matisse. With the help of the Dutch design firm V-2, these sculptures are scanned in Congo and re-created in Amsterdam using imported Congolese cocoa and 3-D printing technology. The cocoa is provided by the Swiss company, Barry Callebaut; Dutch pastry chefs assist in molding the raw cocoa into sculptures. The sculptures on view in galleries and exhibitions tend to be full-body and are produced in editions of seven; smaller sculptures of heads are produced in larger quantities and are available for sale at the price of €39.95. The money generated returns to the Congolese *en toto*. While some questions remain about specific funding sources—how is Martens paid?—all materials and skills seem to have been provided pro bono, yet in exchange for recognition: the Barry Callebaut label, for example, is clearly visible in the gallery (figure 2.3).

Martens's foregoing modes of engagement comprise various projects with different interlocutors, funders, and collaborators. But they all seem to have the same audience, and what they each have in common is Martens himself, as well as what Chris Gilbert calls the "self-institutionalizing" habit of contemporary art.[69] Since *Enjoy Poverty*, Martens's works can be categorized as producing "institutions as art." Likewise, among the interconnecting partners and institutes, sponsors and volunteers, a single project appears: what Martens calls his Congo-based "gentrification program," a process that attempts to reorganize global commodity chains so that monetary value, and its artistic and cultural habits (art galleries, lecture series, "cappuccino bars"), accrue to the Global South, the place where many of the staple commodities of European social reproduction originate.

Still of concern is Martens's understanding of his own role: Why is the poverty of Congolose plantation workers his issue to solve? Martens explains that "if I really want to deal structurally with what I can do as an artist, I have to start my own gentrification program. I have to make sure that I am the one as an artist who takes responsibility for where capital accumulation as a result of artistic critique occurs. So therefore [I initiated] a gentrification program in Congo." He does not necessarily have an answer for that question—*why him?*—and perhaps he doesn't need to. (Why, after all, is this my book to write?) Yet his rhetoric of individual mission and salvation does invite such questions, and the ongoing presence of his own narcissistic involvement leads even some of his collaborators to stress the ambivalence and uncertainty with which they understand his project.

For example, T. J. Demos explains in his own essay on Martens's Congo-

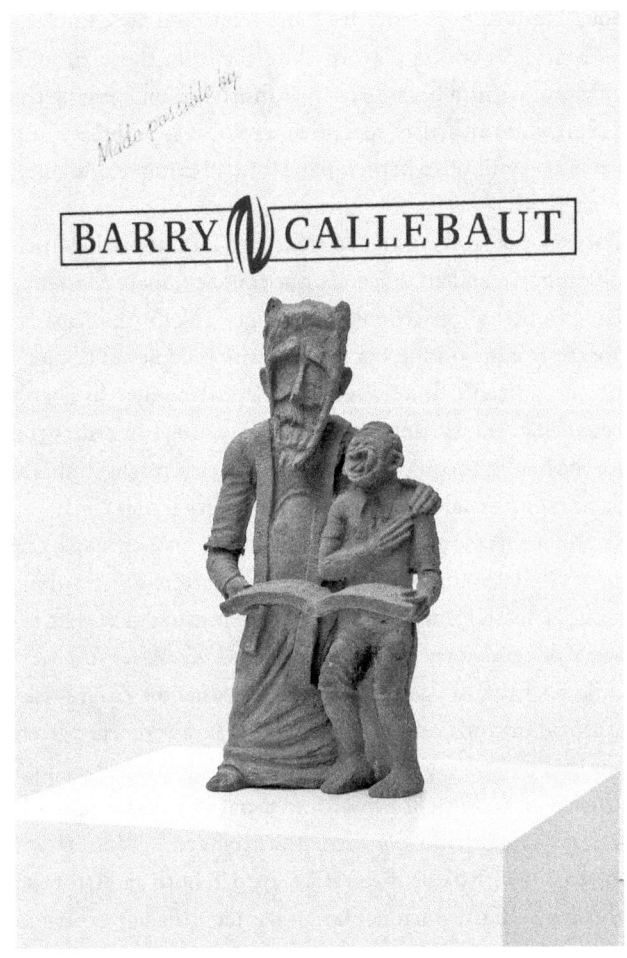

2.3 Cedrick Tamasala, *How My Grandfather Survived*, 2015.
Photograph by Ernst van Deursen, courtesy of Galerie Fons
Welters, Amsterdam, and KOW, Berlin.

based Institute for Human Activities that, "speaking as a participant in the
IHA's Opening Seminar [in Congo], I discovered that, far from some kind of
neocolonial carnival or bad-faith, cynical artistic game—which is sometimes
how Martens's provocative project is (mis)understood—the [gentrification]
programme represented a serious discussion featuring Congolese intellectu-
als, activists and artists . . . and their European counterparts . . . ."[70]

Demos gives away his own initial hesitations; he too was unsure what to
expect. For Demos, Martens's Institute appears in nascent form but none-

theless as "ambitious," "ethically provocative," and "conceptually complex." He concludes that Martens's efforts now *are* different from those "ironic" impulses found in Martens's film because of their insistence on merging the Global South and North into an artists' space that is critical, is profitable, and in which the return of recognition, whether in the form of critique or money, accrues to the Global South.

In this specific sense of borrowing and retrofitting a local capitalist institution toward both capitalist and artistic ends, one could compare Martens's project to the artist Fran Ilich's "Spacebank," an online bank for the Zapatistas and their supporters. This online institution, which copies Citibank's graphic design quite recognizably, functions in all practical manners as a bank and is capable of crediting, transacting, and debiting. Its logo instructs the viewer: "Don't hate the banks, become the banks."[71] Martens might similarly advise: don't hate commodity traders, become a commodity trader.

In terms of its philanthropic mission to alleviate poverty through the transformation of the Global South's poor into artists, Martens's institutions seem to be quite similar to "Kids with Cameras," the organization that resulted from the 2004 documentary film *Born into Brothels*. After discovering the world of child sex work in Calcutta for her film, director Zana Briski founded a philanthropic organization in which child sex workers are given cameras and encouraged to document their lives; these photographs are sold and the money returned in the form of schools and social services for the children.[72] In both Martens's and Briski's projects, the exploited become artists through their involvement with a documentarian. And in both cases, for the project to work, those whom the documentarian has identified as exploited have to work; indeed, they must work as artists.

Finally, in terms of its performance lecture–style presentation, the most germane comparison with which to assess the collaborative ambivalence on view in Martens's gentrification—and crucially, the centrality of the language used to describe it—is found in the anthropologist Elizabeth Povinelli's collaboration with Karrabing, the indigenous Australian film collective. Povinelli has been working with the Belyuen community out of which the collective comes for twenty-plus years, as both an anthropologist who documents this community's struggles with what Povinelli calls "the contradictions of the late liberal state," and as an advocate for that community—one of the contradictions of the late liberal state is that an anthropologist has to certify indigenous land claims.[73] In 2007 this community decided to make films. Povinelli, who refers to herself as "close friends" and "family" with this

community, has been active as a member of the film collective and director of its films. In 2012 Karrabing began receiving awards for its work. The
collective is now frequently invited to tour the international museum and
film festival circuits to discuss its process, its works, the role of indigeneity
in contemporary socially engaged art, and so on. When such invitations are
extended to Karrabing, it is frequently Povinelli who shows up to deliver a
performance lecture.[74]

With both Martens and Povinelli, an established member of an art/critical
community in the Global North partners with a group in the Global South
to produce "socially engaged art" that has as the central orientation of its social engagement monetary remuneration to the Global South. Povinelli and
Martens liaise with their respective collaborators, who cannot leave their own
particular spaces to travel (they can't get visas, they don't have passports, nor
do they have money). Povinelli and Martens present the interpretative frame
of the work, which includes, respectively, translations from indigenous language and the history of Congolese commodity production, without which
not only would the work not be on display in Berlin, New York, Miami, etc.,
but the critical project itself would be unintelligible. And in both cases, the
specific vocabularies make the work: the viewer is told that "the content" of
the art and "the plot" of the films do not matter; the Karrabing produce films
that record late liberalism, whereas the Congolese produce art capable of reverse gentrification. Povinelli is a professor, and her transformation into quasi-
artist might also be seen as an extension of the last chapter, to some degree,
as a consequence of the incorporation of art into universities. Only now we
find it not only in the art department but also in anthropology, particularly
at Columbia University, where Povinelli's colleague Michael Taussing now
collaborates with Francis Alÿs (whom I discuss in the next chapter).

How does Martens's practice challenge our understanding of institutional
critique as it relates to the wage form and to decommodified labor? His work
certainly participates in the kind of "counterinstitutional" and "constructive
institutional" critique that I discussed in this chapter's introduction. Martens
describes his gentrification program as "a research program on what art can do
and what it can be. I think it's some kind of disobedience to the rules by ap-
plying the rules . . . ," an easily recognizable moment of institutional critique.
He then specifies which rules will be applied and which will be disobeyed:
"The tools of analysis will be the dominant rules of the game. So in this case
it's neoliberal economics, so I use neoliberal economics."[75] But as "it" refers to
the "tools" of Martens's "analysis," "it" isn't neoliberal economics—not ex-

actly. Rather, "it" is a combination of the language of Marxist aesthetic theory, neoliberal economics, and critical theory; and when on view, "it" takes the form of a performance lecture with supporting performance documentation.

Martens presents as his framing story the Marxist history of the economic and its converse, the aesthetic. He introduces the terminology of "the plantation" and the "white cube gallery" to frame his history of the opposition between the economic and the aesthetic.[76] This is a history that I recounted in my introduction to this book: namely, how the rise and solidification of capitalism create a more systemic and brutal extraction of value in some places (imperialism, slavery) while creating a more refined and autonomous sense of *not value* (aesthetics, comportment) in other places. Perhaps there is no more concise or famous summation of this dichotomy than that of Walter Benjamin in his *Theses on the Philosophy of History*: "There is no document of civilization which is not at the same time a document of barbarism."[77] Martens locates this global dynamic in Congo: on Congolese monoculture plantations commodities are produced under gruesome working conditions; companies like Unilever appropriate surplus value and "give away" some of their profit to fund "culture" in museums and universities of the Global North. In his insistence that "there is no white cube gallery without the plantation," Martens asserts the truths of primitive accumulation; in his insistence that the pittance the Congolese do get paid only serves to mask the deep inequality of the exchange itself, Martens evokes Marx's critique of the wage.

Yet while he is a Marxist diagnostician, Martens is a neoliberal social engineer. As Martens's Congo-based projects have become more institutional, his language has moved from analysis of the historical condition of possibility to a language of market-based problem solving. Indeed, representing this scene as a problem to be solved is neoliberal in its framing. His use of neoliberal language has additional import in that it designates the project's legacy to institutional critique. The logic of yore — "I will use the museum to critique the museum" — cedes into "I will use neoliberal economics to critique neoliberal economics." In my foregoing discussions of neoliberalism, I focused on the centrality of the loss of labor as a critical concept, one that is then replaced by such concepts as "self-investment" and "human capital." We have already seen this tendency in the vocabulary Martens uses to narrate his film, *Enjoy Poverty*: the Congolese have a "natural resource," their "poverty," which they themselves may "sell." Had this project worked, once their poverty had been purchased on a market, that poverty would have ceased to describe a condition of economic lack and instead would have become a path to potential profit. We are reminded here of the assessment that Cassie Thornton received from a certified financial planner: her MFA constituted a sound investment until the moment in which the investment (her labor) needed to be recouped (sold on a market).

Both cases exemplify the neoliberal insistence that labor is something one *has* and not something one *does*. This transmutation of labor fundamentally alters how labor may be understood to circulate, to be evaluated, and to relate to other labors. Most centrally for our purposes, labor ceases to be a social form and becomes an individual form, a shift that ultimately will have consequences for how we understand Martens as a "socially engaged artist." He introduces into his art practice an economic philosophy that disavows the social itself. When Margaret Thatcher famously said, "There is no such thing as society. There are individual men and women, and there are families," she was parroting this aspect of neoliberalism.

Martens's project thus invites us to consider this aspect of the neoliberal program as it intersects with art production. In turning to what he calls "neoliberal economics," he is turning to "the market." Even as that market remains famously ill-defined by the neoliberals themselves, it does possess certain attributes and features when operationalized.[78] In the words of economic historian Philip Mirowski, for neoliberals, "the market can always provide solutions to problems seemingly caused by the market; any problem has a market solution."[79] In Martens's case, the plight that the Congolese find themselves in certainly has a market-based origin: namely, European desires for commodities. From labor to rubber to Coltan, this imperial accumulation generated for Europeans both sought-after goods and an epistemology of racism that could explain how and why the Congolese find themselves impoverished, starving, living in continual dominion by Europeans. That's the problem. The neoliberal solution to this problem is to integrate Congolese into the global market. As plantation workers, it's true, they could not command a high wage. But—and here is Marten's gambit—as artists perhaps they might.

With the correct construction and administration of markets, the right allowance for pricing, and sensible coordination of externalities and opportunity costs, "problems" such as poverty, racism, starvation, and war crimes become objects of potential investment, sale, and thus profit. Poverty could exchange as a resource; commodification becomes "gentrification" and gentrification becomes "reversible"; social change takes the form of payment: Martens says "we [the Global North] will pay for this [radical inequality]. And we need to pay for it." "Critique" becomes yet another "resource" that can be priced and sold at a profit.

Of all of Martens's neoliberal transmutations, the one that has, understandably, received the most attention in arts criticism is "gentrification." A term most of Martens's viewers and critics will understand as pejorative and equate with the destruction of genuine, multiclass, and multiracial spaces at the behest of commercial "creative" space of the Richard Florida variety, Martens's ironic resuscitation of gentrification clearly aligns him with what he understands as neoliberal economics as well as a critical project *after* institutional critique. If classic institutional critique sought to expand and affirm its object through the critical operation, counter–institutional critique seeks to expand its object through producing its double.[80] Importantly, Demos titles his essay on Martens's institute "Gentrification after Institutional Critique." Martens wants to produce an institutional double of gentrification. That is, he wants to extract the good of gentrification ("art galleries, bars, shops, restaurants," in his words) without the bad (forced displacement, destruction of neighborhoods, loss of higher-wage manufacturing work in favor of lower-wage service work). Martens seeks a "capitalism without the capitalism," as Slavoj Žižek once famously described such fantasies. Can Martens, though, make the fantasy a reality? Can we have, finally, the good without the bad? That is the question Martens asks, indeed almost dares his viewer to engage. But alas, such totalizing opposition between two systematic tendencies rarely yields interesting critical results; it is similar to the static question, Is art a commodity or isn't it?

Rather, the more interesting problem of Martens's work, and the one that most centrally connects his work to the themes of my own book, is the manner in which Martens deploys the terms "wage" and "price," each representative of Marxism and neoliberalism, respectively. Wage is, as we have seen both Marx explain and Martens himself amplify, inherently unequal, structurally unequal, productively unequal. A waged social world both requires and denigrates those who do not receive a wage—as Silvia Federici has argued for years—setting in place an entire global hierarchy of exploitation through shifting constituencies of race, class, nationality, and gender. But price has no such extraneous baggage. Rather, for neoliberals, price constitutes an independent epistemology. Price is asocial. It reflects all available knowledge, and through its transactional efficaciousness it achieves a fundamental correctness.[81] The market, in turn, is the solution any problem (social, political, economic, etc.) because it is "deemed to be a superior information processor, so therefore all human knowledge can be used to its fullest only if it is comprehensively owned and priced."[82] Finally, according to one of the founders of neoliberal economics, Friedrich Hayek himself, "knowledge is the chief good that can be had at a price."[83] Some of the more exceptional moments of this neoliberal discourse of pricing have become infamous: Gary Becker's pricing of children, for example, which we will consider in chapter 4. In the previous chapter, we saw Becker bemoan how the reduction of the pricing for an individual's life to slavery closed out a market for individuals to sell themselves.

Martens's critique turns on the sale and the sale turns on the price. He explains: "We can sell these [chocolate sculptures] for £40 a piece, they cost maybe £2 or £3—so £37 profit." Currently, Martens's Institute for Human Activities "markets these artworks through galleries; it hopes eventually to sell its products through department stores, where the price per pound of chocolate, worth approximately US$0.25 to plantation workers, might soar when transformed into an art object," recounts T. J. Demos.[84] The Congolese need money. Martens insists: the "first step [to help them]: raise wages. Raise wages." A wage in Congo seems to be a price in Europe. In Martens's presentation of the Congolese sculptural self-portraits, the aesthetic efficaciousness of the art transpires through the efficaciousness of price itself. Indeed, an understanding of how price functions in Martens's art will be the key to understanding what and how Martens is ultimately critiquing and whether such a critique is ironic or genuine, representational or ameliorative.

To settle the question that remains central to Martens's oeuvre, the question first seen in his film—Is the "selling it" for real or is it the ironic gesture that signifies his artfulness?—and the question that has now followed him to his institutions (Is his gentrification of Congo for real or an ironic gesture that continues to signify its artfulness?), we must ask, Does Martens produce a critique of price or does he provide an instance of pricing? Is he using neoliberal economics "against itself" by revealing the inadequacies of the pricing of social knowledge, or is he using price for itself by allowing price to remain an uncontested form of knowledge? The moment of institutional critique might be found if he used price to show the limits and possibilities of price. For example, he might show that price is inadequate to convey knowledge about the Congolese. The moment of counter–institutional critique might be found in a new economic relationship that is not price nor wage. We are not yet sure what would constitute this form. But to use "neoliberal economics against itself" would require that price be open to contest. Conversely, what Marxism shows is that the wage is *not* the price of labor. Rather, for Marxism the wage is the price of the continuation of the system of labor extraction.

The manner in which both the Marxist theory of the wage and the neoliberal theory of price intersect with cultural production takes us squarely back to the central dichotomy of my book: How does decommodified labor as it is found in socially engaged art either exemplify or help us to better understand our two most organizing narratives of the economy today: Marxist real subsumption and neoliberal entrepreneurialism?

Both the Marxist formulation of real subsumption and the neoliberal development of cultural economics negotiate how the economy intersects with culture. Marxism worries that art ceases to be an independent space capable of critique and becomes fully integrated into the world market, as Brown has argued; neoliberalism insists that culture can be priced and sold. Martens attempts to combine both. He assumes that culture has been subsumed into capital accumulation and therefore it can now be priced and sold in a "socially responsible" manner. This reading of neoliberal theories of the pricing of culture is indebted to Dave Beech, who asks the question, How does neoliberalism understand cultural production, art specifically?[85] Yet my line of inquiry also repositions the groundbreaking work of Beech. I ask, How does Martens incorporate the discourses of neoliberalism and Marxism into his art, and do those incorporations distill a heretofore unacknowledged feature either of art or of economic discourse?

For all of Martens's hopes in neoliberal pricing, we do know that price has already failed the Congolese once. Martens tells us that the Congolese receive an average wage of $220 a year. But within a neoliberal framework, if they accept such a price for their labor, then that is the worth of their labor. After all, if they were worth more they would get more. Here we see pricing's cruel tautology. To gage whether Martens instantiates or critiques price we then need to pursue the question, What is €40—the price of the sculptures for sale—the price of? When one buys a Congolese-produced cocoa sculpture at that price, what is one buying? What does the price signify?

On the one hand, price becomes the relationship through which Martens's project critiques art. Price is the spread of what might be possible to be changed in Congolese workers' lives. If €40 is transacted in the manner that Martens advises us it will be, their lives will be transformed. On the other hand, €40 is also the price of knowing that price works. For Martens, price does seem to function, as Hayek himself suggests it should, to conduct knowledge to the viewer in the Global North. Price functions faithfully to provide the knowledge that all is not OK. Foremost, €40 is the price art viewers pay to believe that price is an accurate reflection of a global economic reality and that this reality can be changed. Price affirms a feedback loop. Price is self-correcting; it reflects accurately available information. Thus, in its use of price, Martens's art is not simply "socially engaged art"; rather it is an art that demonstrates how art might again be conjoined with the economic in such a way that a claim to the social itself would not be required because in the model he ends up with, there is no social. And this is an art that demonstrates how "social engagement" through its rejection of the social itself can transmute the language of critique into the language of fair price. In providing the Congolese with wages, Martens also provides his viewer with a model of pricing critique. Martens dares us: if you want to transform exploitation, you must abandon your critique of it. We need not assess whether Martens is correct in his claim that price can work in artwork; we need only to assess how and why different economic discourses are required to make this argument. And our assessment has brought us to a place that is not fortuitous. In hewing to the apparatus of neoliberal pricing, has Martens become a neoliberal? We are reminded again here of Peggy Phelan's critique of Andrea Fraser's *Untitled*, in which she engages in sex with a collector in exchange for money: Phelan notes that the work fails through "utter loss of metaphor." Price never achieves metaphorical latitude in Martens's work. Rather, the price remains the price.

Conclusion

Martens and Woolard both craft institutions that seek to enable artists to socially reproduce themselves when they are economically and imaginatively circumscribed by the historical fact of decommodified labor. Woolard accepts the decommodification, as it were. She crafts institutions for artists that can run through the noncommodified exchange of artistic labor. Martens positions himself on the opposite end of the spectrum: He concludes that Congo does not possess a robust enough scene of commodification. Thus he decides that Congolese artistic labor needs to replace Congolese plantation labor, and for that substitution to work, Congolese artistic labor needs to be commodified. As different as these projects are, they both remind us of the fundamental premise of "exchange," what literary critic Franco Moretti calls the "indelible image of bourgeois thought." Moretti outlines the basic parameters of the exchange: "You would like such and such values to be realized? Fine, but then you must accept these others."[86]

Indeed, in 2013 Woolard mounted an installation called "Exchange Café" at the Museum of Modern Art in New York, a project in which she herself attempted to barter, or "exchange," with MoMA (figure 2.4).

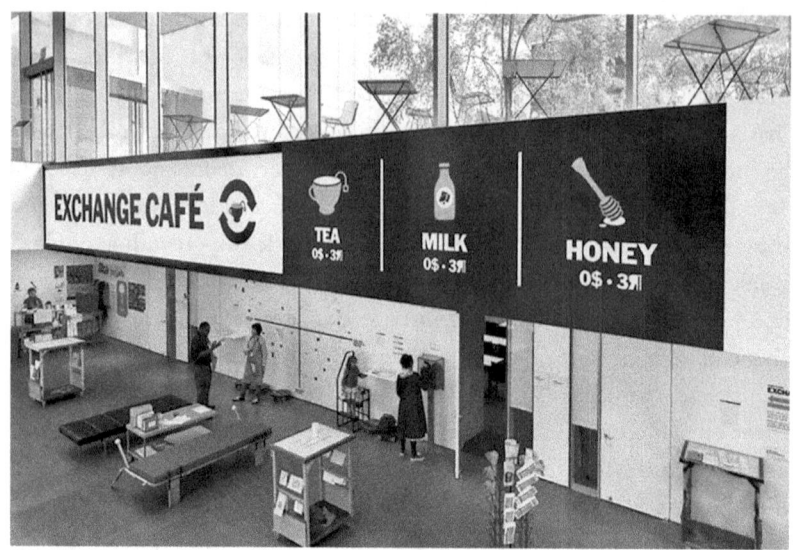

2.4 *Exchange Café*, courtesy of Caroline Woolard.

Exchange Café may be seen as an easy continuation of the themes developed in the aforementioned works. It is a café in which visitors "purchase" tea, but only after inscribing, on notes provided, a "currency" of one's own personal wants and needs. After receiving said tea, visitors then sit along tables. Perhaps they had navigated the scenes and images of "exchange" curated by Woolard from MoMA's archive, which featured such artists as Adrian Piper, Allan Kaprow, and Yoko Ono. Or perhaps they looked at experimental furniture made by Woolard and also based on exchange: a police barricade (ex) changes into a bed, for example. Exchange Café makes a point of including as its art the sourcing of the tea, milk, and honey that populate the café: milk comes from the Milk Not Jails dairy collective, whereas the tea is sourced from the Feral Network, an artist-run courier network that locates artists' upcoming flight routes and asks them to serve as unpaid couriers; the honey was provided from BeeSpace, an urban beekeeping collective. In exchange for their labor, Feral Network couriers meet other artists at the end of their route and thus form a new, global network of decommodified artists.

Martens, too, follows the sinews of Moretti's exchange-based bourgeois imagination: You don't want the Congolese to suffer? Fine, but you must accept price as a form of social knowledge; you must accept both *this price* as well as price itself. Martens's neoliberal aesthetic logic could of course be reversed to provide yet another reading. Mine is a cynical reading of Martens's project, although perhaps no more cynical than that of Martens himself. One could read Martens's various institutes and programs as using the Congolese themselves as a metaphor. One could understand that Martens positions the Congolese as a metaphor for European artists' wages, for the need for them to begin to earn a wage in an era of decreased state funding. In asking for commodification of the Congolese artists, Martens would then be seen as addressing the increasingly decommodifed labor of European artists.

3

Art Worker Animal

Animals as Socially Engaged Artists in a Post-Labor Era

"Where is our zoological Marx when we need him?"
—DONNA HARAWAY, *When Species Meet*

In Sun Yuan and Peng Yu's 2003 installation, *Dogs That Cannot Touch Each Other*, several series of treadmills are placed opposite one another in a gallery space.[1] Each treadmill tilts at a steep upright angle, and atop each treadmill is a dog, itself tethered to a custom-fitted iron buttress. The dogs' lines of sight remain fixed on the treadmill a foot or so in front of them, and thus they stare at another dog in the same position, a dog that stares back. With their musculature excited by the presence of another, they hopelessly race forward, running with speed and determination that they might attack their artistic collaborator. But as the title of the work correctly states, the dogs cannot touch each other, and their futile work generates the force not only of the treadmills' propulsion but also of the artwork itself (figure 3.1).

We cannot but wonder whether this artwork represents human labor. After all, the treadmill is a common metaphor for the futility of our working lives.[2] But if the treadmill is used as metaphor for work's futility, then what metaphorical role do the dogs occupy? One can, of course, "work like a dog," as the simile goes. One can also be "dog-tired" after a long day of work, and a not particularly impressive work might be labeled a "dog and pony show." But how can one work like a dog if one is a dog? Is the vehicle that structures this metaphor an actual vehicle, a treadmill? Is its tenor the dogs' sonorous bark? Is this an "animalwork," to borrow Meiling Cheng's neologism for animal-based performance art, or an elaborate "animetaphor," to borrow Akira Mizuta Lippit's neologism for what he claims is the structural role of animality in generating the "originary metaphors" of which language is composed. Or does lan-

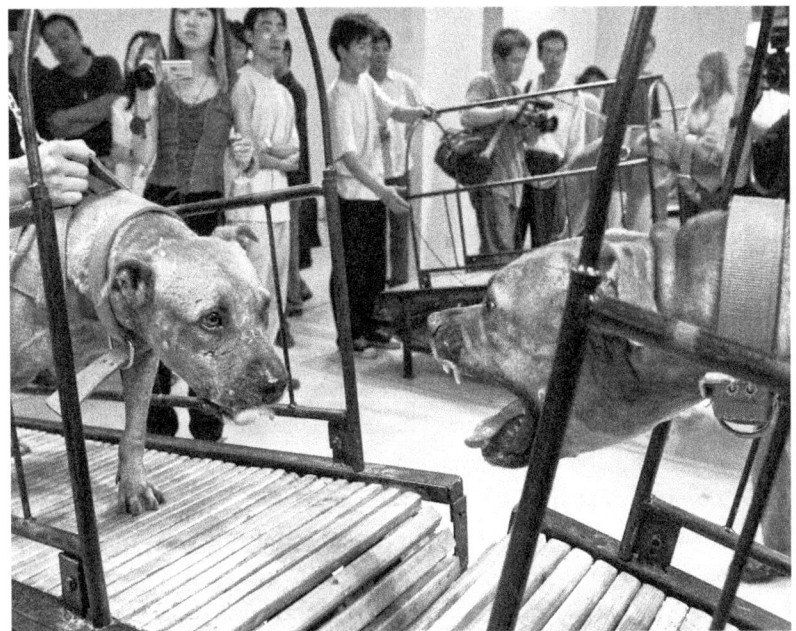

3.1 *Dogs That Cannot Touch Each Other.* Courtesy of Sun Yuan and Peng Yu.

guage, at its root, comprise *animots,* Jacques Derrida's own neologism derived from the French for "animals" (*animaux*) and for "word" (*mot*)?[3] Indeed, one might wonder whether the number of animal-based neologisms proves the point here, including the recent "DerridAnimals."[4]

In this chapter, I consider what animals are doing in socially engaged art, their presence perhaps canonized in the 2006 MASS MoCA show "Becoming Animal."[5] Unlike the previous two chapters, which used studentdom and artist-run institutions to examine how practicing artists have been transformed by decommodifed labor, this chapter focuses on how artists represent decommodified labor. That change in focus, from a modality focused on the existence of decommodified labor to one focused on the representation of decommodified labor, will also change the manner in which this chapter intersects with the central theoretical concern of the book. Namely, how the decommodified labor of socially engaged art may be understood by, and may itself allow for, a different understanding of the two dominant economic narratives of our present: the real subsumption of labor to capital and the neoliberalization of the economy. Both have been considered in previous chapters and both have roles to play here. This confluence is no Hegelian "dark night in which all cows are black." Rather, although the relevant literature is filled with accounts of the effects of neoliberalism on the student and on the artist as an "entrepreneur of herself," there is, as of yet, no declared "neoliberal animal."[6] Likewise, although various artists and critics have used real subsumption's terminology of "inside" and "outside" to critique art's efficaciousness in our current moment, we have no indication of whether "the animal" has been subsumed. Rather, we have, in Steve Baker's influential phrase, "the Postmodern Animal."[7] Thus in this chapter I contend with how the "postmodern animal"—what is better understood, I think, as the poststructural animal—both allows for and disinvites an understanding of decommodified labor in socially engaged art.

The chapter's title, "Art Worker Animal," comes from two important studies and the larger trends they represent. First, I cite Baker's relatively recent *Artist Animal*, which tracks the emergence of animality in contemporary artistic production.[8] While one could begin this genealogy with cave painting, as John Berger famously does, a more appropriate genealogy for my concerns originates with the early entreaties of conceptual art and performance art, such as Hans Haacke's 1969 *Chickens Hatching*, in which a collection of incubated eggs was left to hatch in a gallery, or Joseph Beuys's *I Like America and America Likes Me* in which Beuys spent three days in an enclosed gallery space with a coyote and only a felt blanket, a walking stick, and the *Wall Street Journal* to mitigate his encounters with the animal, Little John.[9] Baker tracks animals in art from the 1960s to our own day's proliferation of animals into a kind of recognizable material with subsets such as "bio-art," "gene-art," "biomedia," "animalworks," and so on.[10] His work on the entry of animality into art and postmodern cultural production may be used to represent a larger turn to animals across the humanities and social sciences, and here I note recent intellectual assemblages such as "multispecies ethnography," "zoo-ontology," and "zoopolitics," all of which compose the nascent field that has been called critical animal studies.[11] In these studies we note that animals shock, please, symbolize, and disorganize the field of culture and our collective analyses of it. Indeed, one of the few activities they seem not to be tasked with is that of being a cultural worker.[12] Until now.

And so the second part of my title nods to Julia Bryan-Wilson's wonderful *Art Workers*, which traces the growing consciousness and institutional cohesion of minimalist and then conceptual art in the 1960s and 70s as artists, including Carl Andre and Robert Morris, began to conceive of themselves as laborers and announced that the *artwork* is made by the *art worker*.[13] Minimalism of the kind Andre and Morris practiced famously repurposed the materials of a soon to be deindustrialized economy into an artistic form, and I will explore whether a similar appropriation has transpired with animals who, for most of human, if not modern, history, have been understood as economic beings and have left us now, in an age of finance, with a vocabulary of "brands" and "stocks."[14] We have already had occasion to consider how artistic labor in the realm of studentdom becomes decommodified at the moment that arts education itself undergoes a sweeping institutionalization and commodification through the rise of the master of fine arts program (chapter 1). We have also seen how artists have attempted to reclaim some of their decommodified labor through the creation and maintenance of their own "institutions as art" (chapter 2).

I now want to explore the relations between the two bodies of work that claim that artists are workers and that animals compose an artistic material.[15] These contentions emerged at a similar time historically, and indeed there is some noteworthy conceptual crossover, if, as of now, insufficient historical causality. Haacke not only produced his *Chickens Hatching* installation as part of what would be delimited as "systems art," but he was also active in organizing the Art Workers Coalition.[16] Beuys not only declared "everyone" to be an artist, but he founded a political party for animals who, he claimed, could not "speak for themselves." (Indeed, Beuys also founded a "grad student party" as well.) Nonetheless, canonical contemporary artists who have worked with animals have tended not to be canonized for that work as such—think of Robert Rauschenberg, Bruce Nauman, or Richard Serra—and the emergent animal-using artists of today have asserted that animals are part of the art, not the work. Indeed, it was Richard Serra himself who first articulated how animals as material might be understood as part of what we have seen Rosalind Krauss designate as the postmedium condition.[17] "Once you find that you're not using paint for its illusionistic qualities or its color refraction but for a material that happens to be red, you can use any material as equally relevant . . . . I did a whole show of 22 live and stuffed animals," Serra explained.[18] Carolee Schneemann simply declared, "the cat is my medium."[19] Other artists from this period are known *only* for their animal work: for example, Kim Jones's sensational 1976 *Rat Piece* in which he burned three rats to death in a gallery under the stage-name "Mudman," or Jannis Kounellis's iconic 1969 *Untitled (12 Horses)* in which twelve horses were tethered to the wall in Rome's *L'Attico* gallery.[20]

Through a reading of the rise of the "animalwork" and several of its contemporary instantiations, I suggest that the presence of live animals in contemporary art and its theorization in contemporary criticism may help us understand the relations between work and artwork, commodities and the aesthetic, the wage and the specter of its decommodification. Animals have emerged as a central force in contemporary art, as artists themselves have been overproduced, underemployed, and indebted. As many of us have become "cultural workers" in one way or another, and as many cultural workers are unable to find cultural work, animals have joined our ranks both to reflect and to constitute a new working reality. "Opera" and "*operaismo*" share the same etymology, but so do "capital" and "chattel." Animals have become crucial sites for representing decommodified labor, and decommodifed labor forms an organizing logic for much socially engaged artwork. Thus we need an account of animal aesthetics in its capacity to organize the production and reception of art as well as the production and circulation of art workers. And while there is plenty of scholarship on labor in art and on animals in art, these two bodies of scholarship have not been brought into conversation.

We do, of course, already have a robust aesthetics of animality. "Perhaps art begins within the animal," write Deleuze and Guattari, whose conception of "becoming animal" remains central to any account of such art as it delimits a "deindividuated, desubjectified mass of otherness" that is available for appropriation but not reification.[21] "The animal is a verb" provides perhaps the most concise summary of this kind of poststructural animal.[22] Giorgio Agamben's "anthropological machine" denotes the ongoing turn to animals to stabilize any conception of humanity.[23] Foucault gave us a biopolitics but never an aesthetic philosophy, even as he did encourage us to think of zoos and gardens as heterotopias.[24] Yet it is Derrida on whom the conceptual leverage of the nascent conversation rests; the DerridAnimal is a reliably discursive one. Both Una Chaudhuri and Cary Wolfe have insisted that, as the field of animal studies aesthetics coalesces, Derrida's *The Animal Therefore That I Am* will "undoubtedly be the most influential contemporary engagement with the question of the animal."[25] In Derrida's account, the animal becomes a site for a recognition of "a subjective finitude" and "a singularity" crucial to the aesthetic as such. Derrida argues that "humans can only produce the autobiography of man by reducing animals (from great apes to silk worms) to a singular group—*l'animal*."[26]

Poststructuralism's centrality in producing a critical animality may be deemed both unsurprising and symptomatic. It is unsurprising in that animals constitute an ideal surface, one whose presumed lack of interiority and tentative relationship to any political efficaciousness parallel the project of poststructuralist reading itself. Ron Broglio's *Surface Encounters: Thinking With Animals and Art* is indicative of this approach. He argues that "depth remains closed off to us and the surface of interactions between humans and animals becomes a zone for thinking."[27] In this tradition animals maintain and are maintained by their inscrutable and intimate otherness to humans, and in doing so they challenge conceptions of humanness itself. But any poststructuralist recuperation of the animal must also be understood as symptomatic in that its propositions of animality recuperate perhaps the oldest recognizable form of capital, the most consistent companion worker—the animal—as a platform to produce a theory of activity and art without a laboring constituent.[28] Nicole Shukin formulates a similar critique: "Critical theory and the emergent field of animal studies have ... tended to sidestep materialist critique in favor of philosophical, psychoanalytical, and aesthetic formulations of animal alterity."[29] Shukin's exacting theory of "animal capital," then, understands the grounds of the aesthetic itself as another "sidestep" of a materialist critique. Yet that need not be the case.[30] The materiality of the aesthetic and the claims that aesthetics capacitate us to make in the world of its opposite, the world of capital and labor, are indeed crucial to any understanding of the shifting composition of value.

As animals have become "complex artistic collaborators" (according to Baker) with their human counterparts, as they have been theorized as "creative agents" in their own right (Brian Massumi), and as they have "formed alliances" (Broglio) with artists, artists as workers have been newly appropriated symbolically and disenfranchised materially. The solution to the problem of an expansion of the category of artists, which, as we will see, now includes animals, and the simultaneous reduction of artists' ability to valorize their labor, is not to place animals firmly within a class of exploited workers, as Jason Hribal has been impressively agitating for years that we do.[31] Claiming that animals constitute the same class of wage laborers as humans is only the flipside of claiming that they are artists: both arguments use animals to index an unassailable real, and both partake in the logic that as animals can be recruited into labor, so can they be recruited in its philosophical opposite: the aesthetic. Neither claim will ultimately satisfy, however. The necessary question, then, is not, Are animals artists? We should rather ask, How do animals in art represent artistic labor? To answer this question, I focus on how animals have been deskilled and reskilled in a variety of artworks.

The path of this chapter, then, is a bifurcated one that maintains my interest in decommodification as an economic problem that might change the scope of the aesthetic. As labor under decommodification becomes a shadow of itself, available for value extraction but not for remuneration, animals become both *representations* of artistic labor and an artistic *form* of decommodified labor. Art that uses animals as its material substrate necessarily represents the decommodified labor of which that substrate is comprised. I am less interested in the fact that artists (or animals) do or don't get paid—after all, commodification cannot be reduced to selling something, and decommodification cannot be reduced to not selling it—than in the fact that artists have begun to represent the nonpayment, the nonremunerated labor of others in their work in the form of live animals. Artists in many cases do not get paid; animals, however, are not payable. So let me take seriously Donna Haraway's question, a question she herself does not adequately answer: Where is our zoological Marx when we need him?

I begin by tracing the tension between "the animal" as an abstraction alongside Marx's understanding of abstract and concrete labor. To claim that animals can now only represent certain labors, I first show that they cannot perform those labors. I then turn to Jannis Kounellis's 1969 *Untitled (12 Horses)*, which was restaged in New York City in 2015. Kounellis's installation, I suggest, foregrounds artistic deskilling. Finally, I read contemporary, socially engaged artist Duke Riley's 2013 pigeon-based installation, *Trading with the Enemy*, which, conversely, foregrounds artistic reskilling. The chapter is less organized around the question of how did certain performance, conceptual, and installation artists turn to animals than it is around the question of how animals became artists. I explore the emergence in the 1960s and 70s of animals as a kind of artistic material, and I trace that emergence into our own present in which journals such as *Antennae* and books such as *Artist Animal* assume an unacknowledged problematic: as animals have been transformed from the material into the messenger, it has become easier for us to think of animals as artists than of artists as laborers.

Working Abstractions

The Labor Abstraction

In this section I trace the abstraction of human labor and its simultaneous reconstitution as concrete work in tandem with the category of "the animal," as it has ceased to denote a household asset or a juridical subject and begun to denote new organizations of meaning such as a spectacle, in the case of "wild-life," or a site of affective cathexis, in the case of a pet.[32] Derrida himself describes this process as one of transformation from "a heterogeneous multiplicity of the living" into "the strict enclosure of this definite article": *the animal*.[33] The labor abstraction and the animal abstraction are not quite parallel processes, but they both partake, if unevenly, in stabilizing an empirical-transcendental doublet that is perhaps the signature move of modern epistemology.[34] We know this move, and thus it is now theoretical common sense to see how Lippit periodizes modernity in relation to a bifurcated animality: "Modernity can be defined," he writes, "by the disappearance of wildlife from humanity's habitat and by the reappearance of the same in humanity's reflections on itself: in philosophy, psychoanalysis, and technological media such as the telephone, film, and radio," he proceeds.[35] His claim is true but contextually incomplete, for it does not account for the causal, originary abstraction: that of labor. The abstraction of work into human labor and the abstraction of animals into the animal do not parallel each other exactly because, as Alfred Sohn-Rethel says, "the concepts of natural science are thought abstractions, [but] the economic concept of value is a real one."[36] I will follow Sohn-Rethel in understanding the order of value to be the primary abstraction from which other abstractions, such as those noted by Lippit, derive. Indeed, as I have argued throughout this book, it is the labor abstraction that provides us, still, with our organizing concept of the aesthetic.

I argue that as abstract labor becomes entrenched as the only value-generating possibility, animals are gradually removed from the population of those who may be economic agents. After that removal, animals may *represent* abstract labor, and we see this still today, from the odd jobs company TaskRabbit, to the endlessly entertaining reality television show *Dogs with Jobs*, to the nascent field of neuroeconomics in which primates routinely represent human economic actors. But while animals can and do represent labor, animals may not function as workers in the abstract, that is, as laborers.[37] Rather, animals are reconstituted as other abstract entities, chiefly "the animal" itself (in Derrida's phase) or as material of linguistic self-reflexivity, as in Lippit's account. So removed from "the economy," "the animal" becomes available for different forms of representation, and its various etymological histories remind us of this transition: "stock" and "brand," "horsepower" and "wild-cat strike" all testify to animals' economic anachronism. Now, as socially engaged artists ambivalently confront the question of their own lack of commodity status, they turn toward the animal as a representative art worker who seems to work, like they do, in a decommodified register. Animals' inability to engage in abstract labor renders them ideally suited to represent decommodified labor.

We need Marx in order to trace this process conceptually and historically. He provides a theory of how value production depends on abstract human labor and a historical archive that follows how animals are cast out of that economic order, how they are cast out of political economy as such. For Marx, what is unique about capitalism as a historically specific social organization is that its form of wealth is value, and value is derived from a system of socialized human activity in which concrete *work* necessarily produces and reproduces an abstract pairing in the form of abstract *labor*. It is within this duality of labor—and only this—in which value may be generated.[38] Value expresses both wealth in the material sense of an accumulation of goods and monies, and a "social relationship" of individual freedoms and coordinated dominations. Marx's exegeses of various facets of capitalism are numerous and many are well-known; I will only rehearse here the two that concern me in this chapter: the form of abstract labor and the exclusion of animals from that regime.

First, however, I want to make a methodological point about the discourse of abstraction into which this discussion must enter. Too often in criticism about the relation between aesthetics and the economy, abstraction is deployed as a freestanding entity so that it can mediate the difference between the two realms. One hears how the economy is "abstract" and how certain nonfigurative media are "abstract." One is told that the nonfiguration of abstract art might best represent economic abstraction even as, much of this writing states, there really is no way to represent an abstract economy. The generalization of "abstraction" renders possible its use as an analogy from one real to the other. And yet, these are in no way analogical abstractions.[39] Postone offers one explanation of the difference: "The category of abstract labor expresses [a] real social process of abstraction and is not simply based on a conceptual process of abstraction."[40] We might say that a conceptual abstraction is made by an individual; a social abstraction is made by many. The result of the positioning of different abstractions as analogues is that abstraction more often than not (and often unintentionally) becomes a metaphor; qualities are transposed from economic to conceptual abstraction without attention to the process of the production of those qualities, a lineage I have traced elsewhere.[41] And yet it is the process that concerns us.

Simply put: what is unique about abstract labor is not that it is abstract.[42] What is unique about it is that its abstract, global qualities are generated daily by local, concrete actions, and that through such actions individuals become radically and unintentionally collective. Again, Sohn-Rethel: "The value abstraction exists nowhere but [humans'] minds but doesn't spring from their minds."[43] When the human activity of work is reorganized under capitalism as value-producing labor, it takes on both abstract and concrete dimensions.[44] Because labor dwells abstractly within capitalism, it possesses certain unchanging features within that system. Labor, for example, cannot be deskilled; work, however, may be. The title of Harry Braverman's magisterial study of twentieth-century capitalist transformation may be seen in this respect to make an argument: *Labor and Monopoly Capital: The Degradation of Work in the Twentieth Century*. As the ratio between technology and labor changes with successive economic moments, what is known as the organic composition of capital, those changes are registered in patterns and organizations of daily work. The work becomes "degraded," but the labor, the abstraction of that work, remains unchanged.

Marx will explain the concrete dimension to us in the most material of terms—namely, those of tissues, hands, nerves, brains, blood, and so on. Most of us will be able to relate to this concrete dimension easily. We know the moments of experiencing our own energy as we begin to conceptualize and move toward a goal. We may feel a sense of ourselves as heightened and engaged or as alienated and controlled. And certainly we all know the moment when those elements of our energy begin to fade and yet we still need to keep working. Perhaps we feel a new distance between our sense of self and what we know is still required of the task at hand; perhaps we become conscious of our new lack of energy or perhaps we enter that dull realm where we are conscious of no longer feeling as attached to certain states of consciousness. One could say humans have been laboring like this for millennia, but Marx himself does not say that precisely because concrete labor changes in conjunction with its abstract dimension in a manner that is only possible under capitalism.

In this discussion, however, Marx feels the need to insist again and again that he is discussing "abstract human labor" or "human labor in the abstract." Marx indeed differentiates human labor in the abstract from animal work, a substance long important in agriculture and long important as a form of property. His insistence, for instance, that value comes from "human labor in the abstract" indexes a historical transition. He claims that "We are not now dealing with those primitive instinctive forms of labour that remind us of the mere animal.... We pre-suppose labour in a form that stamps it as exclusively human." This is a widely read passage in both labor studies and animal studies, less so in animality aesthetics. In a different text, Marx makes a similar claim: "... the result [of the exchange of labor] is that man (the worker) feels that he is acting freely only in his animal functions—eating, drinking, and procreating, or at most in his dwelling and adornment—while in his human functions, he is nothing more than animal. It is true that eating, drinking, and procreating, etc., are also genuine human functions. However, when abstracted from other aspects of human activity, and turned into final and exclusive ends, they are animal."[45] One *has to work*, and work is valuable in that it is nonanimal, but in working one becomes "nothing more than animal." Note the dual use of "animal" in these passages as both noun, "the mere animal," and adjective, "they are animal." In moving from noun to adjective, animal qualities are rendered static and available for representation: animals cease to circulate as capital and become, instead, its representative.

What instinctive forms does animal (primitive) labor take? Marx produces this distinction: "A spider conducts operations that resemble those of a weaver, and a bee puts to shame many an architect in the construction of her cells. But what distinguishes the worst architect from the best of bees is this, that the architect raises his structure in imagination before he erects it in reality."[46] Critics have often read this through the lens of animal alterity in which the passage becomes all too easily aporetic: How are we to know what a bee or spider imagines before undertaking a task? Marx's concern would be better said if the example were offered in an idiom of domination because, while it is conceptual thought that gives humans our unique "species being" (as opposed to animals' "species life"), it is abstract, impersonal domination that gives labor its socially organizing capacity and its value-generating capacity. Imagination here stands in for access to a kind of abstract thought that, contra Brian Massumi, we have no indication of whether animals are engaged.[47]

In reading the literature, one understands that a horse or sled dog seems to respond to the whip and its associated sounds and movements as commands.[48] But they do not seem to respond to those commands without the physical presence of the objects that symbolize them; that is, they do not respond to commands in a manner that is conceptually recognizable to humans. Because animals do not engage in abstract labor they are not subject to abstract domination, and because they are not available for abstract domination they cannot engage in abstract labor. Thus in Marx they now come to represent an obsolete and degraded kind of work. If what is unique about abstract labor is not that it is abstract but that the effect of its abstraction is that humans generate their own unfreedom as a material effect of their work, then we may conclude that animals' inability to labor abstractly and their inability to be dominated abstractly result from the same species-life. Finally, animals also seem to lack a conception of abstract time, which, as Harry Braverman reminds us, is ultimately what the worker transacts in: "What the worker sells . . . is not an agreed amount of labor, but the power to labor over an agreed period of time."[49]

We will not see this kind of labor-oriented genealogy in constructions of the postmodern or poststructural animal. The reason for its absence is that it is precisely animals' inability to labor that draws the poststructuralist to them. What the "postmodern animal" and Foucault-derived theories of neoliberalism that we have analyzed in the previous two chapters have in common is precisely the turn away from labor as a generative concept.[50] Foucault clearly articulates this turn when he claims that neoliberalism theorizes a "breakdown of labor into capital and income," as we saw in chapter 1. Critical animal studies, however, is not so clear in its theorizations about the relation between the animal and its ability or inability to work. Rather, labor disappears as a category of analysis. Meanwhile, in Marxist political economic discourse, the animal likewise vanishes, but for different reasons.

So, as it is Marx's conception of abstract human labor that differentiates him from his predecessors Adam Smith and David Ricardo, it is also his insistence that animals do not participate in this order that can be used to mark his intervention in political economy. Marx turns to animals to periodize capitalism as a mode of production and to distinguish his own method from that of his predecessors. Thus he cites Smith, for whom "'no equal capital puts into motion a greater quantity of productive labour than that of the farmer. Not only his labouring servants, but his labouring cattle are productive labourers.'"[51] Marx issues one of his famous retorts to Smith in *Capital*, volume 2: "How much Adam Smith barred his own way to an understanding of the role of labour-power in the valorization process is shown by [that] sentence, which puts the labour of the worker on the same level as that of draught cattle." And of course, what "a charming compliment" Smith bestows on workers, Marx concludes.[52] Marx might be some distance from Smith here, but they are both quite a distance from Aristotle, who claims that "there is little or no difference between uses of domestic animals and slaves."[53]

In a world made by and for abstract labor, animals are no longer laborers. It is their lack of function that enables them to join another opposite world: the world of the aesthetic. Thus Adorno states that "the constellation of animal/fool/clown is a fundamental layer of art."[54] Because, as Marina Vishmidt concisely reminds us, "anything that is not work can be art."[55] We see this juxtaposition in a variety of animals as they travel from worker to pet or collectible. Indeed, we see it in the development of "culture" itself. Raymond Williams has famously traced how "culture" moves from the verb associated with husbandry to an abstract noun. "Culture in all its early uses was a noun of process: the tending of something, basically crops or animals . . . . Culture as an independent noun, an abstract process or the product of such a process, is not important before C18 [the 1800s] and is not common before C19 [the 1900s]."[56]

Animals do work. Critics from Haraway to Bob Torres agree on this; oddly, Nicole Shukin's excellent *Animal Capital* neglects this element. And they do resist their certain work orders. Jason Hribal rightly catalogues an impressive list of animal "work actions": from cows refusing to be milked to killer whales dictating the terms of their Sea World performances up to and including killing their trainers.[57] But animals do not work abstractly, nor do they resist work abstractly; that is, they do not labor. It is the failure to realize how abstraction itself is redistributed in discussions of animality that generates Donna Haraway's correct concern that "the animal is a . . . humanist abstraction, a universal, an empty, a misplaced concreteness issue, but it's worse than that. It's stripped of all particularity and reality and most of all, from my view, stripped of relationality."[58] In tarrying with animals' status as value producers, Haraway settles on them as a "technology." Bob Torres labels them a "super-exploited living commodity" in his *Making a Killing: The Political Economy of Animal Rights*.[59] Both Torres and Haraway are correct in some sense. Like other technologies, animals seem to be able to generate profit without human work, and yet Marx insists that technological production is in some sense a misnomer: value is a social relationship that cannot be garnered from a machine that, after all, is itself made by a person. And animals may easily be categorized as living commodities that, like humans, are "super-exploited," but the vectors of their exploitation are distinct from those of humans.

My concern with these theories of animal productivity and exploitation is that they do not provide a site of mediation for the production of value through abstract labor. Indeed, this is a doubly worrisome lacuna: First, the omission of the abstract denies the central, value-generating properties of labor as a social system. Second, and more crucial for our purposes, the aesthetic itself derives from a scheme of abstract labor. We need only to revisit the assumptions of why categories such as purposelessness and autonomy remain crucial to any discussion of the aesthetic realm. Indeed, in addition to the animal, the other modern figure who is categorically disbarred from abstract value production is the artist, whose artistic creation as singular and nonproductive arises alongside the history of the animal that we have now traced.

And finally, from this knot of generative problems arise the twin forms of modern reflexivity. Both the aesthetic and labor are self-reflexive: art, as a representative of the aesthetic, generates freedom in its self-reflexivity, whereas work, as a form of labor, generates domination in its self-reflexivity. But crucially, these are two sides of the same coin (literally and figuratively). Animals function as adjuncts to this story. Yet, in their ability to represent abstract human labor because they do not participate in it, animals and the aesthetic do, in a sense, share a similar genealogy. They were waiting for each other.

Becoming Artists

It seems, then, to require only a small conceptual leap that animals should become a material (in artists' eyes) or that they should become artists (in critics' eyes.) In economic history working animals are, like steel, timbers, and bolts of fabric, the material signs of an older economy.[60] In art history, animals bridge the divide between the ready-made of early twentieth-century avant-garde practice and forms of embodiment and theatricality as found in mid-century avant-gardes, from the situationists to Fluxus to early performance art. Animals may be materials to be found, their movements and postures may inspire performance artists, or they may be seen not as performance artists but as performers, a fact to which animals' long history in circuses attests.[61] And like their human counterparts who pursue art, animals' engagements are nonpurposeful in that they act outside of capitalist logics; to remunerate them seems beside the point. If one wants to make money, one would not select the career of artist. Likewise, money itself has a strong representational dimension in that it represents the possibility of being exchanged at another time or place for something else, a transaction for which animals have heretofore demonstrated little use.

While the critical bibliography of how animals became an artistic material and how they became artists is impressive and growing, there is a noticeable dearth on work that concerns animals as a medium. It seems that animals transitioned not from material to medium, but from material to social practice artist. Even as we remember Raymond Williams's prescient 1977 essay, "From Medium to Social Practice," we can only speculate as to what category might be selected to ground the medium concept in this discussion: the "animal" or its instantiation as cat, dog, horse?[62] Or more generic categories such as mammal, bird, reptile, or amphibian? What are the formal possibilities and constraints of a species? Baker, in *Artist Animal*, introduces the compromise term "animal object in art" in an attempt to account for the strange miscegenation of something like medium, material, and subject that the animal becomes. Jonathan Burt offers multiple categories—"animal in art," "animal of art," "animal as art"—to negotiate a similar problem.[63] We would be incorrect to claim that animals could not become a medium: much as anything can be a commodity, anything can be a medium. But animals have not become the site of consistent reflection and institutionalization that would enable the discourse of medium to emerge, and indeed, they entered the art world as a material at the moment the art world was entering a postmedium condition. As we saw, Krauss herself takes recourse to animality in her own historicization of the "post-medium" condition.[64]

By the first decade of the 2000s, with the launch of publications such as *Humanimalia: a journal of human/animal interface studies* and *Antennae: The Journal of Nature in Visual Culture*, the animal had been reconstituted as an artist. Jonathan Burt declares simply that "animals co-create the artwork."[65] Giovanni Aloi makes an argument for why this might be so: "If we consider creativity as the universal originator of all art, then we find that animals are surely capable of displaying that."[66] His argument foreshadows the one Brian Massumi will offer in *What Animals Can Teach us About Politics*: "As we will see, [animal] instinct itself shows signs of elasticity, even a creativity one might be forgiven for labeling artistic."[67] And Lisa Jean Moore and Mary Kosut seek to remedy what they see as the injustice that lack of acceptance of the previous claims has rendered: animals (they write of bees in particular) "have long been giving their labor to the arts without due credit" and are now "being [transformed] into performance artists and sculptors."[68] Baker quotes artist Lucy Kimbell's *Rat Fair* installation, which asks viewers, and rat owners, a question: "Is Your Rat an Artist?"[69] Joseph Beuys had of course said something similar in 1974, not about rats per se but of animals. Yet he did so as provocation to expand the concept of creativity, not to expand the concept of the animal.[70]

Many of the aforementioned theorists are motivated by Deleuze and Guattari's concept of "becoming animal," in which the human trespasses into animal territory and vice versa as "each deterritorializes the other" within the art object.[71] The signal example of such art may be seen in the eponymously titled "Becoming Animal" show at MASS MoCA, staged in 2006 and curated by Nato Thompson. "Becoming Animal" contained multiple artworks that represented the transmogrification of human into animal-hybrid through the adoption of various animal appearances and actions. For example, artist Patricia Piccinini exhibited a transgenic organism developed by the University of Texas and placed it next to various humans, including children, in a series of staged "family portraits" as part of her project *A Young Family.*[72] Yet although such hybridity gathers much attention, one must note that while the central theoretical tenet in criticism of such work is framed through "becoming animal," the viewer is more likely to see animals "becoming artists." The critics I am in conversation with seem to acknowledge this, in fact if not in theory. The subtitle of the *Becoming Animal* catalogue is ambiguous: "Contemporary Art in the Animal Kingdom."

We are presented, then, with an odd theoretical lacuna. Many of these critics have interpreted the problematic of "becoming animal" quite literally as a process that is seeable, sayable, representable. And yet Deleuze and Guattari— Deleuze himself in particular—insist that "representation" is not the level on which their theories are staged. As Deleuze famously says in *Difference and Repetition,* "representation mediates everything but mobilizes and moves nothing."[73] The theoretical distance between animals as representation and the fundamentally antirepresentational practice of "becoming animal" has gone unremarked in much of this criticism. The missing link in such animal-art criticism, I want to argue, is the manner in which animals have been unrecognized as being tasked with performing and representing artistic labor.

Nor is such criticism limited to academic prose. In popular discourses as well, the animal as artist has arrived. In the *New York Times'* "Art That Snorts," a review of Jannis Kounellis's *Untitled (12 Horses),* or its "Cricket Ballet" investigations, which explored how crickets may be seen as modern dancers, the fluidity between animals and contemporary artists is seamlessly asserted. *National Geographic,* meanwhile, has produced article after article with titles such as "Painter-Explorers Turn Animals into Artists," "Brooklyn Dog a Rising Star in New York Art Scene," and "Painting Elephants Get On-line Gallery."[74] Still other trade publications straddle the line between academic and popular, including the bestselling *Why Cats Paint: A Theory of Feline Aesthetics* and the book based on the work of the Russian conceptual artists Komar and Melamid, *When Elephants Paint,* which Dave Eggers introduced and popularized.[75] Animals enter the art world to represent labor at the moment in which, more than ever, art makes money but most artists do not. I have explored the philosophical tradition of the commodity/aesthetics opposition, but there is also the reality to contend with. As we saw in the introduction, 71 percent of all public visual arts commissions in the United Kingdom generate no wage.[76] And as we saw in chapter 2, the artist collective BFAMFA PhD has shown that in the United States, among some 2 million working art graduates, only 8 percent make a living off their art.[77] Artists of-

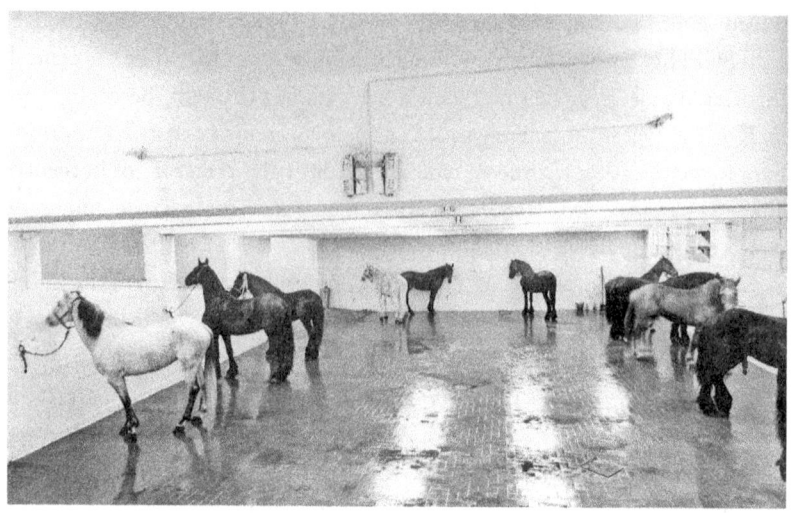

3.2 *Untitled (12 Horses)*. Photograph by Claudio Abate.

ten work in a decommodified register; animals are ideal representatives of an artistic labor that cannot be recompensed. The transformation of animal into artist reveals the changing discourses of art criticism but also, I want to insist, of labor history and thus of the relation between art and labor.

We can trace this development of the animal-as-artist through the life of one canonical animal work first staged in the 1960s and restaged in 2015. Consider the case of Jannis Kounellis, whose *Untitled (12 Horses)* offers perhaps the most iconic image of animality in contemporary art and whose various showings may be used to track the discourse of the unwaged animal as artist. Staged by Rome's *L'Attico* gallery in a parking garage in 1969, Kounellis's installation remains canonical in any genealogy of animals in art and to the local movement out of which it came, *arte povera* (figure 3.2).[78]

The documentation of the 1969 installation provides a striking image: a floor that gleams with a light whose shimmer contrasts with the heaviness of the animals' bodies, with their inability to reflect. Likewise, their well-known ability for locomoting and for producing "horse-power" is here visually circumscribed by their stillness and immobility. They are a potentiality whose number, twelve, resonates with biblical and apocalyptic sentiment, from the twelve disciples of Christ to the four horsemen of the apocalypse. For my purposes, however, the horses were clearly understood as a material that indexed the basic and unrefined commodities of an Italian economy divided between northern industry and southern agriculture. They were in this sense a "poor art" and a material of poverty; as such, the horses represented certain labors including those of craft, of farming, of the field. The horses present, then, as similar to material found in Kounellis's other works, which have included masonry, live birds, coffee beans, and wood cuts. The fact that his works are often untitled only draws more attention to how the material instantiation overrides any description or articulation of itself. For this *Untitled*, horses were selected by Kounellis, who did and still does consider himself a painter, to expand the canvas from so many "Enlightenment" paintings into a third dimension and to enliven theatrically the weightiness and solemnity of the many militaristic and celebratory horse sculptures that punctuate the urban landscape of Rome.

Like so much performance art of the 1960s and 1970s, "decommodification" was an important consideration in the criticism and execution of arte povera, although the term itself was not used.[79] A "poor art," critics such as Germano Celant stressed, should criticize an economic world that produces categories such as rich and poor. In the original catalogue essay for Kounellis's piece, Alberto Boatto suggests that *Untitled (12 Horses)* "forcefully expresse[s] a challenge to the established order of the art market" by "turning the dealer into a stable boy" through a spatial "duality [comprising] living and inert."[80] While there is a certain irony in the fact that an art gallery's roster is often referred to as its "stable," Boatto nonetheless misunderstands a decommodified aesthetic. Such an aesthetic can never be located in the materiality, only in the sociality. Thus his hope, though genuine, may be understood as a moment of "reification," a process by which a subjective relationship is transferred to an objective sphere and then governed by that objective realm.[81]

Kounellis himself remained aware of this tension. When asked in 2011 about contemporary artist Tino Sehgal's supposedly noncommodifiable performances, which eschew all forms of documentation and materiality and which museums, galleries, and collectors have eagerly purchased, Kounellis responded: "There has always been someone who has bought a work . . . This is nothing new, the challenge instead is to remain dialectical."[82] Boatto's catalogue essay ends with the odd proclamation that "if they are horses, they are Kounellis." This is a strange sentiment because throughout the essay, and in much criticism of Kounellis, the horses are clearly a material to be worked on, chosen for their referential connections to other times, places, arts, and traditions.[83] Even Boatto himself suggests that the horse "represents culture more than rustic simplicity." While Kounellis's work introduces "the animal" into art, the animal remains an animal in such art.

It is only with the contemporary restaging of *Untitled (12 Horses)* that the horses emerge from their position as a material into their new standing as crucial participants. In 2015, *Untitled* was exhibited in New York City for the final show at the West Village location of the gallery Gavin Brown Enterprise. It was shown alongside work by Rirkrit Tiravanija and Elaine Sturtevant. The repetitions and reformulations at play here are multiple: from *arte povera* to the now canonized movement of Arte Povera; from radical Italy of the 1960s to financialized New York of 2015; from a Rome where statues of horses populate the landscape to the postindustrial, commercial chic of Manhattan's West Village. In terms of the show's curation, *arte povera* was translated into something like socially engaged art. Kounellis's work was adjacent to Tiravanija's installation, which seems not only to be "untitled" but to in fact have no name; it is referred to in accounts as his "cooking." Tiravanija, a Thai artist hailed in Bourriaud's *Relational Aesthetics*, is well known for such cooking practices. Here he installed a fire pit for roasting a pig and proceeded to hand out pork tacos to gallery goers.[84]

The subtle generic translation from arte povera to socially engaged art is understandable, if awkward. Tiravanija's practice brings the domestic and imminently social act of eating into the gallery space, where one can not only see, smell, and touch, but in fact consume the art object/situation as a digestible experience. Thus his installation is not unlike Kounellis's first staging of *Untitled* in which the smells, sounds, and movements of the horses were received as aesthetic interventions into the stillness and quietude of painterly and sculptural space. Still, differences exist between the larger movements out of which these works come. *Arte povera* sought to intervene in a different public and marshal it toward different ends than has much socially engaged art. As Nicholas Cullinan has recently argued, *arte povera* declared acts, not of social welfare, but of guerrilla warfare, to be the terrain in which "art" and "life" would dissolve into each other.[85]

At Gavin Brown Enterprise, Kounellis's horses indexed the transmogrification of art and life. Indeed, the horses were the focal point of seemingly every question, concern, and demand that this installation provoked: Who is a participant? Who is a spectator? Under what conditions should animals as art exist, both literally (how are they kept?) and conceptually (why are they kept?) In addition to the real materiality of the horses' bodies, the discursive dimension of their being was just as crucial an aspect of the show. Asked the stock question, "What is this about?" gallery owner Gavin Brown responded, "I don't think it's about anything." He added that meaning would be found "more through the coverage than the art."[86] Brown's sentiment is not specific to this work, of course; it only seems to confirm Lane Relyea's argument in *Your Everyday Art World* about the importance of what he calls "networked sociality."[87]

That coverage, as it were, contains a central inversion. Whereas during the 1969 installation, the gallery had *become a stable* and the dealer a *stable boy*, now the hierarchies of placement and belonging were reversed: the success of the work in 2015 was, as the *New York Times*'s Roberta Smith put it, that ". . . the elemental, curative force of animals and their size, and quiet, are felt more keenly in this setting than in a stable."[88] Smith's claim contains a certain redundancy: What is a gallery, after all, if not a place where visuality, dimensionality, and sensibility may be heightened? She noted that the dampening of the acoustics by the black-matted floor rendered still and silent both the animals and the space. Smith's comments included descriptions of the installation's production in an idiom of horse husbandry, and she considered where the horses dwell, who cares for them, how they are constrained in the gallery, and their schedule of return to the stable each night. Each of these might be understood as the now classic questions of duration that so often accompany performance art. This interest in how exactly the horses occupy the gallery was not unique to Smith's article. The installation was well covered and all of the coverage took similar form. "At all times, the horses are looked after by three attentive grooms," declared *artnet News* almost preemptively.[89]

Nonetheless, and as if on cue, protestors too arrived to note, contra Roberta Smith, that a gallery is no place for a horse. *Art Review* describes how protestors "enter[ed] the gallery on the penultimate day of the show with signs that stated 'It's not art, it's animal abuse' and 'Modern Slavery.'"[90] That the protesters decried Kounellis's horses and not Tiravanija's pig roasting and taco assembly stand seems only to confirm the ongoing, distantiating properties of the aesthetic as such: it is the pointlessness of the aesthetic that frames the horses' "abuse." The pig roasting, by contrast, serves a purpose; after all, the tacos were eaten, but the horses do "nothing." Both the critics and the protestors affirm that the frame of the aesthetic is crucial to any assessment of the horses and that it is within that frame where we might see the possibilities and problems of the horses' lives. But it is also the protestors who introduce the question of labor, which had been only indirectly referred to in criticism of the work and which had been presented in terms of worries about the horses' conditions. Whereas in the 1969 staging, the horses were an *arte povera* material to be differentiated from minimalist uses of industrial commodities, now they were viewed as subjects to be cared for, attended to, and worried about. Questions of space, placement, material, light—some of these formal problems are mentioned in passing, but those elements of Kounellis's installation remain overall secondary to the working conditions of the horses.

Except, crucially, those conditions were not referred to as working conditions. They were rather discussed as something resembling "welfare." That the horses were worthy of such consideration shows that they had emerged out of their position as "material." Critics acknowledge that they are doing something that needs protection, that requires their energy and effort, and that "something" seems like "work"—note the focus on the horses' hours. But it is not referred to as work. This ambivalence about how or whether the horses are working is crucial to my argument because it registers a changed status of an artistic labor that these critics intimate but do not address. Rather, the inability to categorize their actions appears as a series of questions: How should these horses be treated? How are their needs different from those of other gallery visitors? How hot is the gallery space? What does matted rubber feel like on a horse's hoof? Do they stand in their own urine and feces? The *New York Times* included the words of one horse expert–visitor in its coverage: ". . . Robert Clemens, who was visiting the exhibition on Friday and has had 17 horses, noted that the setup wasn't at all different from a horse stall where they wouldn't be able to turn around, and the concrete floor covered with rubber for their hooves was likewise much like good horse accommodations. 'There's nothing out of the ordinary going on here,' he said."[91]

The horse-keeper's assertion represents both the utopian and dystopian hopes of any avant-garde: an art in which nothing is out of the ordinary because the bounds between art and life have been dissolved. Only now, nothing is out of the ordinary for the horses as opposed to for the artist or viewer. "Mr. Brown," the *Times* concluded, ". . . has conducted his gallery with a certain largess and a multi-purposefulness that aims to make everyone—even a dozen horses—feel at home."[92]

But where does a horse feel at home? As the discourse–as–painterly space of the installation continued to expand, People for the Ethical Treatment of Animals (PETA) was invited to contribute its understanding of the work as well. If art critics were ambivalent about what exactly these horses were doing and what protections they needed to do it, then PETA offered clarification. PETA senior vice president Lisa Lange noted that "these horses are standing for hours on a hard surface, tethered and unable to exercise or rest." She furthermore suggested that "if people in New York City want to gawk at horses

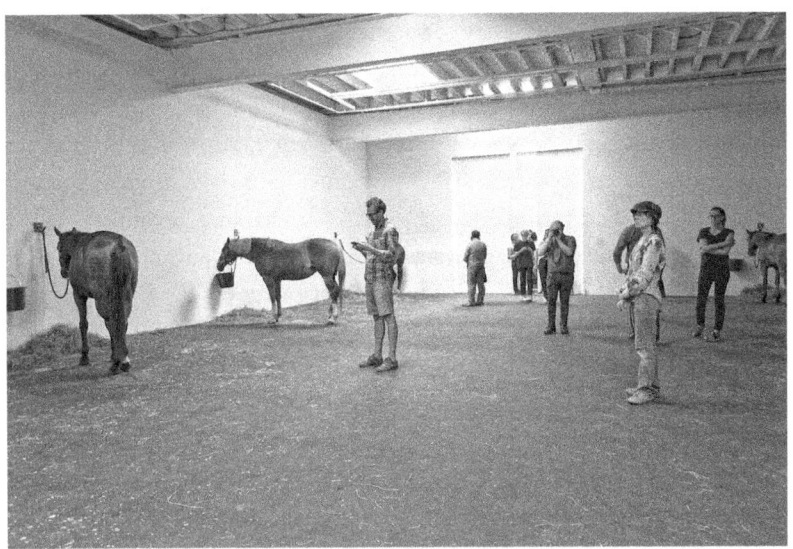

3.3 *Untitled (12 Horses)*. Photograph courtesy of Allison C. Meier.

forced to stand all day long, they can go to the [Central Park] hack line and see the horses lined up in all weather extremes and forced to drag carriages full of tourists around the city."[93] Lange's statement clearly argues that these horses are exploited workers. But her statement also contains a certain irony. If one wants to consume horses as visual pleasure, she goads her interviewer, go look at them working; locate an actual *workhorse*. Of course, her statement also offers an obvious and ethically inflected rhetorical question: Do we really need *more* horses presiding over New York City–based spectacles? We already have the Central Park carriage horses, on whose behalf activists have been demanding an end to carriage rides for years.[94]

And the Central Park workhorses indeed offer the clearest counterexample to Kounellis's horses. The workhorses are governed by the city and described by both activists and the Parks Department in a rubric of employment. The Coalition to Ban Horse-Drawn Carriages claims that these horses have high "turn-over rates," whereas the city responds that there are clear "rules governing the scheduling of their shifts" and notes that, "by law, horses are allowed to work 9 hours a day, 7 days a week."[95] Like many workplace regulations, however, these rules promise more than they offer. "Although they are supposed to get a 15 minute break every 2 hours, there is no way to enforce it," the activists respond.[96] Kounellis's horses, in contrast, undertook six-hour shifts in the gallery; they returned "home" to their stables each night.

Once they enter the gallery space, the horses, then, become something other than workers. But the constitution of that otherness remains unclear. Criticism of animals in art tells us that "the animal" is unmistakably there and real and unable to be symbolized beyond itself in artwork. Broglio writes of an animal-based art in which "we encounter animals as unassailably animals."[97] There is no form besides the body of the animal because, as Baker states, contemporary art "carves out a space where the physical animal can be present as itself."[98] Massumi notes that our categories for discussing animals must be absolutely immanent and explains that we may only speak of "a cockroachity of the cockroach," or "a mousiness of the mouse" (never using that confining, definite article "the").[99] Indeed, the art journalism and criticism I have cited in response to the restaging of Kounellis's *Untitled* would seem to conform to the statements of Baker and Broglio: the horses catalyze and orient the structure of the work as well as the criticism, and they do so *as horses*. We may now return to Boatto's odd claim from 1969: "If they are horses, they are Kounellis." In retrospect, his assessment seems a prescient one, as the horses would soon escape their position as material and be placed alongside, if not surpass, Kounellis himself.

To introduce an arts-theorized language of work into this discussion we might turn to Claire Bishop's notion of "delegated performers," those not-quite-workers/not-quite-artists encountered so often in contemporary art.[100] Bishop uses this construction in *Artificial Hells* to explain "the act of hiring non-professionals or specialists in other fields to undertake the job of being present and performing at a particular time and a particular place on behalf of the artist, and following his/her instructions."[101] Certainly, the "delegated performer" has much in common with the participants of Kounellis's menagerie: the horses are present, they follow someone else's rules, they are bound by the clock. The *Observer* describes their working life as such: "The horses' day starts around 10 a.m., when they are ushered into the space and tethered to the wall, and they spend the day there. At 6 p.m. they are taken to a local stable, where they spend the night."[102]

One of Bishop's examples of "delegated performance" comes from the practice of Spanish artist Santiago Sierra, who regularly employs undocumented immigrants and day laborers to undertake humiliating endurance tasks in his gallery-based installations; such tasks constitute the installation. The titles of his work, which themselves have a central conceptual importance for their economic claims, include *250 cm Line Tattooed on 6 Paid People* and *8 People Paid to Remain Inside Cardboard Boxes*. The fact of the "delegated performers'" economic class functions as an important tenet of Bishop's argument. The artists that Bishop understands to engage in delegated performance "hire people to perform their own socio-economic category, be this on the basis of gender, class, ethnicity, age, disability, or (more rarely) a profession."[103]

And indeed it is the in the realm of economic class, of payment and profession, that Kounellis's installation remains so provocative. The mere presence of an animal should not, of course, be taken to indicate that the animal is working, much as the presence of a human does not indicate human labor. Rather, in keeping with the themes of this book, we would instead suggest that such a claim undergirds the basic position of real subsumption, in which no action could ever exist outside of a regime of the extraction of relative surplus value and that animal-based art, too, participates in this scheme. Sierra's directions, which include people standing awkwardly and uncomfortably in a gallery, do seem to indicate work, however. Yet ultimately it is the word "paid" in his performance documentation that insists that we understand his installation within the realm of wage labor. And it is the presence of the wage that instructs viewers that the "paid people" in Sierra's installations should be considered "delegated performers."

Kounellis's horses clearly occupy an art space. But the description of them is just as clearly as workers, as agents whose activities transform their immediate environment through the exertions of their being. If the horses *are* working as Kounellis's employees, then they are not doing the kind of work one tends to associate with workhorses, including pulling, being ridden, hovering, or corralling. And if they are working, Kounellis's horses are not laboring because, as discussed in the previous section, animals do not participate in the labor abstraction. Finally, if they are working, they are exceptional in the sense that workers are defined in part by their recompense—thus the necessity of the word "paid" in Sierra's installations. The horses are not remunerated and there is no wage-based or language-based confirmation of them as workers. They cannot be paid—because how do you pay a horse?—and if one isn't being paid, how can it be that one is a waged worker? Wage labor requires payment of a wage. It is precisely these negations of the horses as delegated performers or easily recognized workers that situate them to represent decommodified labor.

To understand how the horses come to represent decommodified labor in Kounellis's installation, we must first note that these horses perform an absence of skill, and the distance between their potential skills and their actual repose organizes the work's modest sublimity. The horses' deskilling is then magnified, as it were, into an artistic gesture that produces both the work's grandeur—the possibility of their power and motion—and its ability to generate anxiety: Should they be kept tethered in a gallery? Deskilling itself, as John Roberts notes, is one of the crucial narratives of twentieth-century art history.[104] The concept's importance derives from its ability to mediate between art as a vocation—that which is teachable, reproducible, perhaps even waged—and the fact that no matter how "deskilled" conceptual art becomes, it still participates in "the institution of art."[105] If work is the fungible, adaptable category of labor, then skill could be its equivalent in art. Artistic skill may change, artists may be deskilled or reskilled, but *some* skill, even that of Duchampian nomination or conceptual formulation, will always be required for maintaining art as a category.

The moment of artistic deskilling, then, has similarities with the progressive deskilling of all work under capitalism: it can always be transformed but it can never disappear. Workers are gradually stripped of whatever hard-won craft they possess. They follow the path laid out by Harry Braverman in *Labor and Monopoly Capital: The Degradation of Work in the Twentieth Century*: as technology accretes to capital, it is used to challenge the centrality of the workers' ability to control the production process and to interrupt workers' control of their own energies.[106] Deskilling minimizes but does not deplete workers' ability to valorize their labor. Kounellis's horses are represented in the gallery space as deskilled workers. They are also represented as deskilled artists, and these two deskillings index different historical processes. Roberts argues that, "despite the artist's would-be loss of all-around artisanal skills and the enforcement of her social alienation, there is no comparable loss of artistic autonomy; other skills directed towards self-motivated and creative ends fill the gap...."[107] We may interpret Roberts's claim as an argument that artistic deskilling may be used to represent all deskilling precisely because artistic labor is labor of a different sort. Roberts thus claims that "the demise of traditional artistic skills is not the result of a coercive process of control and division."[108]

Transformation in skill does not fundamentally reorient what constitutes art, but it may transform the aesthetic judgment about such art. Sianne Ngai has called the problem of the aesthetic evaluation of work a problem of the "gimmick."[109] For Ngai, a literary or artistic gimmick produces a certain anxiety: that there is either too much work in an art object (think Proust or Joyce) or not enough work (think of the ready-made). The anxiety produced through

Kounellis's horses is not unrelated to Ngai's "theory of the gimmick." And yet the anxiety found in response to Kounellis's horses seems more ontological. The question is not, Are these horses working too little or too much? but, Are they workers? In fact, we must see these horses as representing decommodifed labor. What Steve Baker understands as the "postmodern animal" or the "the artist-animal" I understand as the "art worker animal," a construction that comes into being in a neoliberal, ostensibly post-labor era.

The wages of art may have been decommodified, but when represented by the art worker animal, such decommodification becomes a site of critique of all artistic labor in its contemporary forms. Indeed, the horses are probably not the only members of Kounellis's entourage or Gavin Brown Enterprise's staff to whom we might pose the question, Are you working? Think of the gallery interns. Think of the other artists. In *Untitled (12 Horses)* the proposition is doubled because the horses are categorically excluded from the wage. They are nonwaged workers who represent the nonwaged labor of the aesthetic itself. In that sense, their work is more conceptually challenging than Sierra's series of payments, foremost, of course, because horses cannot be paid. The horses are "not really" workers because the one thing that defines workers as such is the wage and a horse, or any animal, is "unwageable." They may be given food, shelter, water, care, but they do not receive a wage.[110] Yet the definition of decommodified labor, as explored in depth in the introduction, is that which either forgoes or is disbarred from the wage.

The horse has become an artist. The artist can be paid but is not paid. The horse is not payable. The horse-as-artist is, then, doubly decommodified and that conjunction has been misread in the critical literature as an essential "thereness" or a haecceity of the horses that cannot be mediated. In fact, animals in art come to us as already mediated by their aesthetic wagelessness and their ability to be stand-ins for the art workers whose socially engaged art aims at a redistributive aesthetic. Finally, it is from the work of Harry Braverman that Howard Singerman takes his influential notion of the "deskilled" artist in his book *Art Subjects* to note that by the mid-1990s an advanced art degree did not provide any level of craft and instead provided a study in the personality, conduct, and what we might call the self-fashioning necessary to inhabit the role of artist. The contemporary artist must, according to Singerman, have the ability to manipulate and reshape not material forms but social relations. That skill the horses still possess.

Trading with the Enemy

We have seen how Kounellis frames the problem of decommodified labor by withholding the horses' horsepower in order to represent their deskilling, which then, ironically, reaffirms their ability to represent the decommodified labor of artists. Duke Riley's 2013 *Trading with the Enemy* reverses the problem, as it were: Riley "reskills" a flock of homing pigeons and sets them on a similar conceptual, if different literal, course: these pigeons fly from Cuba back to their coop in Florida carrying Cuba's famous contraband cigars and recording their journeys as they go. In Riley's performance, the pigeon as "art worker animal," will again place animals in a position so that they may represent the decommodified labor of socially engaged art.

On view at the Brooklyn Museum in October 2014, *Trading with the Enemy* sat nestled in a corner.[111] Three video screens were mounted on a wall, displaying what appeared, depending on how long one stared and when, to be footage at various levels of visual abstraction: some of it aerial with the built environment, horizon, and sky visible; some of it conversational; some of it so nonfigurative it was impossible for the viewer to contextualize (figure 3.4). Earphones under each screen invited the viewer to add sound to their experience, but for the most part what a viewer heard was a mechanical whirring noise, repetitive and atonal enough to not have a precise origin. It is not until various pigeons appear in the footage that the narratives implicit in the video reveal themselves. Together with Riley, these pigeons are documenting their collective flight, a collaboration between them and the artist.

Once she ascertains that relationship, the viewer might pivot to the right to see a house-like wooden structure. She might hear a similarly irregular noise or smell something rather unusual. A wooden pigeon coop sits several feet from the videos. One needs the wall text to string together with some coherency sound, moving image, coop, and pigeons. Unlike Haacke's *Chickens Hatching*, which captured processes that unfolded or not with little assistance from the artist or gallery staff, *Trading with the Enemy* required skilled training and execution from the artist and the pigeons themselves. Riley equipped a group of homing pigeons, some with customized cigar holders and others with customized video cameras, and set them on course from Havana to Key West. The training of the birds took several years; certain pigeons made the journey in days, others in weeks, others haven't been heard from since. And unlike Kounellis's relationship with horses, Riley was intimately involved in the birds' lives and welfare. He trained them and lived with them in a shared

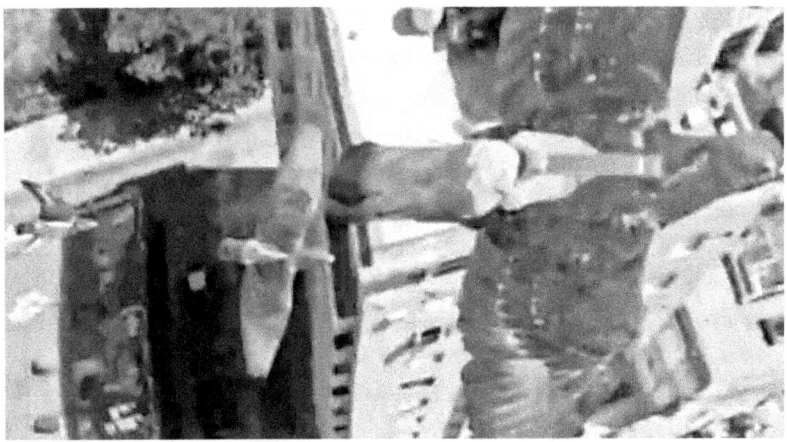

3.4 Still from *Trading with the Enemy*. Courtesy of Duke Riley.

coop. Intimately familiar with their individual bodies, he retrofitted digital cameras using bra strap–based harnesses so these apparatuses would be light enough and comfortable enough for the pigeons to both make and record their ninety-mile journeys.

Riley is known in the New York and socially engaged art scene (the latter through his relationship with Creative Time) for his historical re-creations and his bird artistry. He has re-created a Revolutionary War–era ship, run a speakeasy, and given many a bird tattoo. Indeed, he makes his living as a tattoo artist, not a socially engaged artist. Unlike Kounellis, Riley is, at present, not a canonical artist, a fact that necessarily modifies my own methodology of critiquing his work, as it changes the critical bibliography with which my analysis engages. Yet, perhaps more than any working artist today, his work exemplifies and problematizes the "artist animal." That stature results from Riley's more recent, and also pigeon-based, installation *Fly By Night* (2016). A spectacular performance staged nightly over the course of six weeks in which Riley flew some two thousand pigeons, each with LED lights strapped to their ankles, in formation over New York City's harbor, *Fly By Night* garnered international attention along with features in the *New Yorker*, the *Wall Street Journal*, and the *Guardian*.

Trading with the Enemy introduces itself through its wall text and through the early text-based moments of the video as a kind of subterfuge. Riley manifestly invites his viewers to witness a sleight of hand through his assertion that "millions of dollars" are spent annually by the U.S. government on surveillance and border enforcement. He then rhetorically wonders whether "nature," to use an imprecise but perhaps necessary word, can circumvent the technology of the U.S. state; he wonders whether the view from the drone can be replaced by a bird's-eye view. If, as Haraway asserts, "working animals" should be understood as a kind of technology, then Riley's performance pits the obsolete technology of the carrier pigeon against the emergent one of the drone to ask how we see various economies. The artist tells us that we are in the world of smugglers and counterhegemonic movements, both locatable on a flock of homing pigeons on whom Riley bestows names befitting their actions.

This initial categorization through the types of action various birds are tasked with performing produces a now familiar conceptual division between animal as material and animal as artist. In the *New York Times'* coverage of Riley's work, the distinction is captured as such: "The cigar-carrying birds were named for notorious smugglers, like Pierre Lafitte, of New Orleans, and Minnie Burr, from Memphis, who transported supplies under her skirts during the Civil War. The documentarians were named for directors who had trouble with the law, like Roman Polanski and Mel Gibson."[112] That is, those pigeons that carry cigars are "cigar-carrying birds" while those that carry video cameras are simply "documentarians." The *Times'* story is ambivalently titled, "Avian Artistry, with Smuggled Cigars" so that it remains productively unclear whether "avian artistry" refers to the birds or the artist.

If we do approach the animal-as-material with any kind of protomedium specificity, then we must note that pigeons are animals of a different sort than horses. While the horse commands grandeur, either respectfully or fearfully, the pigeon has been transformed into a kind of universal nuisance, one that has recently had its story told in Colin Jerolmack's surprising ethnography, *The Global Pigeon*.[113] The horse harkens back to a majestic, imperialist history but the pigeon has no such lineage, and we are far from the days when Darwin's editor famously urged him to devote *The Origin of Species* to the bird and claimed that "everyone is interested in pigeons."[114] Yet as an artistic readymade, the pigeon seems more inviting than the horse. The pigeon is a castaway species, an overlooked species, one more akin to a urinal or shovel. At the margin of utility, the pigeon seems an obvious choice for an artistic engagement: "Pigeons are no longer useful to most societies as messengers or as sources of food and fertilizer," Jerolmack asserts. Jerolmack conveys this uselessness in a language of objective progress and subjective deskilling. "They [pigeons] have been replaced by cheaper and more efficient alternatives," he continues.

And finally, he stresses the kind of dialectical tension that we would expect of a made-by-human, natural kind: "Today, the pigeon's docile demeanor, its fecundity, its nitrogen-rich feces, its proclivity to always return home, and its easy adaptability to human environments—traits that humans once valued and intentionally enhanced—are exactly the traits that bother modern urbanites."[115]

Jerolmack's wonderful ethnography is itself interesting in this discussion for the manner in which it may be used to highlight the race, class, and gender dynamics of socially engaged artwork in its specific relationship to animals. Even as some anthropologists have turned to what Eben Kirksey calls "multi-species ethnography," Jerolmack keeps his sights trained on the mostly working-class Puerto Rican, Dominican, and African American men who keep and fly pigeons in Brooklyn.[116] Along with the changing demographics of Brooklyn, an older generation of Italian pigeon-keepers has now been replaced, and the current generation of Latino and black ones seems to be vanishing. "The once ubiquitous rooftop [pigeon] coops of New York are now as scarce as the longshoremen who often built them," Jerolmack claims, clearly tying pigeon-flyers to older forms of industrial work and to an expiring industrial masculinity.[117] The angle of analysis that foregrounds the class and race of New York pigeon-flyers has been absent in discussions of Riley's work, even as his pigeon works could certainly be understood as an appropriation of their craft.[118]

On the one hand, were the men of Jerolmack's study in an art gallery, were they differently educated, were they white, these pigeon-flyers may well have been considered socially engaged artists. Instead, in the ample popular commentary on Riley's work, the working-class and often black and Latino history of the skills Riley possesses disappears, and it is the pigeons that emerge as the artists. Jerolmack urges us to realize that, similar to certain strategies of minimalism that we saw with Richard Serra in chapter 1, Riley's work reproduces in the aesthetic realm a waning economy and in particular the racial and class dynamics that economy has bequeathed. While the pigeon-flyers of Brooklyn discuss with Jerolmack the gradual deskilling of their various trades and the fact that pigeon-flying is "hard work," Riley uses the accumulated communal, social knowledge of this community to craft a performance in which the nexus of the artist working with a reskilled animal represents yet another dimension of decommodified labor.

The argument I want to make is that *Trading with the Enemy* gives us an example of how animals in art may represent decommodified labor in two dimensions: First, in its use of animal as material, the pigeons are the sensual and conceptual backbone of the installation. Second, the installation offers a representation of the "art worker animal" as an ambiguous worker. It's not only the *New York Times* but also Riley himself who calls certain of his flock documentarians. What we see in the video component of *Trading with the Enemy*, what we see in the gallery, are representations of the pigeons' time and energy as they transit through different economic formations: capitalist, socialist, transnational. *Trading with the Enemy*'s focus on reskilling as opposed to deskilling may in fact be seen as a response to Kounellis's vision of the art worker animal. Riley's installation accomplishes such critique through its representation of multiple economies and multiple labors, all limned by the boundaries of U.S. law.

We can begin simply by locating the many economies and many labors that compose this work. Cuba may be an "enemy," but what that means in economic terms is hardly straightforward. For sixty years or so, Cuba was the great site of American-run foreign economic crime. (Remember the island's appearance in *Godfather II*: "All this is ours," Hyman Roth says to Michael Corleone as they survey Havana's shimmering harbor.) It was the central haven—out of the country but in the same time zone, as the saying goes—for American capital flight along the eastern seaboard.[119] When Cuba ceased to host American money laundering through its radical socialization of land and labor during the Revolution of 1959, it became the United States' economic enemy.

Riley could in fact be citing this economic history in *Trading with the Enemy*, and the work must be said to contain socialist labor, too. The birds left from Havana, and no doubt Riley had various dealings with support staff there. Riley has pointedly declined to discuss how the birds arrived in Havana or how they were released from their coop while in Cuba. "How those birds got to Cuba I cannot say," he has offered.[120] Indeed, whatever Riley's economic dealings in Cuba were, we can assume that he broke American law by "trading" money in exchange for labor with "the enemy." We can also assume that any Cubans he worked with were in violation of Cuban law for selling their labor on Cuba's expansive but illegal informal market. That Cuban labor, like most Cuban labor, is not precisely decommodified, but it is not precisely commodified, either. The common saying in Cuba to describe the official, state-run market for labor is, "They pretend to pay us. We pretend to work."[121] Fantasy and disavowal suture this economy, like most others.

Riley transacts with Cuban workers, but he does not bring Cuban commodities back into American economic space. Rather, the pigeons are responsible for such actions, and it is they who visibly trade with the enemy. Nonetheless it is Riley, not the birds, who might ultimately be prosecuted, and it is here that we may locate a parallel of artistic labor to the pigeons' representation of decommodified labor. The birds work but cannot be paid, just as they break the law but cannot be prosecuted. U.S. federal code reads as follows: "Regulation does not limit travel of U.S. citizens to Cuba *per se*, but it makes it illegal for U.S. citizens to have transactions (spend money or receive gifts) in Cuba, under most circumstances. The regulations require that persons subject to U.S. jurisdiction be licensed in order to engage in any travel-related transactions pursuant to travel to, from, and within Cuba."[122] Only persons, citizens, are subject to enforcement. Yet another wrinkle in the law is that academics and artists (because their work is not considered to produce value) are able to conduct themselves professionally in Cuba, and any American is able to bring back from Cuba unlimited "artwork and informational material." As nonpersons and noncitizens, the pigeons are free to come and go. As "artists," the pigeons are free to carry whatever artistic cargo they choose. But in their artistic production, they are transporting the most illicit and desired of Cuban commodities, the Cohiba cigar. In *Trading with the Enemy*, we watch them carry their cargo.

The moving visual abstraction and figuration that compose the pigeons' documentary footage slowly absorb the viewer. As the birds' flight commences, the bright colors of Havana's facades and rooftops give way to the monochrome blue-grey of sky and ocean, only to diversify into bright blues and pinks as the pigeons land in their coop in Key West. When the birds fly together, one of the documentarians might record a cigar smuggler. When they fly solo, the view is often only of sky and sea meeting at horizon. At other times their wings, breast, or neck will frame the images. The sound of their wings flapping in the wind is oddly similar to a plane's propellers, droning and constant. Certain of the pigeons' videos might evoke Rothko: blocks of color succeed each other in orderly fashion. Others are edited in Warholian fashion: bright images, backlit and electric, grab the viewer's attention. One clip showcases a pigeon's situationist-like intervention. The pigeon takes a detour and lands unnoticed on a charter fishing boat as Jimmy Buffet is heard crooning in the background. Landing on the boat's mast, the pigeon eavesdrops, surveys the vessel, and records the conversational chatter below. Ultimately, it is spotted by a passenger who notices but cannot identify its harness and camera. "It's got something on it," this passenger observes. "It's got a bomb on it!"

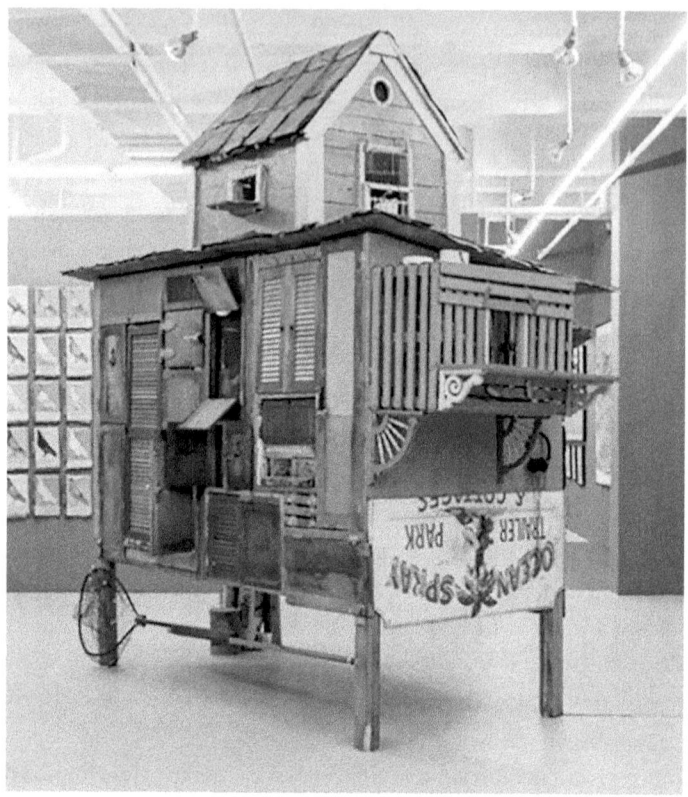

3.5 Installation view, *Trading with the Enemy*. Courtesy of Duke Riley.

another of the boat's passengers exclaims in a worried tone. As if sensing the danger from its trespass, the pigeon continues on its journey.

During the work's museum installation, the three videos loop and at any time the viewer can see the real that the videos index: the pigeons that stand, coo, flap, and sleep in solemn testimony to their work. They do so in a colorful coop that Riley fashioned from discarded nautical and industrial material that he pilfered around Key West (figure 3.5). In the museum, the pigeons sit in close proximity to the mounted video screens, and the immediacy of their bodies along with the time compression of the four-minute video modifies how the nature of their work is represented. While Riley and the pigeons trained for years, their journey took, on average, two weeks. (Riley claims a "well-trained bird" can complete the ninety-mile distance in eight hours.) The looping videos are roughly four minutes each. That the time of the pigeons' skilling and the temporal unfolding of that skill evaporate into the performance has the effect of obscuring the pigeons' work and of producing the questions of duration that organize so many discussions of performance art. Nonetheless, we have no trouble recognizing the pigeons' work. Why is that the case? How does the visibility of the pigeons' work relate to the question of how decommodified labor in art understands and responds to discussions of neoliberalism, with its conceptual disappearance of labor, and real subsumption, with its durational extension of labor?

Again, the pigeons must be understood as representations of decommodified labor. They themselves work but do not labor. Yet in their representations they do offer a contribution to a theoretical understanding of our contemporary political economy. Kounellis's horses might be said to frame a neoliberal approach to the economy. Their work seems, and indeed was, difficult to locate. Riley's pigeons, by contrast, are easier to characterize as "workers" because of their motion, their energy, the fact of their destination, and because of the viewer's knowledge that Riley has extracted from them their documentary footage. They did something for him. Their work, however, seems uncomfortably close to what these pigeons would be doing were they not working—namely, flying. Doing something that one would be doing anyway creates a different type of work. Perhaps their work has a certain similarity to what sleep constitutes for Jonathan Crary in his recent book *24/7*.[123] Both sleep for humans and flying for pigeons must and will be done, but now that doing extracts value for someone else. The pigeons' work, then, might be said to represent labor under real subsumption. As we saw in this book's introduction, Antonio Negri claims that real subsumption is "exemplified by the inability to distinguish measure from substance ... [and] the inability to distinguish the totality of life from the totality from which this life is woven."[124] As we have seen, this running together of life-spheres Negri says produces a kind of "tautological time."

The pigeons' work conforms to but also critiques tautological time. Flying becomes art through their work. Thus the pigeons' actions may be seen to partake in tautological time. But flying remains flying, and many, indeed most, of Riley's pigeons refused incorporation into his art. "It never occurred to me that they would take breaks," Riley commented in response to reviewing their hours of footage. Indeed, some of these pigeons took more than breaks. Most of them never returned to Riley. They left the scene in which they could be understood to have been subsumed. The risk of Riley's skilling of these pigeons is that they would refuse participation in his art and that the installa-

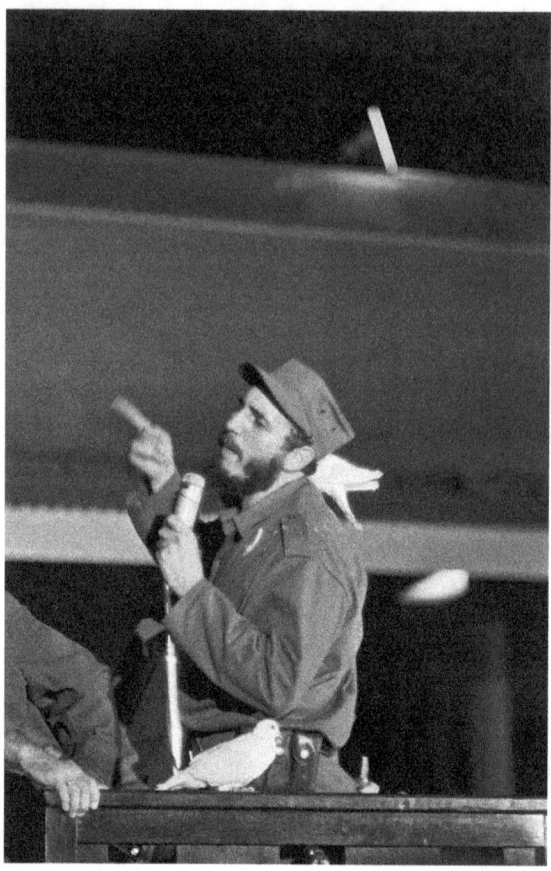

3.6 Fidel Castro, 1959, address with doves. Credit:
Tor Eigeland/Alamy Stock Photo.

tion would not be able to be completed or repeated—a seeming refusal of the
repetition inherent in tautology.

The birds' skilling produces a certain singularity even as *Trading with the
Enemy* itself potentially includes several forms of reenactment. During the
speech announcing the plan of the Cuban Revolution, several doves famously
landed on Fidel Castro's shoulder, an event treated with great symbolism and
iconicity in Cuban lore (figure 3.6). Cuban socially engaged artist Tania Bruguera (herself persecuted by the Cuban state) restaged that event in her work
Tatlin's Whisper #6, in which audience members play Fidel and a bird lands on
their shoulders (figure 3.7).[125] And, indeed, perhaps the first enactment itself

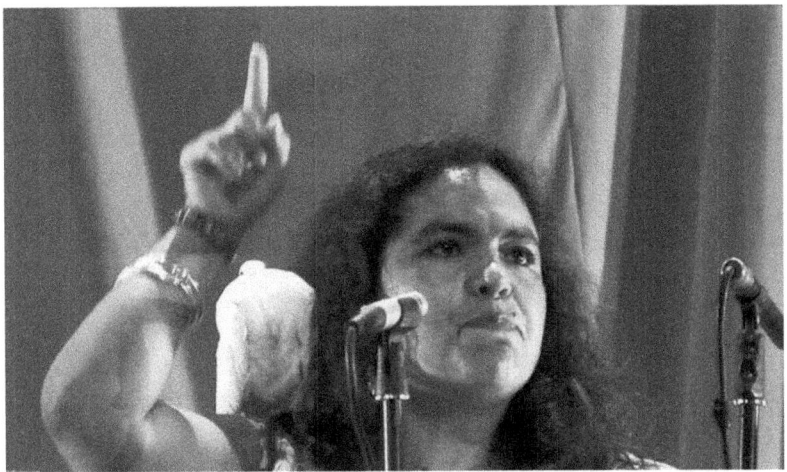

3.7 *Tatlin's Whisper #6 (Havana Version)*. Courtesy of Tania Bruguera.

was a restaging. Some have suggested the doves and their dramatic landing on Fidel's shoulder during his most important national speech to date were a staged act, and thus those birds have already been understood as performers.

So, *Trading with the Enemy* may in fact be a kind of historical reenactment, which would keep with other aspects of Riley's practice such as his *After the Battle of Brooklyn*, in which he restaged a Revolutionary War encounter in a handcrafted submarine. Such reenactments might place him in the company of artists such as Jeremy Deller, who famously reenacted the 1984 British coal miners' strike in his own *The Battle of Orgreave*, which we turn to in the next chapter. But what precisely is being reenacted in *Trading with the Enemy*? The pigeon landing, a symbol of hope and prosperity for a postrevolutionary Cuba? The beginnings of a new socialist society? Or perhaps, because Riley meticulously trained his pigeons, the artificial nature of Fidel's own socialist art worker animal performance? Finally, because trade does figure prominently in the title and accompanying text, perhaps Riley has in his sights restaging the various Cuba-based laundering and smuggling operations that came before the Revolution and the many surreptitious departures that have transpired since.

Whether it is the illicit movement of commodities, money, or people, if we focus on the trade in *Trading with the Enemy*, then this work must be deemed ironic, because movement between the U.S. and Cuba has been and still is illicit, and those who engage in illicit transactions tend to eschew documentation. Often the illicit must be imagined fictionally—I already did this myself by citing Francis Ford Coppola's film *Godfather II*. Whether in Riley's performance or more practical smuggling, the "trade," as it were, only transpires because a certain aspect of it, either the capital gains or the documentation thereof, is disavowed. So the immediate ironies that subtend the installation are the visibility of the performance and the centrality of the performance documentation itself.

The more structuring irony, however, is that it is the pigeons who are doing the recording and it is the pigeons who are conducting the trade. Pigeons cannot be prosecuted for violating the embargo. But they also cannot, in any semantically consistent way, be beneficiaries of the fruits of their trade. They cannot sell the cigars on a black or legitimate market, nor can they receive a wage from Riley for their collaboration in this work. Related to their inability to receive a wage is the fact that the pigeons' actions will be disavowed as causal whether they are located in a criminal or an economic realm. Indeed, a reporter from the ever-reliable *New York Times* called the Treasury Department to solicit a comment on Riley's work for their "Avian Artistry" piece. The reporter informed the Treasury official that "eleven homing pigeons have flown from Havana to Key West; some arrived with Cuban cigars strapped to their bellies." "Ooookkkaaaayyy" was the federal government's response, phonetically reproduced in the pages of the *Times*.

Thus the pigeons' actions are discounted as economic and instead understood as purposeless, that hallmark of the aesthetic. But does the disavowal of their labor result from the fact that as animals they are not laborers? Or does it result from the fact that as animals they are really artists? These questions orient the installation's central tension. The model for flagrantly violating the law and not being prosecuted is an artistic one, after all. We know this both from art historical studies such as Jonathan Eburne's *Surrealism and the Art of Crime* as well as from other artistic reenactments.[126] Think of Francis Alÿs's eponymous *Reenactment*, a work that consists of him purchasing a handgun and walking through Mexico City with it loaded, only to be arrested, freed after paying a bribe, and then engaging the arresting officers in a re-creation of the event—all of it videotaped. The pigeon performers of Riley's installation are given similar latitude.

What we are faced with in Riley's work is animals representing decommodified artistic labor. To communicate this, the installation moves through and combines various economic formations: socialist, capitalist, legal, illegal.

In each of these formations, we note a disavowal of money-as-wage. Labor doesn't count as labor when artists are doing it; work doesn't count as labor when animals are doing it; trades don't count as trades when illicit goods are exchanged—they are not represented in gross domestic product, nor are they aggregated. We reach, then, a similar conclusion to the one we arrived at in critiquing Kounellis's work.

All of this amounts to an understanding of why in much of the critical literature it now seems easier to conceive of animals as artists than of artists as laborers. I do not mean "artist" in the sense that, for example, we find in Vitaly Komar and Alexander Melamid's training of chimpanzees to take and sell tourist photos in Red Square or teaching elephants to paint in a Thai jungle and sell their wares online, as *National Geographic* reported.[127] Rather, I mean "artist" in the sense of those who occupy a certain category of nonpurposeful production. We can read Riley's installation as turning to a place where the art worker animal may critique the artist animal precisely because labor cannot be evaluated or remunerated on multiple, economic levels: What is the price of cigar smuggling? What are the transaction costs of a pigeon breaking the embargo? How does one pay a pigeon a wage?

Thus we are led into the reductio ad absurdum that these pigeons are artists. Indeed, the critical literature I have cited throughout this chapter, along with the many books and associations, is devoted to documenting the "artist animal," in Baker's phrasing. Yet we should, finally, reject this claim that has at its root the imposition of an ethics and a subjectivity over a representation and a value. To insist that animals now conduct a kind of artistic labor ricochets off and reclaims the structural disavowal of labor as such in much socially engaged art. In *Trading with the Enemy*, the process unfolds in transnational space of "the embargo" or "*el bloqueo*," a vexed space in which commodity circulation is both deeply entrenched and always already impossible.

Conclusion

Famous as an annoying presence in London's Trafalgar Square, pigeons were also memorialized there in November 2004. The City of London unveiled a sculpture of dogs, horses, elephants, and pigeons meant to honor their presence in Britain's various twentieth-century wars, a monument simply called "Animals in War." The inscription read, "This monument is dedicated to all the animals that served and died alongside British and Allied forces in wars and campaigns throughout time. They had no choice."[128]

But artists always have a choice. That, indeed, is the freedom implied in the very category of the aesthetic. In the Trafalgar monument the pigeons are conscripted workers; in *Trading with the Enemy* they are free artists. It seems sensible to understand Riley's pigeons, when compared to those in "Animals in War," as genuine "collaborators," as artists in their own right. But to do so is to foreclose the already threatened transformative economic criticality of art.

The Artwork of Children's Labor

Socially Engaged Art and the Future of Work

"Does not the true character of each epoch come alive in the nature of its children?"
—KARL MARX, *Grundrisse*

When artist Koki Tanaka happened into the News from Nowhere used bookstore in Liverpool, England, he found the inspiration he didn't know he was looking for: photojournalist Dave Sinclair's 2014 book, *Liverpool in the 1980s*.[1] In a series of black-and-white prints, Sinclair presents Liverpool in that decade as a place of disappearing work and factory closings, but also as a place of labor organizing and revelatory social agitation. Now Tanaka, who had been commissioned to do an installation for Liverpool's 2016 Biennial, was interested in continuing the kind of participatory installations for which he had become known and adapting them to the Biennial's local context. In Sinclair's book of images, Tanaka located what would become his piece's subject: the 1985 children's strike against the Thatcher government's compulsory and essentially unpaid teenage work program, the "Youth Training Scheme."

The 2016 Liverpool Biennial billed itself as offering "the first comprehensive commissioning programme for artists to work collaboratively with children."[2] Following closely Sinclair's visual history, Tanaka produced a collaborative work entitled *Provisional Studies: Action #6, 1985 School Students' Strike* and invited Liverpool's once-child-strikers to sit for interviews with their own children and to restage their militant street action. Using video, installation, and Sinclair himself as a photographer, Tanaka recorded their conversations and documented their restaged march, now comprising a small group of soon-to-be retirees carrying protest signs as they marched through Liverpool's streets. Their placards proclaimed, "Fight to Protect your Future,"

"No Scab Labour," "Jobs for Our Future," and so on. Tanaka's artistic intervention may be located in the fact that the strikers' future, Liverpool's future, labor's future, appeared in his work in retrospect: the child-strikers were still present, but they were no longer children.

Despite the prevalence of university student strikes both historically and indeed still today (in Europe, Canada, and Puerto Rico, but not in the mainland United States), we are less accustomed to secondary school students engaging in such actions. What orients the positionality of their strike, after all? They are not workers striking for wages. Nor are they fee-payers striking against tuition. Rather they are "children," one of the great liminal categories of the modern epoch. On the verge of so much, children are, by definition, poised to inherit the various freedoms and constraints of adulthood. But they also, by definition, are capable of so little: children cannot consent to sex (i.e., adult freedom), and they cannot contract to labor (i.e., adult constraint).[3] Situated on that long threshold of potential, children have, throughout modernity, symbolized the future, as youth itself is regularly called on to represent, in Franco Moretti's words, "an uncertain exploration of social space."[4] By incorporating children into his art practice in order to index social temporality, Tanaka joins the ranks of a broad group of contemporary artists—including Carsten Höller, Tino Sehgal, Mel Chin, Candice Breitz, Caitlin Berrigan, the collective Mammalian Diving Reflex, and Bob and Roberta Smith, among many others—who attempt to harness the ludic, exuberant indifference of children and marshal it toward artful ends.

And as children have come to be ever more present in socially engaged art, the paternalist question of how they are doing there—and of what art is doing to them—has unsurprisingly emerged as well. "Children are having a bad time of it in today's art," critic Hettie Judah writes. "Abandoned, drilled, exploited, rendered hauntingly blank, or engorged with sapid youthiness ready for the tasting, their burgeoning presence in galleries, museums, and art fairs is, by turns, cautionary and disturbing."[5] Here the critic ethically evaluates the palate of potential representations for children along an axis of availability as exploitability. Shannon Jackson takes a more historical approach but locates a similar breadth of the possible effects of introducing children into art. "From the nineteenth-century vaudeville house to the twenty-first century art house, the child is riveting because of her potential to destroy the aesthetic frame . . . she is a walking threat to the divide between art and life."[6] Indeed, children's appearance in socially engaged art seems to have almost become generic. Artist Ernesto Pujol pleads with other artists to avoid "another art education initiative," whereas Claire Bishop bemoans a roster of socially engaged art that includes "a predictable slew of children's workshops."[7]

As children have arrived on the contemporary socially engaged art scene, a quite different but no less timely or dichotomous conversation about children has emerged in critical theory. That spectrum of debate is structured around the question of whether the future that children represent promises social continuity or augurs social disruption. Some critical theorists, following Lee Edelman's *No Future: Queer Theory and the Death Drive*, have argued that children are made to bear society's most normative promises to itself.[8] Others have suggested that "the queer child" (in Kathryn Bond Stockton's phrase), the child of color, the trans child, or the differently abled child may refuse certain normative categories and thus might conduce a radically different future, perhaps even a utopia.[9] That queer child does not have the normative pleasure of linear progress at her disposal. Rather, she refuses social narratives through her lateral or "sideways" movement.

These twin entrances of children into socially engaged art and critical theory have transpired almost simultaneously, and even though they at times cross-reference each other, they have not been put into sustained conversation. Although the representation of children has been identified as a dichotomizing presence across art practice and critical theory, in this chapter I focus on a different historical contradiction that draws on both conversations but remains sutured to the wage form: namely, the child as worker. Children do sometimes engage as political actors—throughout the American Civil Rights movement, for example—but not economic ones. Throughout the twentieth century in capitalist democracies, modernity's children have been both forced to inhabit and prohibited from inhabiting the identity of waged worker. To engage this contradiction, I track children into socially engaged art by reading a series of artists who put children to work as artwork. And yet, as critical theory—from the Frankfurt school of the 1930s to the queer theory of today—reminds us, children are children by virtue of the fact that they cannot work. Rather, children play, and it is all too tempting to let what Joseph Weiss rightly calls "the bad dichotomy of work and play" come to structure our discussion.[10]

To isolate this tension, Sianne Ngai, in her turn toward what she calls "vernacular aesthetics," introduces a category of aesthetic judgment that almost certainly undergirds our appreciation of children: that of the "cute." For Ngai, cuteness "indexes the uncertain status of performing between labor and play."[11] In Ngai's derivation, the very category of cuteness interrupts a certain logic; it's not that children are cute because they dwell between labor and play; rather, those beings located between labor and play will be judged as "cute." Children could be said to occupy that category in this chapter, as could animals in the previous chapter. Indeed, whether in art or critical theory, often where we find animals, we find children. While Ngai links the formation of her aesthetic categories to developments in capitalism that allow for an "increasingly intimate relation between the autonomous artwork and the form of the commodity" and that question "the future of the long-standing idea of art as play as opposed to labor in a world in which immaterial labor is increasingly aestheticized," I examine a more local, economic category as I look at how children in socially engaged art instantiate and critique decommodified labor.[12] Like animals, children have transitioned from productive workers to sites of affective investment. Unlike animals, however, children have shown themselves to be capable of experiencing labor as a dominating, coordinated social abstraction. And even if they do not fully grasp this logic when they are young, "youth does not last forever."[13]

Childhood's expanding duration, what it prohibits and what it relies on, has its own history. Before the Progressive Era movement to outlaw child labor in the United States, and ultimately the passage of the Fair Labor Standards Act of 1938, which set a minimum national working age, children were "unquestionably economic assets."[14] Once prohibited from working, however, children began to occupy a radically oppositional identity: far from being economic assets, they became, in Viviana Zelizer's incisive vocabulary, "economically useless and emotionally priceless."[15] Indeed, the prohibition of child labor in the United States in 1938 stands as one of the momentous historical realizations of labor's formal decommodification, what Zelizer calls "the expulsion of children from the cash nexus." Even as that expulsion was uneven in terms of race and nationality, it has gradually had the effect of transforming children into a potential class of decommodified laborers who can subsequently represent as well as function as decommodified labor.

Some of the artists that I critique herein ironize this fact and install children in the gallery as philosophers, prognosticators, and financial advisors precisely because children cannot be paid to work. Other artists use children's unemployability as a site for interrupting social norms: they place children in art installations and pay them to work as artwork. If Kathryn Bond Stockton is correct that children's "lack of money makes them more vulnerable" to exploitation, then perhaps artists who pay children have located a site of enfranchisement befitting of socially engaged art's general orientation toward social betterment. Tanaka's installation takes yet another approach: today's adult workers reminisce about and re-create the very childhood fear that many of them now live—they have become exploited workers, and as wages continue their long decline, their own children will have it worse. In their attempts to expand painterly space, sculptural space, theatrical space, the space of the museum and gallery, even the kind of species who may participate in such artwork, socially engaged artists have turned to children as a material to be worked on, as collaborators to be worked with, as participants, as new audience members, even as critics. Indeed, children have become a "burgeoning presence in galleries, museums, and art fairs" as artistic labor has been decommodified.[16]

The generative exclusion of much of the art I analyze herein revolves around the fact that children can work in art as artwork precisely because they cannot be waged workers. In such artworks, children are often interpreted as a marginalized population that artists seek to represent and engage so that they might lessen the experience of that marginalization. Playgrounds are built; schools are constructed; afterschool groups are formed; educational games are initiated. Of course, as a disempowered constituency—one that is legally barred from exercising the rights we associate with democratic freedoms—it seems reasonable enough for children to make an appearance in an art that seeks to redistribute modalities of power and agency. Furthermore, because those who attempt to redistribute social power usually desire that their redistribution have some historical longevity, the involvement of those members of society who constitute its future seems not only warranted but necessary. As Paolo Virno reminds us, since the eighteenth-century dreams of Jean Jacques Rousseau, "revolutionaries and reformers" have sought to "make the infant's training conform to the ideal of a more just society."[17] Perhaps the most famous revolutionary call of the Enlightenment, *The Communist Manifesto* (1848) contains precisely two realized demands from a list of ten that includes "abolition of property in land" and "abolition of the right of inheritance." Those demands that have come to pass, and that have become bedrocks of democratic capitalist societies, both involve children: "Free education for all children in public schools [and the] abolition of child factory labor in its present form."[18]

The impulse of turning toward children in order to harness a better future is not new, then. Neither is the artistic engagement of that impulse, and social practice artists are not the first to incorporate the childhood world of play, the language of games, or even the goal of educational utility into their artwork. Allan Kaprow claimed to have modeled his Fluxus Happenings on his own children; artist Alison Knowles's *Child Art Piece* (1964) left two- and three-year-olds alone on stage for as long as they—and the audience—could bear it. One moment of 1970s Viennese Actionism, under the auspices of Otto Muehl, had children as art in pursuit of an intergenerational free sex commune (Muehl was convicted of abusing them). Still other art movements have used the language of childhood play to describe their own practice.[19] André Breton explained that Surrealists engaged in a "persistent playing of games," whereas Dadaist Hugo Ball called the Zurich Dada workshop a "playground for crazy emotions."[20] Furthermore, philosophers have consistently linked the aesthetic to play itself. Nietzsche extols that "in this world only play, play as artists and children engage in it, exhibits come-to-be and passing away, structuring and destroying, without any moral additive."[21] Perhaps the most well-known philosophical claim of play is found in Friedrich Schiller's dictum that "man only plays when he is in the fullest sense of the word a human being, and he is only fully a human being when he plays." Indeed, play has been a crucial idiom in which to articulate the noninstrumental freedom of the aesthetic.[22] But—contra Nietzsche—children have not always had a monopoly on play.

It was only once children shed their productive lives that they could come to represent play as a form of the mimetic elaboration of labor and as a critical possibility of a life beyond labor, a notion that finds its most idealized home in the Frankfurt school. And as play itself is reconfigured into something that children uniquely engage in, critical theorists turn to children to resituate the playfulness of the aesthetic itself. Such a conjoining is not without risk. Both Adorno and Benjamin repeatedly evoke the figure of the playful child, though the former does so with characteristically more suspicion than the latter. For both, children become unwitting critics of "the law of labor," in Adorno's words; in their play one is offered a glimpse of life beyond the commodity form.[23] And yet no sooner do children emerge as antilabor than we face the crucial tautology that underpins this aesthetic child: if children, by definition, cannot *work*, then they may also by definition not *not work*. Because children cannot work but only play, and because children's play shows how not working might appear, artists and critics alike put children to work as representations of not-working. Thus, this separation is a tenuous one. Yet another problem with this dichotomy now appears in an age of decommodified labor in which the evacuation of the wage form itself necessarily changes the coordinates of a critique of labor.

What draws artists and critics alike to children is that they mimic adult things during their play. When playing in art, however, one of the things children might mimic is mimesis itself, a term we have yet to consider. Mimesis is that "non-sensuous similarity" by which art captures the truth of its object. Benjamin claims that "in mimesis, tightly interfolded like cotyledons, slumber the two aspects of art: *Schein* [semblance] and play."[24] For my project, mimesis reminds us of what could be called the mimetic elements of decommodified labor itself: like work but not work, potentially critical and potentially regressive. Thus we want to avoid an argument structured around a work–play dichotomy and in its place examine a pairing of decommodified labor and mimetic mimesis. In the examination of decommodified artistic labor that structures this chapter, we will see children "playing at work."

Because the commodity's two structuring characteristics—made by wage labor, sold on a market—are difficult to locate in the gallery, it is unclear who is working and who is not. We have the intern, who is probably unpaid; the artist, also most probably unpaid; the audience, absolutely unpaid; the student, who might be paying to work in order to receive college credit; and finally, the animal, who cannot be paid. How can the addition of an unpaid child to the mix function as critique? By having them make pronouncements about their alienated labor, as Tino Sehgal does in *Ann Lee* (2013)? By having them read work by Michael Hardt and Antonio Negri, the latter of whom I have cited throughout my book as the key philosopher of real subsumption, as Mikhail Karikis does in *Children of Unquiet 2013–14* (2014)? By having them give advice about retirement, as both Caitlin Berrigan does in *Lessons in Capitalism* (2012) and Candice Breitz does in *The Woods* (2011–)?

To answer such questions is to note that the possibility of the child ambiguously "playing at work" as artwork becomes possible only under conditions of the decommodification of artistic labor in general. I begin with works by Berrigan and Bob and Roberta Smith that negotiate the boundaries of the child as worker, the child as artist, and that explore what kind of art the child produces. Wedded to the child as the one who *cannot be waged*, these works index the historical reversal noted by Zelizer and Edelman alike: to the extent that the child cannot be waged, she may be a repository for some kind of adult fantasy or "investment," to use a neoliberal idiom. I then turn to Tanaka's installation, *Provisional Studies: Action #6, 1985 School Students' Strike* (2016), and to *Haircuts by Children* (2007–) from the collective Mammalian Diving Reflex, two pieces that question the normativity of children with regard to the wage form by imagining and instantiating the waged child. These final pieces not only put pressure on the kind of art we have seen throughout this book;

they also put pressure on the concept of decommodification itself. By paying children to work as art, and by showing how children themselves organize against work, these pieces, and indeed through them this book, might be seen as asking, In our current economic moment, is not *commodification* the most desirable state of aesthetic and political affairs?

Lessons in Neoliberalism

In this section I read two works that may or may not be "lessons in capitalism," to borrow artist Caitlin Berrigan's redolent phrase. In these installations, the child is part of the artwork and the child's identity as a child is unquestioned in the artwork through the work's and the viewer's shared presumption of the child's wagelessness. The viewer knows the child is a child because she participates in the art installation by making childish art about adult work for free. From that place of secure identity, the artwork seemingly invites its viewer to follow the child, who mimics adult work through the organization of certain forms of play. We ultimately want to question the basic hermeneutic organization of these pieces by including an assumption of decommodified labor, but for the moment, we will approach them as they asked to be approached.

Berrigan's 2012 *Lessons in Capitalism* performs a tension between the economic knowledge of adults and the artful play of children, offering each constituency a chance to experience the differently aged other. Berrigan's installation revolves around the insistent confrontation with scale already evident in her piece's title. A lesson is a discrete and repeatable form, particularly compared with the more expansive concept of "education." The growing character of the bildungsroman does not succeed through mere lessons; rather, he is transformed through the long arc of *Bildung*, through educational self-cultivation. Capitalism, that global totality of social relations, seems well beyond the scope of the lesson, and this radical juxtaposition organizes Berrigan's piece.

Visitors enter a gallery and meet their intermediary, a professional-looking "business consultant" who offers to convey visitors' financial questions to a group of financial advisors who are installed in the space but initially are out of sight. Gallery visitors have produced questions ranging from how to manage one's Roth individual retirement account (IRA), to those about bond yields, to those about the professional constraints bequeathed by student debt. The business consultant transcribes these questions and delivers them to one of the several financial advisors at work in the gallery. Said financial advisors are children, spanning ages five to ten years, who, still out of sight of the gallery's visitors, proceed to answer the visitors' questions on eight-by-eleven pieces of paper by using magic markers to create "free-form drawings." In Berrigan's own description, "I have teamed up with the Carpenter Center and Harvard Business School affiliates to operate a free financial advice booth during scheduled, participatory performances.... *Lessons in Capitalism* leverages the realm of play, and the imaginative capacities of children, to encounter the language and structures of finance with fresh eyes .... How do we learn the language of capitalism, finance and money? Can insights into the process of learning capitalism also teach us how to *unlearn* it?"[25]

Berrigan's distinction between money and finance orients the gallery visitor to multiple constructions of value and to a difference between the two these forms. Money has value *now*; it is a contemporaneous economic form. By contrast, finance is a future-oriented economic form. One uses financial instruments to invest money *now* and realize the gain from investment *later*; the time-space between the now and then of finance constitutes the nonidentity that makes profit or loss possible. The etymology of "finance" demonstrates this ends-oriented logic: it derives from the French *fin,* "the end," and the associated verb *finir,* "to finish."[26]

Lessons in Capitalism reorganizes the *now* and *later* of financial transactions through its use of the *now* and *later* of "growing up." It negotiates the distance between children's and adults' relationships to their own, and to each other's, economic futures. For example, one question submitted by a gallery visitor asks, "Should I invest in stocks or real estate? Investment amount: $250,000." The choice of verb, "invest," presumes a future return on the principal. In the performance documentation, a photograph of a perhaps eight-year-old girl answering this question shows her from behind, her pigtails dangling on either side of her head, and her hand drawing a series of unidentifiable objects. The hoped-for profit from investment will take upcoming years to realize; likewise, it will take years for the "advisor" to be able to offer anything approximating advice. The child's presence might be said to figure a kind of analepsis and prolepsis, both of which offer the viewer access to a different past and perhaps a different future. In the documentation of this question-answer, the child draws with a black marker; beside her drawing sits a collection of colored markers, suggesting that she is only mid-creation. There is more work to be done. But what kind of work will it be, children's work or artwork?

After the gallery visitor has her question documented, and after the question has been delivered to the child-advisors, she is invited to turn a corner and view answers to previous questions, which hang off the gallery's wall in elementary school–like fashion. That hall leads to the children's room in which the viewer may witness the actual advisors in the process of producing their responses. What one sees, of course, is a group of supervised schoolchildren responding to visitors' personal finance questions with magic markers, a tool whose proximal etymological relation to "market," and to the accounting strategy of "mark-to-market," conveniently resonates throughout.[27]

Some of the "answers" the children provide do offer a possible referential response to the question asked. The response shown in figure 4.1, for example, ignores the "how" of the question, "How should I allocate my Roth IRA contributions?" but engages the second question—"Does it even matter?" The answer is a declarative "no." Of course, the general "no" could also be read as a negation of the entire prompt and thus not a response to "Does it even matter?" because we may safely assume that a child possesses no knowledge about the risks of allocation in a tax-deferred IRA. Other answers not only refuse to engage the specifics of the question, they refuse language as a medium for doing so. In place of a response to a question about bond yields, a child produces a green, Godzilla-like footprint, accompanied by two smaller stick figures sitting at a desk, suggesting a representation of desk the child had been sitting at during its composition.

Perhaps the most common response to *Lessons in Capitalism* would be to question the contemporary, and highly profitable, service industry of financial advising. When this work was staged in 2012, a few years after the global credit crisis of 2007–8—when, in economic historian Philip Mirowski's words, "an entire academic profession [of economists] got everything wrong"—ideas of the limits of economic knowledge would have been fresh in gallery-goers' minds.[28] If economics professors at the world's leading universities cannot predict the movement of financial markets to the point of missing a once-in-a-century crisis, how could "personal financial advisors," who often work out of franchises and on commission, be expected to do so? Indeed, the tendentious knowledge of the "financial advisor" has already made one appearance in this book: Cassie Thornton considers a financial advisor's knowledge in chapter 1—and Thornton's advisor provides her with drawings as well.

While a perfectly valid interpretation, the focus on the knowledge generated by the child-advisors must be accompanied by a consideration of the "playing at work" in which the child-advisors engage. The tension between image and language, the possible reduction of "capitalism" to a "lesson," the irony that a child—a future worker—can see what path finance, a future-oriented

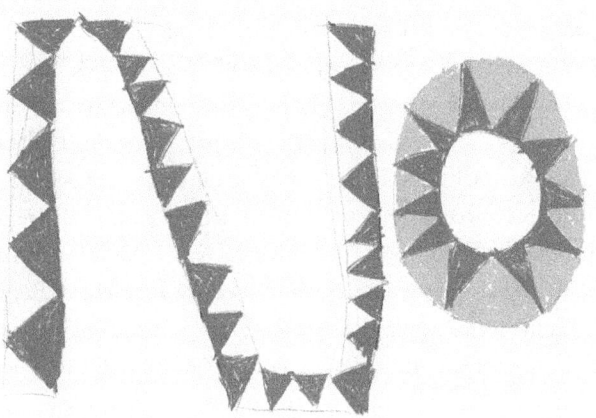

4.1 *Lessons in Capitalism.* Courtesy of Caitlin Berrigan.

economic form, might follow: all these pairings only become possible because of the ambivalent status of children's labor and specifically the relation between that ambivalence and artwork. Berrigan's installation only works because the children do. But what do they actually do? Are they undertaking labor? Or are they mimicking labor as play? Or has play become labor? I use the phrase "playing at work" to hold together these questions, with the caveat that play and work must be posited at different levels of mediation in any given historical moment. On the one hand, we must recognize why Marx said that "labour cannot become play," as the internal division is itself a site of profit.[29] On the other, we must allow for some conceptual movement of these terms, and we know that in our contemporary moment theories of neoliberalism, following Becker and Foucault, have suggested that labor itself is an obsolete economic construction, whereas theories of real subsumption have argued that play very much can become labor, as the neologism "playbor" makes perfectly clear.[30] Which of these assumptions does Berrigan's work assume and critique?

From a child's perspective, what the child–financial advisors are making is very much artwork, not in spite of, but because they are, mimicking financial advisors. Their productions have all the stylistic markers of their indigenous art: the eight-by-eleven paper, presented in serial form and affixed to the wall with Scotch tape; the awkward overlay of magic marker color, with its strange inability to combine one shade with another; the quite distinct alternation between literal and figurative and elements of representation. From the adult's perspective, what Berrigan presents through her use of children is artwork not because of the children's productions but precisely because children as a category cannot work. Rather, the children "play at the work" of being a financial advisor, and in the gallery context such "play at work" becomes art.

This kind of mimetic child's play as a model for artistic mimesis has its own history. Benjamin understands that "in using [adult] things [children] do not so much imitate the works of adults as they bring together, in the artifacts produced in play, [the] materials of widely different kinds in a new intuitive relationship."[31] And this cataclysmic combination of adult and child life-worlds seems very much the hoped-for moment of Berrigan's work. Can children's mimetic play deliver some new knowledge, some new organization of finance for the adult viewer? For Benjamin, the child's imagination knows no bounds: "Children's play is permeated everywhere by mimetic forms and behavior; and its realm is in no way limited to what one person can mimic about another. The child not only plays shopkeeper or teacher but also windmill and railroad train."[32] Perhaps here the child not only will play financial advisor, but will play finance.

Ultimately, of course, what is always already being both imagined and unimagined in child's play as a critical model is the ability to see social freedom where there is, as of yet, none: in the world of labor. Adorno is more clear, if ultimately more pessimistic, on this insistence: "To the child returning from the holiday, home seems new, fresh, festive. Yet nothing has changed since he left. Only because duty has now been forgotten . . . is the house given back this Sabbath peace . . . . No differently will the world one day appear, almost unchanged, in its constant feast-day light, when it stands no longer under the law of labor, and when for home-comers duty has the lightness of holiday play."[33] Thus, for Adorno, the child can experience the repetition of return, the sameness of place, as freedom, not drudgery. In a different idiom, Paolo Virno notes that children "are repetitive without being habitual."[34] It is this capacity to experience the same differently that achieves a special status in children's games.

Like his compatriot Benjamin, Adorno devotes special attention to children's toys for their ability to conjure a mimicry of a labor whose dominating tendencies will ultimately be refused. "Their little trucks travel nowhere and the tiny barrels on them are empty; but they remain true to their destiny by not performing, not participating in the abstraction that levels down that destiny but instead abide as allegories of what they are specifically for."[35] Here we see a similar relation to repetition and difference as when the child returns home from holiday. Adorno's insistence on the "nowhereness" and "emptiness" of children's play evokes the aesthetic's fundamental refusal of purpose. Both Adorno and Benjamin offer an aesthetic child who, by his very childishness, sees, imagines, and indeed instantiates what the adult cannot: "to see the new anew."[36] The child offers a window into this possibility through the very fact of her childishness, what Kevin Floyd calls simply "the importance of being childish" for Adorno, although it most certainly applies to Benjamin as well.[37] As Susan Buck-Morss notes, "no modern thinker [with the exception of Jean Piaget] took childhood as seriously as Benjamin."[38]

While *Lessons in Capitalism* certainly subscribes to an idea of child's play as critique, as developed by Adorno and Benjamin, the installation also interrupts those thinkers' curious, ahistorical tendency to consider children always at play, as though children *and* play do not each have their own histories. The Frankfurt school child is, perhaps unsurprisingly, thoroughly male and bourgeois. Perhaps a bit more surprisingly, though, as Bill Brown notes in his own reading of Adorno's understanding of the child as capitalist critic, it is a child fully imbricated in the market. Brown comments that "only the modernization of childhood—the mass marketing of toys that represent the mass market—will enable the child to perform a subversive repetition of modern life."[39] For Brown, Adorno's is a "despatialized child"; I see a more dehistoricized one. Even as Benjamin wrote a history of children's toys, he seems to neglect that children did not always play and, even more so, that toys were not always instruments of capitalist manufacture that could represent capitalist manufacture. My own historicization of childhood has at its root Philippe Ariès's magisterial history of the subject—one whose central claim is that "childhood" itself is product of capitalist modernity.[40] It is rather remarkable that Benjamin and Adorno did not engage this fact.

Indeed, during the 1920s, the moment when the Dadaists and Surrealists in Zurich and Paris turned their art into "playgrounds," reformers in New York were agitating to create actual playgrounds.[41] Children were no longer free to play in streets, which had begun their own transition into becoming mediums for that ur-commodity of monopoly capitalism, the car. Rather, children would be placed in new child-only spaces where play could be contained and protected. But for children to make use of these newly constructed playgrounds, for them to play with mass-manufactured toys, they needed not to be *at work*. And indeed, as children historically metamorphose into those social beings who come to be defined by their inability to contract (for work) and to consent (to sex), they also become obsolete economic material. Rendered useless and obsolete, precious if resource intensive, now they can, like so many industrial warehouses, be reclaimed.

To be properly historical, Adorno and Benjamin would be better served by claiming that children in capitalism develop a monopoly on the representation of play, rather than positioning children as essentially playful. Such a qualification would allow for play and childhood to remain historically contingent. *Lessons in Capitalism*, and indeed, each of the pieces I will read in this chapter, acknowledge that representational element by placing children within the confines of the art object itself. For Adorno and Benjamin, child's play is like art because children's mimicry of labor is like mimesis itself (nonsensuous identity); for the artists I read herein, child's play may become art because labor itself has become a more permeable category. The latter understanding, then, relies on the fact that both labor's theorization and its circulation have developed beyond their conditions of monopoly capital. Once *in art*, as opposed to *like art*, we must ask, Does child's play maintain its critical capacity? Does it still do so in a world of decommodified labor? Children mimic work through play, but under conditions of real subsumption there would be no mimicry of work; there is only work. In a neoliberal economic world, there would likewise be no mimicry of labor because there is no labor. Rather, all parities are organized around the deployment of human capital. In that scheme, children are differentiated from adults in that they more often serve as receptacles for the investments of others rather than as investors themselves.

Lessons in Capitalism is permeated with the idioms and gestures of investment more so than of labor. In part, the predominance of that language derives from Berrigan's own decisions in framing the work, but perhaps in equal part it derives from the hegemony that such language has achieved in our current economic discourse. Of course that does not mean that people aren't working, but it does mean that, in a fashion similar to that of Renzo Martens, Berrigan seems to adopt a neoliberal vantage point in hopes of critiquing neoliberalism. Gallery-goers orient themselves through a vocabulary of "leverage," "money," "finance," "capitalism." Questions produced by the audience hew to a certain trend: investment, debt, returns, and interest. And that, of course, may be understood as proof of a "neoliberal moment," because in a neoliberal moment we are encouraged to understand ourselves not as workers, but as owners of human capital who have opportunities to leverage, finance, and invest in ourselves. Berrigan's installation not only adopts such a discourse; in its use of child as investment to critique investment, it parallels some of the neoliberals' conceptualization of childhood.[42]

In Berrigan's *Lessons*, children mimic that action of giving investment advice. In Gary Becker's early work on neoliberal economics, children *are* investments. Indeed, Becker's seminal paper on the "Interaction between Quantity and Quality of Children" may be placed in dialogue with Zelizer's periodizing comment that after the prohibition of child labor in the twentieth-century United States, children became "economically useless and emotionally priceless."[43] In his work on "the pricing of children," Becker argues that more money allotted toward fewer children will result in higher-quality children. Conversely, less money allotted toward more children will result in lower-quality children. Children, quite simply, are for Becker nascent forms of human capital that can be differently cultivated with different amounts of investment. In Becker's theorization, labor is twice abjured: First, children do not work; rather, they receive investment. Second, parents do not work to raise children—there is no social reproduction—rather, they invest forms of human capital in their children.

As Foucault reads Becker, he stresses that all forms of attention directed toward the child should be considered an investment in the child. Foucault reads the neoliberals as such: "The neoliberals lay stress on the fact that what should be called educational investment is much broader than simple schooling or professional training and that many more elements than these enter into the formation of human capital."[44] The sought-after result, as with any investment, is to have more capital than one had when one started. Here, capital is specified as human capital. Perhaps Foucault might have better read this through the lens of what Lee Edelman calls the "Ponzi scheme of reproductive futurism."[45] In a Ponzi scheme, more investors must put in capital for fewer investors to receive a guaranteed return. A Ponzi scheme is not really an investment, then; rather, it is a transfer of assets framed in the discourse of investment.[46]

Berrigan's work doubles down on the idioms and fantasies of neoliberalism: the child as "investment" critiques "investments" by offering a kind of useless financial advice, a critique only made possible because children "play at work" rather than "work at play." Throughout this installation, adults worry about how their money will or will not extend into the future. And of course, it says something about our own historical moment in which the most repeated questions about finance at a Creative Time–sponsored event of socially engaged art are all but guaranteed to include investment strategies for either dealing with debt or more commonly, preparing for retirement.[47] Perhaps the idioms of neoliberalism are required, then, to engage the audience. But for the engagement to happen, labor must disappear, and here it is the presence of the child who grounds that disappearance, one only possible under conditions of decommodifed labor.

If children's status as neoliberal investments allows them to ironize investment advice, then that same status must sacrifice a critique of their possible labor and indeed of labor itself. Berrigan's is an ultimately ambivalent work, then, because of its relation to the tension between "investment" and "labor." This lack of resolution, however, might be read as a comment on the potential meaningfulness that socially engaged art wants to ascribe to its subject. If children occupy the position of "investment," then they do not necessarily need the redistributive aims of such art. Indeed, they are a kind of investment that, as Becker states, may undergo forms of redistribution as quality assumes a new relation to quantity.

The next installation I read follows a similar logic in that it both uses and questions the use of socially engaged art's incorporation of children into the artwork as economic actors. Bob and Roberta Smith's *Art Amnesty* (2014) reorganizes the uncertain status of children "playing at work" to question why—or whether—"artist" should remain a professional category.[48] In the installation, children's ambivalent status as workers is used to warn their grown-up counterparts that one should avoid art as a career precisely because artistic labor has been and continues to be decommodified. Although *Art Amnesty* does not contain the kind of data about artistic careers that we saw in chapter 2 through Caroline Woolard's work, the assumptions of the same economic reality structure the installation. Woolard makes her claims through statistics; Smith makes his through declaration. Among the advice he offers viewers is the direction for artists to, "'Get Real' [and] ditch [the] life of poverty and precarious self-employment" that an art career offers. The installation's documentation is quite clear on the ends of an art career: "Many artists delude themselves into believing that they are promising, productive artists when they would live much more fulfilled and useful lives engaged in proper employment. I PROMISE NEVER TO MAKE ART AGAIN provides a baptism of necessary real life . . . ."[49]

Like other socially engaged art we have surveyed in this book, *Art Amnesty* reflexively orients socially engaged art's insistence on community back onto the art community itself; here the hope for community betterment comes in the form of the abolition of art as profession. We all know of the avant-garde instruction to abolish the divide between art and life; here that negation becomes oriented toward art's professional ends.

On view at PS1, *Art Amnesty* both makes use of children as artists in the installation space and engages the one normative social narrative about children we might be forgiven for making—namely, that they will grow up. The problematic around which the work is structured asks whether art facilitates or retards that process of growing up, a process that must necessarily encompass growing into one's role as a worker or a possessor of human capital. Like Berrigan's installation, *Art Amnesty* stresses the neoliberal assumptions of human capital more so than real subsumption's insistence of constant work.

Viewers walk into a gallery that can only be described as cluttered. Groups of objects are scattered inconsistently around the several-room installation space. In addition to the objects being inconsistently spaced and curated, they are themselves inconsistent with regard to shape, size, texture, color, and so on. The installation presents a motley collection, and what connects specific objects is not an elusive formal attribute but rather the fact they have all been "amnestied," or released by their makers from the category of art. They are now free to dwell in the way the viewer will likely see them, a kind of detritus of papier-mâché, poster-board, randomized ready-mades, painted canvases in all styles and in stages of repair. Some of the items are heaped together and intrude on each other; other items are so divorced from their surroundings that they appear as unexpected solos. *Art Amnesty* might evoke comparison to the Salvage Art Institute, made famous in Ben Lerner's 2015 novel, *10:04*. Yet, although irreparably damaged, the nonart on view at the Salvage Art Institute was once famous and thus valuable and insured. Indeed, it is still famous, even in its state of disrepair; imagine a broken Jeff Koons sculpture sitting beside a ripped Ad Reinhardt canvas. The art presented in *Art Amnesty* is decidedly not famous, was never insured, and indeed only was considered art by virtue of its once nomination to the category. Likewise, it has now been freed from that category by similar nomination: viewers and participants are invited to "throw your art away."

As disparate as the objects on display are, each has a placard in front of it, filled out in a noticeably different handwriting, which serves both to identify the artist and to index the particular piece's amnesty. The viewer now understands she is not in the gallery to praise these works but to bury them. Anyone is welcome to join the show by contributing their own art and thus having it become amnestied. Those who wish to discard a single work of art are asked to sign a pledge that reads: "I NEVER WANT TO SEE THIS WORK

AGAIN." Those participants who are more committed to the process of recusal from the art world may pledge: "I PROMISE NEVER TO MAKE ART AGAIN." After completing that pledge, they receive a badge that states: "I AM NO LONGER AN ARTIST."[50] The installation, then, is structured around physically and conceptually jettisoning art. Participants turn their art over to a museum and ultimately to a dumpster. Through that act emerges the work's possibly cruel irony: every working artist's dream, to have a piece in a major museum, is made realizable on the condition that the art itself will be consigned to the trash. John Baldessari destroyed his art in *Cremation Project* (1970) through its immolation; in different measure, Lee Lozano enacted her *General Strike Piece* starting in 1969 in which she withdrew herself from the New York art world. Smith here will destroy everyone's art.

The installation is participatory in that any artist can donate their work to it. By doing so, however, artists become material for a larger political economic claim that the installation makes: namely, that artistic labor *already has been decommodified*. Artists know this, of course. How could they not? But perhaps they imagine that a show in PS1 would ameliorate their economic problems. Smith guards against that hope by including the film about his own professional life, "Make Your Own Damn Art," concurrently with the installation. The film opens with Smith himself bemoaning his lack of pension, lack of professional security, and the ongoing precarity he confronts at age fifty.[51] Even if one has a solo show at PS1, he insists, art does not provide economic support for the artist.

Art Amnesty conceives of art, then, as both an object and a career. As the installation tracks this expanded life cycle of art's ontology, it moves between staging the expiration of the art object and of the artist herself. *Art Amnesty* provides a sense of sequence: as art becomes amnestied, art becomes uncertain former art object; likewise, the child-artist becomes the adult artist becomes the dead artist. The realizations of these different stages are simultaneous rather than progressive, and they are staged in situ and in textual addenda. Smith writes in the performance documentation that "the personal journey for most artists starts with enthusiasm and joy, and ends, if the artist does not have huge success, in embarrassed children taking their dead parents' work to the dump." Thus the many representations of the stages of the artist's life and the artwork's life come to "explore the full arc of the life of an artist."[52] These two trajectories—art's life and artist's life—homologously balance each other during the six-week duration of the installation. Both trajectories, rather normatively, begin with the child.

To make its claims about the economically depressed world of art as profession, *Art Amnesty* grounds itself in children "playing at work," even as it insists that art is a professional milieu where perhaps work should be made obsolete. In Hamlet-like fashion, children are encouraged both "to be" and "not to be" artists; adults, given less latitude, are encouraged to free themselves from the very category of "artist." Children appear in the gallery space to stand in for the artist's and for the art object's beginning. The installation opens with an

> Art Party at MoMA PS1, at which children will be encouraged to make art with their families using art materials available at the event. Beginning at the Art Party and throughout the run of the Art Amnesty, a ... pledge form will be available for signing, which states I WILL ENCOURAGE CHILDREN TO BE ALL THAT THEY CAN BE. CHOOSE ART AT SCHOOL. These pledges will be collected, along with "first drawings" children make and wish to contribute, and mailed to local politicians to encourage arts funding and arts education.

"Be all that you can be" was, from 1980 to 2001, the official advertising slogan of the U.S. Army, here repurposed for art school. Children ground the party—"the Art Party"—because children are assumed by the work to represent a malleable future. Sometimes they represent the future life of an artist and other times they represent the future life of an artwork. "Was Joseph Beuys an idiot when he said everyone is an artist?" Smith wonders in textual addenda. The installation suggests an answer to this question through its presentation of children's ambivalent status as art workers: "everyone" might be a practicing artist, but few practicing artists should attempt professionalization. "Everyone is an artist" only if art is not a profession.

We saw how both Adorno and Benjamin used child's play as a model for art's fundamental, nonpurposive playfulness—how children's mimicry might rise to the level of mimesis. The child in play transforms objects—"bricks that are coffins, cacti that are totem poles, and copper pennies that are shields"—and in doing so refuses to accept the division of use value and exchange value.[53] For Benjamin, finally, the child grounds a utopian vision of the manner in which "human labor will then proceed in accord with the model of children's play ... play as the canon of a form of labor that is no longer exploitative ...."[54] Yet while for Adorno and Benjamin child's play is a model for the adult's engagement with the libratory power of the aesthetic, while it provides a model for the liberation of labor, *Art Amnesty*'s exploration of the relationship between art and children acknowledges that play has become constricted. First, it has been reduced. Child's play does not stand in for art's potentiality; rather, children now make art. Play itself has been narrowed as a category. In *Art Amnesty*, what is unique about child's "play," now only realizable as art, is that children can make art outside of the professional liabilities of being an artist. Quite simply, children cannot work, whether as laborers or artists. And that, not their playful mimicry, becomes the basis for their ability to, as Adorno famously says, "unconsciously rehearse the right life."[55]

It is they who offer a lesson in capitalism. However, *Art Amnesty* has none of the drama, or fun, of Berrigan's *Lessons in Capitalism*. On the one hand, there is a definite language of arts advocacy—so prominent in socially engaged art. On the other hand, the advocacy is used to advocate against art as a profession. *Art Amnesty* further suggests that children *do* need the redistributive ends of socially engaged art, but ironically, that the most important lesson such art can provide is a professional one: do not become artists. Art and its professionalization are cleaved apart, and choosing art must be disassociated from the choice of becoming an artist. This is a polemic, one enabled by children's ambivalent status as workers.

Because they cannot work as waged laborers as children, children are capable of making art without working as artists. Both Berrigan and Bob and Roberta Smith rely on this distantiation. These artists, we might say, assume the neoliberal child, the one who can be invested in—with knowledge and attention, if not money—and who will grow up following the contours of that investment as opposed to the child who could be put to work. As a consequence, *Art Amnesty*'s critique assumes the neoliberal child, the one who cannot work. One gets the sense that it hopes for a world of art education in place of professionalization: let children represent decommodified labor through their art (for adults), but also let them do so on the condition that they don't become yet another generation of decommodifed artistic laborers.

Wages for Artwork

The child may only enter art as an ambivalent representation of "playing at work" after the decommodification of child labor, but she would only be called to do so under conditions of the general decommodification of artistic labor. In an age of decommodified artistic labor, both child and animal arrive in the gallery. Once there, however, children tend to inhabit one of the two economic orientations that we have seen throughout this book. The child might be conceived of through a neoliberal frame as the bearer of future investment—the *fin* (end) to whom the future of *fin*ance is necessarily oriented. Or she may be placed in the frame of the real subsumption of labor to capital. In that case, she will be productive whether she likes it or not. These next two works may be understood as engaging the questions of real subsumption because they are concerned not with the return on invested human capital but with present, waged productivity. The question for art that uses the latter becomes, How does that child engage with her position as uncompensated producer of surplus value through her role as and representation of decommodified laborer? As we will see in the works I read here, sometimes the child embraces her unpaid productivity and sometimes she does not; sometimes such unpaid productivity empowers children and at other times it debilitates them. Both pieces I examine share an insistence that in an age of decommodified artistic labor, using decommodification to critique capitalism must remain suspect. Thus, I have chosen to conclude with them in order that my own guiding concept throughout this book might too be subject to art-based criticism.

As I read these works, I remain conscious of Melinda Cooper's astute assessment that, "in general, leftist demands for the decommodification of social life or the protection of kinship relations all too readily lend themselves to the social conservative argument that certain forms of (domestic, feminized) labor should remain unpaid."[56] Cooper suggests that within capitalism itself, the commodification of labor, more so than its decommodification, tends toward a more equitable field of social relations. That concern cannot be easily dismissed. As the economist Joan Robinson noted, "the misery of being exploited by capitalists is nothing compared to the misery of not being exploited at all."[57] Robinson's is a pithy but perhaps true observation, an economistic translation of Adorno's own epigraph of capitalist impossibility: "The wrong life cannot be lived rightly." Both Koki Tanaka's *Provisional Studies: Action #6, 1985 School Students' Strike* (2016) and the art collective Mammalian Diving Reflex's *Haircuts by Children* (2007–) question toward what ends the fact and representation of decommodification in socially engaged art move, what meaning they impart and what meaning they refuse. Importantly, both pieces question whether children occupy a unique position from which to critique decommodified labor, as they themselves are part of a class of decommodified laborers.

"Strike To Protect Your Futur [sic]"

Tanaka's *Provisional Studies: Action #6, 1985 School Students' Strike* sprawls through time and space. His previous work, while "socially engaged," would not indicate an interest in labor history or indeed in labor itself.[58] Rather, it seems that Tanaka became an unintentional interlocutor of labor's decommodification, a history that his own style of socially engaged "encounter" seems particularly apt to record. Using many of the forms so common to socially engaged, participatory art, his work often coordinates dialogue between various community interlocutors. For example, his "1946–52 Occupation Era, and 1970 Between Man and Matter" (2014), considers militarism in a post-fascist Japan through the staging of conversations among young community members about necessary war and unjust war. Commissioned to do a piece for the Liverpool Biennial, his selection of the children's strike intersected with several of the "episodes" through which the Biennial was organized, including "Children," "Flashback," and so on. In restaging the children's strike, Tanaka's piece might resuscitate this rather idiosyncratic labor action and critique socially engaged art's most well-known labor restaging: Jeremy Deller's 2001 *The Battle of Orgreave*. Tanaka would not consider unionized workers on strike—as Deller so famously did—but rather children on strike from schooling. Any potential "lessons in capitalism" will here be given new form.

Tanaka's installation makes obvious reference to Deller's spectacular *Battle of Orgreave* through its site specificity in the same country; its historical referents, which consist of the same time period; and most importantly, the same insistence: labor will not capitulate to Margaret Thatcher's dismantling of British social democracy in the 1980s. It was Thatcher of course who made the now iconically neoliberal claim that "there is no such thing as society, only men, women and families."[59] Thatcher's rejection of "society" was multifaceted, but like many neoliberals, she worked toward dismantling organized labor and subsequently toward a broad-based wage reduction. And even that was a medium, not a goal: "Economics is the method," she said, "but the object is to change the soul."[60]

Thousands of people were involved in Deller's re-creation of the miners' strike, a scale that produced a certain monumentality. By contrast, Tanaka's installation settles on a scalar intimacy. Even as it is estimated that upward of thirty thousand children went on strike in Liverpool in 1985, perhaps only fifty or so were present for Tanaka's restaging. Thatcher herself had labeled the striking miners "the enemy within" and as engaged in a form "mob violence," and Deller's reenactment sought to demonstrate the falsehoods contained within both assertions. In contrast, Tanaka's work presents itself as more open to contingency. It explores possibility more than it refuses facts. The miners' strike, and their loss, was perhaps the most spectacular and pivotal display of Thatcher's neoliberalization program. The children's strike seems almost picayune in comparison. But they won.

The motivation for the strike, and consequently an important consideration of Tanaka's piece, was the British government's introduction in 1985 of a compulsory "Youth Training Scheme" (YTS). The scheme would have paid a stipend to local businesses to train those sixteen- and seventeen-year-olds who had left school. But the scheme would not have paid those same sixteen- and seventeen-year-olds for their labor. Yet they were obliged to participate in YTS if they wanted to remain eligible for social welfare. As the *Guardian* explained, the Thatcher government "planned to remove unemployment benefits for 16 and 17-year-olds and compel those who could not get work, or pursue further studies, to attend YTS. The aim was to reduce unemployment among young people and provide them with training and skills."[61] Many youth interpreted Thatcher's YTS as a form of forced, uncompensated, and nonunionized labor. In response to its planned initiation, children and teenagers nationwide staged a strike from school, a one-day walkout. The largest concentration of strikers was located in Liverpool, one of the country's most militant cities, and the effect of the event was to postpone implementation of the scheme for several years. The scale of such an action, its necessary coordination and militancy, was made possible by the organization of school-based coalitions of Young Socialists through the youth wing of the Labor Party.

Likewise, this children's labor history as visual history was available for Tanaka to access only through the work of another artist, the socialist photographer Dave Sinclair. Tanaka restaged not simply the children's strike, but also Sinclair's visual documentation of it, which was subsequently republished in Sinclair's small folio, *YTS School Children's Strike Liverpool 1985*.[62] Using Sinclair's history as his guide, Tanaka invited grown members of the Young Socialists to sit for interviews with both him and their own grown children. Tanaka's installation displayed in situ Sinclair's original photographs, journalistic documentation from the 1985 event, as well as Tanaka's interviews with the grown strikers, visible on mounted screens throughout the gallery.

Perhaps unsurprisingly, the participatory climax of Tanaka's installation was the reenactment of the children's public demonstration. After his interview with the original strikers, Tanaka, Sinclair, and whomever else—it was a public event—restaged the strike as it left Liverpool's St. George's Hall and meandered its way through the city to the port (figure 4.2). In the 1990s, this port had been a site of the Liverpool dockers' strike, one of the longest in British labor history; today it houses the art gallery that hosted Tanaka's installation, the Open Eye Gallery. Before the restaged march began, Rachel, still remembered for her work as the teenaged organizer of the strike in 1985, ad-

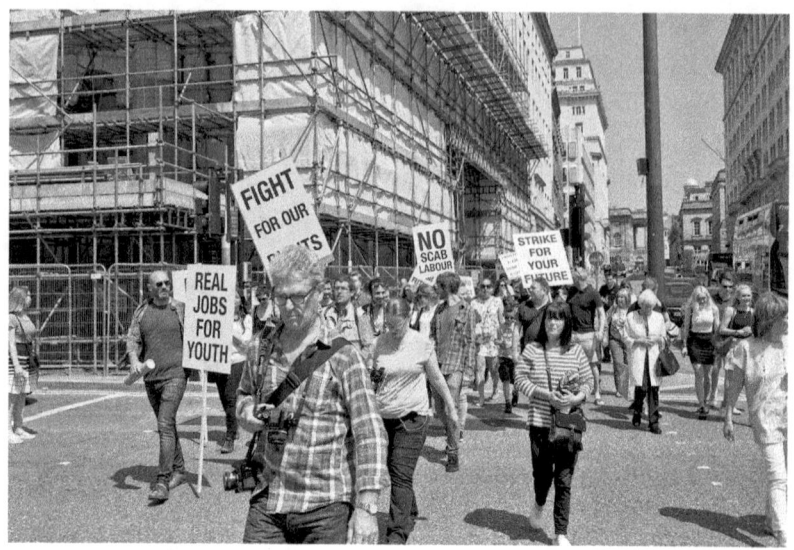

4.2 *Provisional Studies: Action #6, 1985 School Students' Strike.* Courtesy of Koki Tanaka.

dressed the perhaps fifty or so people who had assembled for the re-creation. "Liverpool has no Tory MPs" she proudly proclaimed, "and hopefully it never will."[63]

The historical and affective distance between the then and the now of the children's labor action organizes the work's tone. It asks, What did they do then? What do they remember now? Can the affective charge of those memories, as brought about through a restaging, critique labor today as the action itself was a critique of labor in 1985? As they speak in 2016, the now-adult child-strikers often surpass the bounds of Tanaka's generic questions. Although the viewer is only privy to some of Tanaka's provocations, she will certainly notice that the Trotskyists, the Socialists, the collective politicization of labor as staging ground for individual and social reproduction, appear nowhere in Tanaka's own language. Tanaka, rather, indicates an interest in collective memory, national memory, and restaged memory more than the particular content that those memories index. A question such as "What did you learn?" elicits the answer, "Being part of the Young Socialists meant that I got a political education." The question "Why did you stage this event?" generates the answer, "You'd be doing a proper job, forty hours a week, but you're not being paid." Likewise, "How do you see things now?" provokes the answer from a middle-aged woman who speaks with her two adult sons: "I'm

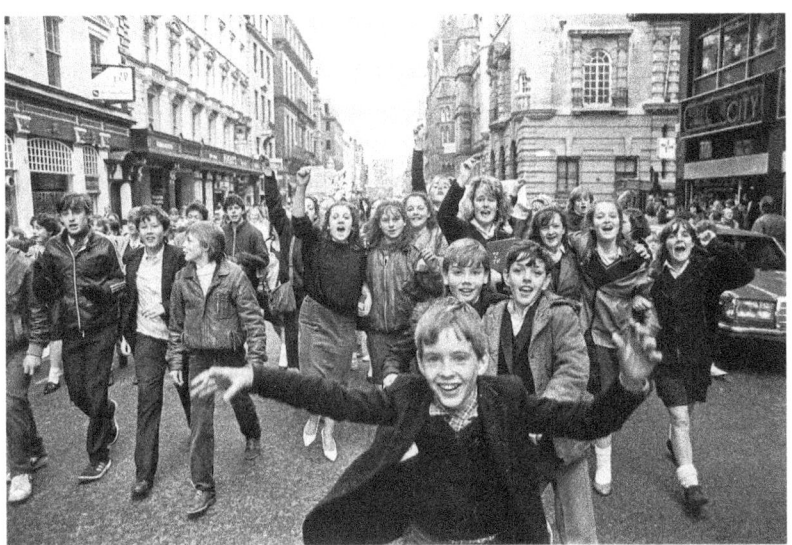

4.3 *YTS School Strike*. Courtesy of Dave Sinclair.

very cynical now. When I was fifteen, I was full of hope." When Tanaka asks, "What was the day [of the strike] like?" one adult child-striker, Emy, reminisces: "All demonstrations [in Liverpool] started out at the same place, St. George's Hall[,] and ended at the pier. And [the walk] would usually take about seven hours. [The children's strike] took about twenty minutes because the children were all running . . . they didn't take the designated route. They just ran all the way to the finish" (figure 4.3).

As Emy speaks to Tanaka, the memories of the child-based exuberance of that day transform his tone, and he seems to feel again some of its possibility. Indeed, he still seems surprised by that day's intensity as well as his ability to reproduce some of that intensity through recollection. It is in the affective scene produced by the adult child-strikers' reminiscences more so than the "reenactment" that *Provisional Studies: Action #6* comes to life as it connects a past and present of what I want to argue was a refusal of decommodified labor *then* and a showcasing of decommodified labor as crucial to socially engaged art *now*. The affective charge of the refusal was necessarily inflected by the subject-position of the agitators: children. The strike was a strike, of course: children of all ages set about refusing the prospect of conscription into an unpaid labor scheme. But it was also, for them, a day off school. Likewise, the demonstration was a demonstration; it departed from the place in Liverpool where demonstrations began and it was organized to follow the prescribed route. But it was also a race to the finish line. In both moments, the fact of the children's childishness becomes a forceful, political critique of labor. The photographer Dave Sinclair sits for an interview with Tanaka and he too becomes part of the work. Like Emy, Sinclair notes the speed with which the children's march transpired. "They announced the march would be beginning, but the kids just ran. They ran straight down to the pier head." Conjuring both the social and physical sense of the word "movement," Sinclair notes, "When we get such a movement of young people, you're optimistic. You think: it can't be bad. The main feeling of the day was optimism. Joy and optimism."

In recalling this joy and optimism and thus reproducing it, Emy and Sinclair seem to recall the path that Marx himself laid out in using the metaphor of the child to understand art's relations to periodization. When considering why certain epochs produce certain art, and why ancient Greece—a not-advanced society, according to Marx—could produce such wonderful art, Marx comments that "a man cannot become a child again or he becomes childish, but does he not find joy in the child's naïveté, and must not he himself strive to reproduce its truth at a higher stage? Does not the true character of each epoch come alive in the nature of its children?" In Marx's conception, ontogeny recapitulates phylogeny but it does so politically. As the child grows up, so humanity grows up. Yet that is not the sole concern for Marx. Rather, he wonders, what enables Moderns to continue to enjoy ancient art? He suggests that "the Greeks were normal children. The charm of their art for us is not in contradiction to the undeveloped stage of society on which it grew. [It] is [the] result, rather, and is inextricably bound up, rather, with the fact that the unripe social conditions under which it arose, and could alone arise, can never return."[64] In other words, Marx locates a generalized historical nostalgia that art, as representative of a period, can both provoke and assuage.

For the adult child-strikers in Tanaka's installation, there is a similar personal and social distance from the strike as well as a similar appreciation. These now-adult child-strikers wonder whether workers, particularly their own children, might ever return to the level of labor organization found in the 1980s. Individually, they cannot return to their own childhoods. Yet Tanaka has their own children sit with them during their interviews, and together they peruse Sinclair's images. And through their children they do experience some form of childhood again but in a setting that combines socially engaged art and organized labor. Each category on its own—art and labor—is not generative enough to achieve the work's sought after tone of energetic nostalgia.

As now-grown strike-leader Rachel notes of art's ability to reflect its own conditions of production, "the 1980s were a very politicized time in Liverpool. But I think they would prefer not to remember it in the museums." And as Emy concludes of organized labor, "for good reasons young people have switched off mainstream political action . . . . I think they feel that [our] form of democracy is very limited. What's the answer? I don't know. I'm encouraged by France and Spain where there are protests organized and led by young people."

Perhaps an answer might better be located in a different understanding of what the children did then in their critique of labor and how Tanaka captures that critique now in his art. As we have seen, for Adorno children present not a metaphor for aesthetic periodization, as they do for Marx, but rather they offer a prehistory of division between the playfulness of the aesthetic and the drudgery of its opposite, the world of waged labor. Children function not as a scaled-down humanity but as soon-to-be wage earners who have not yet succumbed to a life of abstract labor and its forced equivalences, a life in which everything is qualitatively equal to everything else because it can be bought and sold with varying quantities of money. Adorno explicitly notes the need for the commodity to render all equivalent and claims that children are preternaturally suspicious of it: "The unerring child is struck by the 'peculiarity of the equivalent form,'" he writes.[65] Children are, for Adorno, dissenters from wage labor, and that dissent is registered through their play. "In his purposeless activity the child, by subterfuge, sides with use value against exchange value," Adorno writes.[66] His reading offers a compelling understanding of adults' appreciation of childish "naïveté," but it is likewise one that *Provisional Studies: Action #6* interrupts.

Crucially, Tanaka's installation is structured through a representation of children demanding a wage. It uses the protected wageless frame of the aesthetic to remember and repeat an event during which children's playful mimicry of work made a demand for waged labor, when these two spheres converged and when we could, even if only momentarily, reject Marx's own claim that "labour cannot become play." In making a demand for a wage, their play becomes something more than play's accepted normative dimension of the "experience of a non-purposeful state."[67] From its rejection of the accepted wagelessness of the aesthetic to the worklessness of the child, Tanaka's installation, then, realizes a crucial resituating of the work–play dichotomy, if not of real subsumption itself.

In this resituating, I locate the category of decommodified labor: a form of labor that may circulate as a commodity but is presently not circulating as one. Here it takes the form of child's play and becomes a force that is both oppositional to wage labor and consistent with it. Furthermore, I suggest that such a resituating might change how we approach children's playful *mimicry* and its relation to art's mimesis in an era of decommodified labor. Children playing at mimesis reminds us of what could be called the mimetic elements of decommodified labor itself: like work but not work, potentially critical and potentially regressive. In this piece's critique of decommodified artistic labor we see children "playing at work," an activity that might or might not become labor; but if those actions are not ultimately realized as labor, it is unclear whether they may be realized as "play." Rather, the installation succeeds in suspending this dichotomy.

How, for example, do we understand that Tanaka's piece twice affirms the fact that the children raced to the finish line? A demonstration seeks to absorb and reconfigure public space through its expansive temporality and spatiality. It is not fortified by moving quickly or directly. Yet, as Emy notes with some amazement even today, "they just ran." In seizing the destination of the strike as more meaningful than the slow occupation of public space, the children in fact transformed how the strike against work would transpire through the very destinationless nature of play. On that day in 1985, the ludic, destination-less aspect of play took hold of the destination itself. In racing to the desig-nated end, the designated end disappeared. In that moment, their moment, the striking children never had to ask, "Are we there yet?" This action reveals the larger structure of refusal in the day's events: children, those for whom la-bor is officially proscribed, refused to be unpaid laborers. That transformation may be understood as their critique of work, an inversion that we can read as related to the specter of decommodification.

Tanaka refuses the metaphorical distance between child and adult, work and play, mimicry and mimesis. The children were not mimicking a strike. They were on strike. Their strike used work's opposite, play, to make a de-mand that they become waged laborers. Perhaps here we see a glimpse of Ben-jamin's own utopian hint, itself a commentary of Marx's understanding of children as periodizing, that "the most extreme concreteness for an epoch . . . appears now and again in children's games. . . ."[68] Through its investigation of whether children in art may do more than play, Tanaka's piece, as well as the one to which we will soon turn, asks whether Benjamin's "game" remains or whether it has become compromised. Children demand a wage for work and yet they cannot work. In Tanaka's re-creation, the demand to work becomes art, which is categorically opposed to work. In a time of decommodified labor, these two can coexist. Perhaps there can be wages for artwork. From this position, the child-striker's demand to be compensated through a wage, to be treated as a worker, itself becomes the utopian demand. The child-strikers refuse the binary that enables Adorno's reading of childhood as itself a refusal of the waged life.

Almost against its own inclination, Tanaka's piece pulls together the twin economic narratives that organize this book. As he records this period of neoliberalization of the U.K., the once-children-now-adult strikers insist on their labor. They insist on labor itself. As they were doing so, in the 1980s, children themselves became objects of neoliberal investigation both because they offered a longer duration of what course the investment in human capital might take and because they were clearly a site to investigate human capital not understood as labor. After all, they don't work. Of course people are entirely capable of renarrating their experience of labor as investment; that possibility inheres in the very existence of discourse. But for that understanding to become hegemonic, the shift will need to be managed and organized on multiple levels. Indeed, as a program, neoliberalism has proceeded to both attenuate state services and to promulgate certain discourses about those services.

In the case of the Youth Training Scheme, the child-strikers refused that narration. They understood state-ordered but private sector–based "training" to be a kind of "labor." Indeed, they seem to have understood school to be a kind of labor as opposed to an "investment" they should make in themselves. While neoliberalism seeks to limit the conceptual breadth of "labor" to the point that it disappears entirely into "human capital," the student strikers made a claim for themselves on an entirely different level: they refused to work. In one of Sinclair's images from 1985, two girls hold a Young Socialist placard that aims to declare "Fight to Protect Your Future," but spells "future" first as "futer," only to have the "e" traced over and become a misshapen "u." The final declaration: "Fight to Protect Your Futur." On another sign from Sinclair's archive, Thatcher's countenance appears somewhere between ghost and clown—a white face with dark rings around deep, hollow eyes. This sign presents an imagined dialogue between the child-strikers and the Iron Lady. "Thatcher says 'I deplore this action.'" Directly below her image and comment appears the students' retort: "School students say: 'Strike for your future. All out on Thursday April 25.'"

The next piece I examine goes a step beyond the re-creation of children's de-mands to be waged. *Haircuts by Children*, by the artist collective Mammalian Diving Reflex (MDR), pays children to work as artwork. In his "Childhood and Critical Theory," Paolo Virno argues that "the meaningless and parasitic nature of wage labor becomes particularly evident in light of the game prac-ticed in the preschool period in which the absence of a goal and an experi-mental inclination coexist."[69] The collective seems to have accepted Virno's insight and transformed it into a kind of challenge: Can children not expose the wage, but play with it, and if so, will the wage retain its organizing force? Will the child retain her playfulness?

Haircuts by Children has been staged globally over the course of ten years, and in each of its iterations children become—for a few days, anyway—wage laborers. In the performance, MDR collaborates with a hair salon and a pri-mary school over a series of weeks to train a group of between twenty and thirty children in the skill of haircutting. After a series of workshops about the history of socially engaged art, in which they will soon be partaking, as well as vocational training with hair stylists, the participating children take over a haircutting salon for a weekend, during which they commit to four-to five-hour staffing shifts.[70] Publicizing their availability with hand-drawn posters, the children and MDR make available free haircutting appointments to an adult public who shows up and allows their hair to be cut by a group of children.

Like other socially engaged art that provides an encounter with difference, often along lines of race, class, nationality, or geography, here an encounter with a different age structures the work.[71] Adults and children meet each other and the adults' appearances will be modified as a result. The collective selected hair for their object of practice because few aspects of our person are as easily modifiable (both to get rid of and get back) and as revealing of our own narcissism. Jenna Winter, one member of the MDR collective, recalls her early participation in *Haircuts by Children*. "The first time I got my hair cut [by children]: I was like: oh my god! For artists [it's] ok, but for other people, they have to live in the world and go to their jobs."[72] This risk or temptation that one might look weird could explain, in part, why certain adults consent to have their hair cut by children: that they too may be read as artists. Yet MDR reports that a substantial portion of their haircutting audience are senior citizens who might have to live in the world but do not have to go to work.

If business gets slow the children resort to cutting each other's hair, a process that tends to result in "a lot of crying."[73] *Haircuts* is not simply about hair, then, but rather concerns itself with social risk, gendered risk, generational risk, and the self-transformation that might accompany the taking of each.

The piece is documented through photo, video, and text, and—for a brief period, anyway—through the transformed appearance of the participants who allow their hair to be cut. In one of the collective's many videos that accompany the performance, salon owners and managers are interviewed as to why they would turn over their business to a group of eight- to twelve-year olds. "Publicity" and "fun" are among the answers; "working with artists" is also mentioned. Patrons, too, are interviewed as to why they would turn over their heads, their appearances even, to a group of recently trained children. Their answers are similar: "fun," "experience," and "free hair-cuts." The collective also interviews its own members: Why do they do it? Here, their message of social engagement comes to the fore. They understand child-adult interaction outside of circumscribed, usually familial, and thus racial contexts as exceedingly rare. If adults have children, then of course they interact with them and their friends. But most adults do not encounter different populations of children across the bounds of class and race, much less share a public space with them over the course of twenty or thirty minutes (figure 4.4). And adults rarely touch nor are they touched by children other than their own or their family members. MDR understands this piece as an activist intervention into the boundary that separates adults and children into disparate populations. That intervention is structured through the art-based interruption of one of the definitional exclusions of the child in capitalist democracies of the Global North: children do not work.

Critics often locate socially engaged art on a genealogical map in a position that postdates Fluxus and that considers it as the inheritance of 1960s and 1970s performance art. A piece such as *Haircuts by Children* can be easily compared to Fluxus artist Geoffrey Hendricks's 1976 piece, *Unfinished Business: Education of a Boy Child*, in which multiple acts of haircutting, beard-shaving, and "educational activities" were staged in New York over a several-day period with performers who included Hendricks' son, Bracken, as well as leading Fluxus artist George Maciunas.[74] Hannah Higgins has aptly, for this chapter at least, offered the term "Fluxkids" to refer to the many children, including her, who dotted, if not motivated, various Fluxus performances. Its use of a similar demographic notwithstanding, *Haircuts* both borrows from and modifies a piece such as *Unfinished Business* by scaling up and depersonalizing

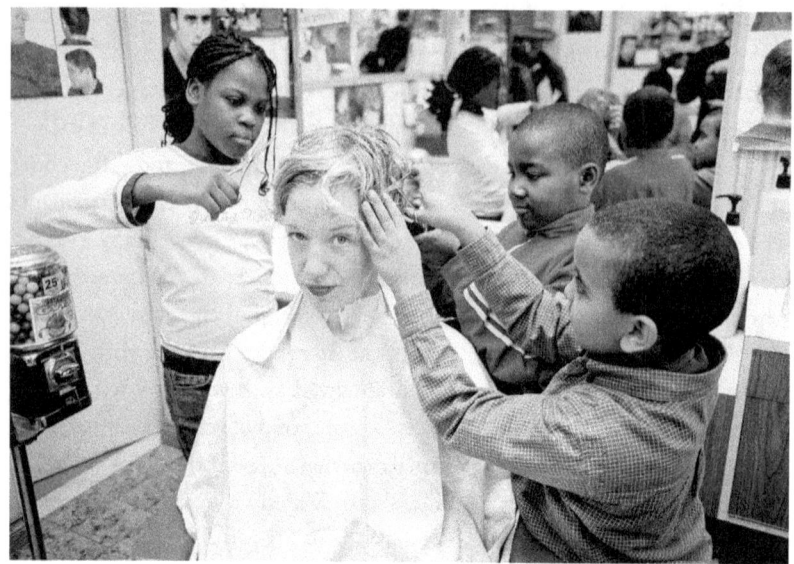

4.4 *Haircuts by Children*. Image courtesy of John Lauener.

the act of cutting of hair. *Haircuts* is structured to include more participatory possibility and in that a repeatability. There is no equivalent of a George Maciunas here; there are many children, many patrons, many haircuts. The children are trained in a trade, they advertise their availability with their own drawings, they cut the hair, and they are paid to do so.

Certain resonances exist, then, with *Haircuts* and both Berrigan's and Tanaka's child-based installations. As in Berrigan's work, there is an assumption of an adult trade by the child; as in Tanaka's, there is a refusal to let the child simply stand in for an economic actor. Perhaps most importantly, like Tanaka's project, *Haircuts* assumes a world of real subsumption in which we are all always already working. It makes this assumption over and against a logic of neoliberal self-capitalization in which a subject's self-investment in human capital now might produce a return later. There is no deferred investment in the children; rather, their wage renders their labor a commodity in the here and now.

The collective does not assume that viewers, much less children, know the history of child labor prohibitions. Why, precisely, are children prohibited from working? David McNally has claimed that the plight of children's factory labor in nineteenth-century England may be understood as one of the "first moral panics of capitalism."[75] But we are surely a long way from the mills of Manchester. And indeed, worries about children's safety are today narrated in a quite different moral panic—namely, that of the child's premature sexualization. To consider one moral panic, the piece will necessarily need to consider the other. Included alongside the installation's documentation is the text "Protocols for Working With Children," authored by MDR collective member Darren O'Donnell. The publication functions as both an explanation of and justification for works such as *Haircuts by Children*. "Protocols" might be read as a manifesto of sorts. It declares, "In the future, every child will be given a pair of scissors and invited to shape our destinies. In the future, every child will be granted full citizenship rights; [they will be] encouraged to vote, run for office and drive streetcars. In the future, children will teach and adults will learn. . . . In the future, children will be powerful creatures able to cross the street without looking both ways, and hold their breath underwater forever and ever and ever."[76]

Scissors function as a metaphor for access to shape a collective social world through work. But they also cut hair, an action that is initially fun for the children and that, through its repetition, might become a form of skilled trade. This literalizing of social power through the refusal of a distinction between the toy and the tool also extends to the wage form as a refusal to distinguish between commodified and decommodified labor. Each child who participates in *Haircuts by Children* is paid for her labor. The children don't simply mimic work, they are compensated for working. Yet children cannot work. Thus their actions must be understood somewhere between mimicking and doing in art, a place where no one works. Finally, in returning to and questioning a historical capitalist moral panic that has become common sense—children do not work—the piece must confront a contemporary moral panic: nonrelated adults and children should not touch each other.

Thus MDR's public declaration of a methodology is particularly important for *Haircuts* because the piece confronts the two structuring prohibitions that, according to Bond Stockton, in fact constitute contemporary childhood: the exclusion of paid labor and the exclusion of shared sexuality—even if only nonfamilial touch—between children and adults. "Childhood" as an invaluable and protected space depends on the circulation of the fictions and fantasies found in these prohibitions. To perform this work in places such as the United States, Canada, and the United Kingdom is to trespass not only on laws against child labor but on forms of cultural normativity that define children as "priceless" and fundamentally noneconomic actors who possess little agency. Because they have no agency, because they are not sullied by the economy, they also have a certain "innocence," which then, in a predictably Foucauldian dialectic, both invites and discourages their sexualization by adults. According to Bond Stockton, these two prohibitions are not easily disentangled. And indeed she suggests through a series of novelistic readings that "what may be children's greatest vulnerability . . . involves not sex but money. If children were to have more economic power, would they be less vulnerable to adults, in some contexts."[77] In the genealogy that Bond Stockton, Zelizer, and Ariès all trace, as children are deracinated from a wage labor that is itself becoming increasingly dominant, they become newly vulnerable, newly innocent, newly violable. Indeed, before Foucault's introduction of the repressive hypothesis in *The History of Sexuality* volume 1, Ariès had already noted that as childhood becomes more clearly defined over the course of modernity, adults' perception of children shifts from "immodesty to innocence."[78]

MDR confronts this knot of taboos directly: the collective pays children to work touching adults as artwork. Each child receives a wage of $10 for participating. Yet there surely exists a reason why all Western democracies outlaw child labor. No one favors a return to the days when "little hands" were considered "ideal for weaving," or when the future of the United States' economic growth and national character were narrated with the claim that "the work of the world has to be done, and these children have their share . . . why should we place emphasis on prohibitions . . . ? We don't want to rear up a generation of non-workers, what we want is workers and more workers."[79] Of course such a sentiment was hardly borne equally by all children; class and race have always had as much influence on whether modernity's children worked as did their age.

MDR must answer the twin questions of how one should work with children and why children should work. Their "Protocol for Working with Children" borrows from a rights-based discourse. For example, it includes reference to the United Nations' Convention on the Rights of the Child. Children have the right to "relax and play, and to join in a wide range of cultural, artistic and other recreational activities." Because this treaty is global in reach and includes signatories in both the Global North and Global South, we also find in it an acknowledgement of children's work. "The government should protect children from work that is dangerous or might harm their health or their education . . . Children's work should not jeopardize any of their other rights, including the right to education, or the right to relaxation and play."[80] *Haircuts by Children* exerts a certain sense of restitution, then. Children, in exile from so many adult worlds in the capitalist democracies of the Global North, are welcomed back into the public sphere that has always been, whether liberalism acknowledges it or not, at the same time a commercial sphere. The rights to play and to protection from work are not mutually exclusive; rather, they might be conjoined. In the Global North, that conjoining will appear in art where labor is already difficult to discern. In the realm of art, decommodified labor seems at home, and it is here that children's labor will be recommodified, as it were, as a site to critique the commodity status of all labor.

But in an unintentional demonstration of the soundness of Bond Stockton's argument in *The Queer Child*, to pay children, to enfranchise them through work, is to pass through the specter of child sexual abuse. In demonstrating this consequence, the performance exceeds the rights-based discourse that it itself champions. Children, for their part, are told to be wary of "stranger danger." MDR uses this term repeatedly in its texts and discussions to indicate the pervasive fear to which children are instructed to adhere: adult strangers should be avoided. Conversely, adults are told to be wary of being perceived as too interested in children, lest that interest be perceived as sexual. Anyone who has ever visited a playground in New York City will recall the signs that adults are not allowed on its premises unless they are "accompanied by a child," and anyone who has ever worked with children has likely been instructed never to be alone with a child. Each is taught to fear the other. This space of mutual, sexualized fear—the reverse command to see children as sexual through the policing of all interest in children as potentially sexual—is foundational to what James Kincaid calls "the culture of child molesting" in his remarkable book with a subtitle of the same name.[81] *Haircuts by Children* is motivated by and must respond to the reality of such fears.

Foremost, the problem of "stranger danger" is one that this work both invokes and distances itself from. In declaring that they will not be subject to this moral panic, the piece enacts what studies such as Kincaid's and Bond Stockton's can only insist on—namely, that "strangers" are hardly the "danger."[82] *Haircuts by Children* risks an interaction between adults and children who do not know each other. And indeed, a haircut requires a specific engagement: the communication of wants, the vulnerability of vanity, and finally, repeated touching. During the performance's duration there transpires sustained physical interaction between adult strangers and the children who attend to them. These children place their hands on the adult's head, shoulders, perhaps even face. This is a haptic work, then, one whose medium is touch.

It involves the mediation of individual and collective proprioception through its insistence on cross-generational touching, which is simultaneously artist-audience touching. Jennifer Doyle, in her reading of performance artist Adrian Howells's 2006 *Held*, has suggested that the haptic is usually a sign of gravity. Howells worked toward what he called "accelerated intimacy" by inviting viewers to meet him in a hotel room and be held by him for a period of time. *Held* has certain similarities to *Haircuts by Children* in that it revolves around an appointment structure in which artist and audience agree to meet and engage in sustained touch, working through a medium Doyle calls "the affective density of the interaction between artist and audience."[83] *Haircuts by Children* is likewise "affectively dense," yet its content is not grave. It is not private, nor does it contain the slow duration and intentional progress of *Held*. Rather, its density comes through speed, temptation, and excited pleasure. Like the children ran to the pier on the day of the children's strike, as recounted in the recollections of Tanaka's interviewees, here they are eager to "shave everyone bald right off the bat."[84]

Fittingly, a hair salon is a place of mirrors, where things are not only seen from one angle, or two, but from many, as mirrors reflect other mirrors. As the scissors offer the literal possibility of reshaping both hair and social relations, the mirrors offer multiple perspectives with which to see the present. A salon is a business, which will, at least for a few days, be run by children: appointments will be made and kept, reception will be staffed, floors will be swept, instruments will be disinfected. *Haircuts by Children* transforms the salon into what Benjamin described as the Saturnalia-like environment specific to children's theatre. "Everything is turned upside down, and just as master served slave during the Roman Saturnalia, so during the performance, children stand on stage and teach and educate their attentive educators. New Forces and new impulses appear."[85] Children at play may be "representatives of paradise" according to Benjamin, but their utopia is a delicate one. On the one hand, utopia may be found in the neighborhood hair salon, a declaration of the imminent possibility of the transformation of social relations. On the other hand, the nearness of utopia is also fleeting, as the salon becomes a site of frequent breakdown: children refuse to rotate tasks, some avoid clean up and the maintenance work of running the salon, everyone desires to control the scissors.[86]

But these children working as art differ from Benjamin's children as representations of not working—or utopia. And part of that difference may be located in the decommodified labor that artists do and that children have, since 1938, been formal representatives of. Combing both of these historical variations of labor, the piece offers a critique of each. Children do not represent the possibility of art through play; rather, they are the art as they "play at work." The work that they play at is artistic labor, and that labor has been decommodified. Here a decommodified population of workers undertakes commodified labor in art.

Tanaka's piece was structured around the "then" and "now" of decommodified labor: the decommodified labor of children then is brought to bear on the decommodified labor of socially engaged art now. *Haircuts* refuses the play-versus-work dichotomy by refusing other dichotomies—namely, tool versus toy and children as commodified versus decommodified laborers. In *Haircuts by Children*, what Virno suggested was the "meaningless" and "parasitic" nature of wage labor—its repetitive temporality, its monotony of task, the inelasticity of the wage itself—becomes the site of play. It becomes fun. Furthermore, the absence of wage labor found in the child's world of immediacy and intensity is paired with the seeming mimicry of the wage itself: the children are paid to "play at work." Through the payment, the mimicry is refused. The piece refuses to let children function as or represent decommodified labor.

But if the prohibition on receiving a wage in part defines the boundedness of childhood, then its violation must have some consequence. Indeed, with its refusal of children's decommodified labor, with its redistribution of the wage within the piece, the piece suggests another form of potential redistribution—namely, of childhood as an affective state. Alongside a distribution of the wage to now include children—itself made possible by considering and dispelling the worry of "stranger danger"—the piece then seeks to redistribute the affective density of childhood itself.

Importantly, the collective never makes the move of considering the literal social efficaciousness of *Haircuts by Children*—a move we saw in chapter 2 in the work of Renzo Martens. There is no empirical metric for children's enfranchisement or for adults' enjoyment of their interactions with children. These children are not being transformed into artists or into entrepreneurs. Unlike a host of socially engaged practices that serve a clear purpose, bringing something to the community that was clearly lacking—forms of education, forms of medical care, transfer of resources, and so on—MDR provides haircuts, hardly a necessary social good, and one whose duration is variable. Hair always grows back.

Rather, children are instructed in how to be aestheticians, in all senses of the word. They learn to cut hair at the salon, but they also learn about contemporary art from MDR members who coproduce the project with them. In one video documenting the performance, the collective explains "socially engaged art" and "relational aesthetics" to the children as they present to them an image of Francis Alÿs's video *When Faith Moves Mountains* (2002). Set on the outskirts of Lima, Peru, the piece choreographs some five hundred volunteers who labor for hours with shovels in order that they might collectively move a 1,600-foot-tall sand dune 4 inches. Alÿs's work is meant to provide to the children an example of the kind of collaborative, socially engaged artwork they will undertake during their running of the salon. To me, this is an odd pedagogical choice. Indeed, a reading of Alÿs's piece provides a site to distinguish the unpaid volunteerism so present in socially engaged art from a critique of decommodified labor, an accomplishment of *Haircuts by Children*.

Here I follow Grant Kester, who remains quite unmoved by Alÿs's piece and argues that a crucial difference exists between "collaboration" in socially engaged art and allegories of it.[87] He suggests that the local Peruvian volunteers, many of them students, "have been summoned by Alÿs not as collaborators but as bodies to illustrate a social allegory about [the economic] failures of Latin America."[88] Kester argues that the allegory is subtended by "wasted labor," what he calls the piece's "medium and vehicle of symbolic protest."[89] Against this presentation of labor's futility, Kester then suggests that "there are other possibilities of course, other ways of working, in which the experience of collaborative labor is seen as generative, not simply symbolic, improvisationally responsive, rather than scripted, in which the distribution of agency is more reciprocal."[90] Of course, Kester does not think this situation will be remedied by simply paying volunteers. Such an action would be both too literal and facile. Think of Santiago Sierra's "8 People Paid to Remain Inside Cardboard Boxes," (1999) whose accurately descriptive title has already been used to make my point (in chapter 3).

Kester's understanding of the construction of Alÿs's allegory and its "ethical" weaknesses ring true. But his reading of labor could be more nuanced. It's not that labor needs to be shared differently, or that volunteer labor is not fundamentally inequitable; both claims are certainly correct. Rather, in order to critique labor in socially engaged art, we must locate other valences of labor. The use of "volunteerism" needs to be substituted as Kester's necessary site of critique. *That* volunteers are not paid produces an ethical critique; *how* socially engaged art understands labor is what is required to move the charge from ethics to one of critiquing value, which, after all, is what labor indexes.

On the one hand, *Haircuts* avoids the charge that Kester quite appropriately makes toward Alÿs both by avoiding volunteerism and by inverting the possibilities and exclusions of the wage itself. Alÿs asks adults to work in his art without pay. They can be paid but Alÿs refuses to pay them. MDR takes children who cannot be paid and pays them. On the other hand, in refusing to let children function as decommodified labor, the collective holds open a site of that labor's critique, especially in socially engaged art. But for this critique to be possible, labor must be understood as containing multiple dimensions— one of those is its ability to dwell in a decommodified state.

In positioning children to undergird its critique of decommodified labor, how different *Haircuts by Children* appears from Tino Sehgal's or Carsten Höller's collaborations with children. In their recent works, either work or play predominates so as to easily criticize, and stabilize, its dichotomous other. Sehgal's *This Progress*, staged to great acclaim at the Guggenheim in 2010, involved the training and participation of children of all ages. (Adults underwent training to participate in the piece as well). As we would expect from Sehgal, *This Progress* orchestrated a series of conversations between the audience and the piece's child and adult "interpreters," who were stationed throughout the museum's famous rotunda. In her reading of the piece, Shannon Jackson argues that the children's participation appears as though it is "bent on proving that ephemerality cannot in fact resist commodification."[91] In fact, the reverse is true—commodification cannot resist ephemerality. But regardless, it is not the children's presence but their labor that indexes the so-called ephemeral. We see clearly the importance of the children's labor in the *New York Times*'s feature on *This Progress*. We should also note the neat similarity to the *Times*'s depiction of animals as unpayable artists, as seen in the previous chapter. Like Kounellis's horses, which could be worried over but could not be workers and thus could not be paid, the *Times* isolates the children's lack of wage and their overwork. It reports that "the schedule could be grueling even for much younger interpreters, who, unlike their elders, were unpaid. (They did receive a hat, bag and a museum membership; adults were paid $18.75 an hour, teenagers $7.25 an hour.) Solomon Dworkin . . ., who was one of the oldest children in the piece, said many of the younger ones had trouble with the pace of 40 to 50 interactions a day, 60 to 70 on weekends. 'They had a workload breakdown,' he said."[92]

According to the *Times*, the commodification of labor is the piece's ultimate horizon: who gets paid, who doesn't, how much, and with what consequences. Children are paid nothing; teenagers, something; adults, more. *This Progress* is described in a language of pure work; children are present to insist that even work has an end. Even if, as they themselves insist, they are exhausted. The joke, of course, is that the children aren't really working both because they can't and because art isn't really work.

Cartsen Höller's productions with children take the precisely opposite approach. Children occupy a site of all fun and no work, and conversely, his piece *Gartenkinder* (2014) has been interpreted as pure play. The *Financial Times* reports that "children play at the opening of artist Carsten Höller's installation 'Gartenkinder,' in which he has transformed the Gagosian Gallery . . . into a children's playground."[93] The British *Art Daily* explains the piece as "a new form of children's playground with walls and floor in red, green, blue and yellow . . . [which also] includes a large-scale dice that children can crawl inside [and] a giant mushroom that rocks like a roly-poly toy . . . . The installation emphasises the importance of play."[94]

It seems that Höller has staged what used to be known as a playground. I do not make this comment dismissively. Rather, I want to suggest that critics do not yet have another language for the decommodified labor that they witness in Sehgal's and Höller's artwork. Without such a language, their pieces are interpreted as either all work or all play. With regard to Sehgal's expansion of work, children are used absolutely normatively to critique both too much work and to assure the viewer that even work ends. With regard to Höller's expansion of play, we should heed Weiss's reading of Adorno's own worries about the overrepresentation of play. "If play attributes too much capacity to itself, [it] weighs down . . . its own development. If it conceives of itself as the sole avenue of relating to the world's disenchantment . . . play actually becomes closer to sport."[95] Adorno elsewhere calls the potential consequences of such overrepresentation of play a "regression to sport"—that frequently nationalistic, capitalist spectacle. Adorno states, "Art that seeks to redeem itself from semblance through play becomes sport."[96]

Conclusion

In accordance with our definition of "the aesthetic," art remains a site where adults access play. Yet the meaning of such access has itself been modified, and the artists who populate this chapter seem less interested in adults playing like children and more interested in children working like adults. That work happens in artwork, within the realm of the aesthetic—in the gallery or museum—which by definition is a place of the suspension of work. If chapter 3 was structured around animals as historic workers who, having lost that status, may now represent decommodified labor, this chapter has taken a rather inverse approach. Children, as historically once and soon-to-be-again individual laborers, here are captured aesthetically at the moment of their nonutility and put to work. The child, defined in part as she who cannot contract to work, enters the gallery to represent work, while the adult, she who works too much and cannot access play, enters the gallery to suspend work. There their paths cross and in doing so, put pressure on the wage form. But what kind of pressure should be brought to bear? More work? More play? Or a refusal of the very difference?

There, at the moment when they cannot work, in the space where work itself cannot happen, children's arrival in the artwork must now be understood as one response to the decommodification of artistic labor. In every example but *Haircuts by Children*, children are asked to work without a wage so as to buttress a demonstration of economic inequality. Unsurprisingly, then, it is Mammalian Diving Reflex's "Protocols for Collaborating with Children" that ventures to describe "decommodified labor," even if that term is not used. It claims that "we feel that it is important to point out that recent developments in the world of work and the locations where value is produced have put children at the centre of the work world, often in ways that are not yet acknowledged or, for that matter, fully understood."

There is a certain irony here. Children stand as one of labor's major historical decommodifications, one that is historical and visible as well as deeply moralized, raced, and gendered. In addition to that fact not being acknowledged or understood, the collective argues that "this is a new frontier for the generation of value, and it's important that children are recognized as important content and, in turn, value providers, who remain uncompensated."[97] They do not say that socially engaged art may be understood as both cause and effect of this frontier; they turn instead to "creative" enterprises such as Facebook and other sites of "playbor." But certainly the fact that art offers both a seamless site of continuation and a possible site of restitution may be read as an argument in their work and in this book.

Of course, one cannot scale art—perhaps the physical manifestation of the unique ability of aesthetic judgment to think the particular under the universal—and the point is not to begin paying children to be children, something that certain neoliberals have in fact suggested (similar to basic income).[98] Rather, the point is to demonstrate that as artistic labor has been decommodified, artists have begun to incorporate populations of decommodified laborers into their work. Those incorporations have followed a range of strategies and tones—some critical, some celebratory, some polemical. This range of approaches to critiquing children as representatives and potential critics of decommodified artistic labor is crucial to understanding socially engaged art's relations to the economy.

Epilogue

Liberal Arts

"Am I reaching for happiness? I am reaching for my work."
—FRIEDRICH NIETZSCHE, *Also sprach Zarathustra*

In 2013 the Swiss artist Urs Fischer mounted a show at the Geffen Contemporary in Los Angeles's Museum of Contemporary Art. With a declaratory title of *YES*, the sprawling installation was the result of the work of over one thousand volunteers who responded to an open call and were subsequently invited to produce whatever they wished during the weeks leading up to the opening. They made their art in the Geffen itself, using both the clay Fischer provided through a sponsorship by Laguna Clay Company and their own energy. While it seems that live animals were not among those producing the clay sculptures that would ultimately populate *YES*, children, students, artists—the very populations I have described in this book—functioned as generators of the show's artistic content, which quickly became a kind of who's who of decommodifed artistic laborers.

It is not surprising that the installation was less discussed for its final form—thousands of figurative clay sculptures and the detritus of their production in all sizes and states of repair—than it was for the process of its rendering. The museum claimed in its publicity materials that the show had been staged by "Urs Fischer with the help of 1,000 people from L.A." In its feature on *YES*, the *Los Angeles Times* highlighted the fact that all the art on view was completed by unwaged workers. Responding to the reporter's prompt that "[you don't] mind doing this work unpaid?" one collaborating artist responded, "Not at all. It's amazing to say I have a piece at the Geffen. And it's free material—it's every artist's dream."[1] This artist seems to be referring to her own possibility of accessing the clay at no charge and then placing her work on view in such a prominent locale. But from Fischer's point of view, she herself is the "free material" of "every artist's dream"; indeed, she herself as unpaid worker is what is on view at the Geffen. It is *Fischer's* show, after all. In the article, Fischer, too, weighs in on the lack of payment given to his installation's myriad artists and notes that chefs were on site to provide complimentary gourmet snacks. "We can't pay people, but we want to do our best," he explained. From Fischer to its interview of a college student, the article then jumps to another artist, "Theo Taplitz, [age] 10, a Wonderland Elementary student on spring break [who] didn't care so much about the perks."

Fischer differs from most of the artists I have discussed in this book. Few would describe his work as "socially engaged," for example, and he shows with the blue-chip Gagosian Gallery. Indeed, he might in fact make money through his artistic labor. And yet the percolation of both the themes and forms of decommodified labor—from art student to amateur to child to content generator—means that it is now seen far beyond its autochthonous province and locatable in leading museums and galleries. Such diversity of presence only serves to confirm decommodified labor's fundamental role in art production and criticism today.

I have claimed throughout this book that decommodified labor reveals a heretofore unnamed component of labor and provides a way to think labor after financialization. I have likewise showed how decommodified labor has become present in socially engaged art to the point of overdetermining much of this art's production, if not yet reception. This art understands itself as historically new, as constituting a break from previous mediums and disciplines located in fine art and performing art. That real historical newness has both been made possible by and serves to critique decommodified labor. In arts practice, then, decommodified labor is a changed labor, and art is changed by its emergence. Artists thematize this labor, they are formed by it, and they have turned to other populations of producers—who are likewise decommodified—to assist them in rendering decommodied labor not only historically present but also historically critical. For me to show how this labor has changed art, other categories—centrally the aesthetic itself—have had to remain more normative.

But I have not addressed the converse: namely, does decommodification change labor?[2] Does decommodified labor belong in the interstices between Marx's own characterization in the *Grundrisse* of "labor" and "really free working" for example?[3]

Is decommodification a better state of affairs? Such questions must be answered on several levels, of course. One answer resonates empirically, and the other dwells within the protected sphere of the aesthetic.

At the level of the empirical, we must argue that decommodified labor exists in art and elsewhere—it is fundamental to the culture industry, from sports to museums to television to social media—and that it indexes a continued evacuation in the content of the wage form; that is, it diminishes the substance that waged workers need in order to reproduce themselves socially: money. At that level, decommodification does not move us from labor toward "really free working." Indeed, if some people are getting paid, then those not getting paid will probably remain anchored in labor's long unfreedom. That unfreedom takes many forms, and the gambit of my book has been to focus on how labor's unfreedom is organized in capitalist democracies of the Global North in places where the presumptions of formal work remain.

It is there that we find that formal work's odd double—not housework, not affective labor, not immaterial labor—appears as an awkward combination of something like work but not waged. That configuration both derives from and perpetuates the uneven commodification of labor. In developed capitalist democracies, where the presumption is one of commodified labor, we find a correlation between labor's uneven commodification and social inequality. In the countries with the highest index of social equality, fewer people work without a wage—what Cuba appropriately still calls "volunteer labor" but what we know in developed capitalist democracies as "volunteering" or "community service." The United States, one of the great leaders in social inequality, has one of the highest levels of volunteer labor. Think of the parent-teacher association meetings that run schools; the internships for college credit; professional sports, including what one reporter calls the Professional Golf Association's "secret army" of "unpaid labor"; the museum docents; the firefighters and EMTs; the hospital volunteers. The list goes on. As one friend of mine said when I told him about some of these more social scientific findings—many of which did not make it into my manuscript—"the reserve army of labor is already employed, they're just not getting paid."[4]

If some are paid to work, then all should be paid to work. Throughout this study I have counterposed the receipt of wages with a lack of wages, but that is hardly a utopian dichotomy. Wages are already a compromise, and a structurally imbalanced one at that. A wage is as much a material demonstration of what the worker is not receiving as it is of what she does receive. Thus Silvia

Federici's fundamental claim contains at its root an opposition: the struggle we confront is one of wages *against* housework.

In art, however, the situation might be different. As it partakes in the aesthetic, art was already against the wage before artists lost their wages, and as we just noted, wages themselves distill a conflicted form. Some of the artists I've presented in the foregoing study, Woolard and Thornton in particular, seem to locate some liberating moments in their own decommodified artistic labor and that of their respective arts communities. But in our current conjuncture, such an embrace of wagelessness is not scalable; it is not a solution. But then again, art is not supposed to be scalable. In its early modern Kantian formulation, aesthetic judgment allows one to think "the particular under the universal."[5] That is of an order quite different from scaling an efficacious action from particular to universal. Other artists, such as Martens and the collective Mammalian Diving Reflex, understand decommodified labor as much more constricting, and indeed, in need of amelioration, even as they take radically different paths toward achieving such an end. Martens himself precisely attempts to use art at scale in order to increase wages. One response might suggest: At scale? For pay? Then it's not art.

It does seem fair to claim that one interpretation of socially engaged art's logic might be understood as solving social problems, but not at scale. Perhaps then it's also fair to call socially engaged art a *liberal art*. As I was finishing this manuscript, I happened across Geoff Mann's remarkable book on the historical arc of economic liberalism, *In the Long Run We Are All Dead: Keynesianism, Political Economy, and Revolution*.[6] In a book that veers between Hegel and Keynes, largely omitting a certain prominent German philosopher by the name of Marx whose life neatly bisects those of this pair, Mann attempts to explore the intellectual and material limits of liberalism. He posits that economic liberalism of the Keynesian variety has become our collective horizon—materially, politically, historically. And it remains a no less compromised project. The basic charge against liberalism, of course, is that its separation of the political and economic creates a whole host of generative contradictions that frequently take the form of seemingly unsolvable sites of social cruelty. Mann writes that "a separation of the political and economic realms, and the liberal capitalist civilization that depends upon it, tend inescapably toward disintegration because the liberal 'freedom' they cultivate and celebrate—yield-seeking, entrepreneurial atomicity—inevitably and endogenously produces scarcity and poverty, both of which make the separation difficult to maintain."[7] And yet it is maintained because, Mann concludes, "poverty has no proper place."[8]

Art might very well have become one of the many improper places for poverty. But what, then, is the proper place of Marxist cultural critique of art? Might it be understood as partaking in the aesthetic? As considering not a material (re)organization of social life, but of producing a space apart from that material organization that enables reflection on it divorced from a need to act? Might Marxist cultural critique be seen as an interpretative schema that offers a sense of "purposefulness without purpose?" We do indeed seem conceptually and psychically far from Marx's famous dictum in his *Theses on Feuerbach* that "The philosophers have only interpreted the world in various ways; the point is to change it."[9] Idealized and analytical—think of the book you've just finished—Marxist cultural critique struggles to offer a way into or out of the material problems of liberalism. For Marxism, liberalism is not radical enough, and yet because radicality is not possible within the confines of liberalism, Marxists cannot act radically. But we should not leave that contradiction untouched; we must embrace it and pressure it.

By some readings, art emerges from this space of critical nonpossibility. For Bürger, art is compensatory. For Adorno, art contains the resulting paradoxes and through that containment provides "negative knowledge" of the actual world. For still others, art offers a potential utopian jolt of recognition out of such a scenario even if the jolted soon regain their composure. If liberalism maintains the conceptual space that in some sense delimits art, then we have to ask how a nonliberal art would appear. Indeed, we might need to ask whether a nonliberal art *will* appear. In the language I have used throughout: Why would real subsumption not subsume art? The answer is, it would; it will. I have made this argument about literature elsewhere.[10] Both Nicholas Brown and Peter Osborne have made it about art specifically, each with their own terms. In this book I have let the aesthetic—and within it art—present as ideal to explore the permutations of the wage. I have likewise left the category of the wage somewhat abstract from the three categories that largely organize the structure of work today on a global scale: race, gender and nationality.

We often conceive of the aesthetic spatially as a sphere or logically as category. Maybe it is better thought temporally as a pause in accumulative time, just as I have suggested decommodified labor might be seen as a pause in commodification. It is not commodified presently—*now*, a category with its own philosophical uncertainty—but it may be sooner or later. Decommodified labor reclaims the sense of tautology of real subsumption: always kind of working but never really working and thus receiving less of a wage. Socially engaged art distills this process, both incorporating it and representing it. In making this claim with different artists working through their own media and practices but always returning to the uncertain status of their labor, I hope to have followed John Roberts's injunction, first cited in this book's introduction, that "we need . . . a rereading of capital that captures labor for aesthetic theory."[11] Of course the converse—that we need a rereading of capital that captures aesthetic theory for labor—is just as true.

Notes

Introduction

1 Mark Brown, "Not Paying Artists Deeply Entrenched in Gallery Culture, Research Suggests," *Guardian*, May 26, 2014, https://www.theguardian.com/artanddesign/2014/may/26/not-paying-artists-gallery-culture-publicaly-funded-exhibitions/.

2 For a nice summary of the cultural neoliberalization of Berlin, see Quinn Slobodian and Michelle Sterling, "Sacking Berlin: How Hipsters, Expats, Yummies, and Smartphones Ruined a City," *The Baffler*, no. 23 (August 2013), https://thebaffler.com/salvos/sacking-berlin, accessed October 2018.

3 Lutz Henke, "Why We Painted over Berlin's Most Famous Graffiti," *Guardian*, December 19, 2014, https://www.theguardian.com/commentisfree/2014/dec/19/why-we-painted-over-berlin-graffiti-kreuzberg-murals/.

4 The genealogy of the emergence of "affective labor" is impressive. See, for example, Patricia Clough, ed., *The Affective Turn* (Durham, NC: Duke University Press, 2007); see also Michael Hardt and Antonio Negri, *Empire* (Cambridge, MA: Harvard University Press, 2000) for their cognate term "immaterial labor" as well as their own genealogy of "affective labor."

5 See Ted Purves and Shane Selzer, eds., *What We Want Is Free: Exchange and Generosity in Recent Art* (Binghamton: State University of New York Press, 2009).

6 See Sharon Zukin, *Loft Living: Culture and Capital in Urban Change* (New Brunswick, NJ: Rutgers University Press, 1986), 97.

7 We can put this tension in conversation with, for example, Karl Polanyi's "double movement" of capital as theorized in his *The Great Transformation* (Chicago: University of Chicago Press, 1944). Giovanni Arrighi interprets the same problem as a spatialization of Marx's formula for capital,mcm,' or Money, Commodity, Money (of altered value) in *The Long Twentieth Century: Money, Power and the Origin of Our Times* (London: Verso, 1994). For something totally different see David Graeber on alternating cycles of credit-money versus specie-money in *Debt: The First 5,000 Years* (New York: Melville House, 2012).

8 For deskilling in labor, see Harry Braverman, *Labor and Monopoly Capital: The Degradation of Work in the Twentieth Century* (New York: Monthly Review Press, 1974). For a necessary recent take on deindustrialization, see Sven Beckert, *Empire of Cotton: A Global History* (New York: Penguin, 2014).

9 "Decommodification" is given its most complete consideration in Gøsta Esping-Andersen's *The Three Worlds of Welfare Capitalism* (Princeton, NJ: Princeton

University Press, 1990). I explore this in detail in the section "Economies of Art Criticism" in this introduction.

10 "Avant-garde" is no doubt a contentious term. I like John Roberts's *Revolutionary Time and the Avant-Garde* (London: Verso, 2015) for its consideration of this term "as a historically open-ended research programme."

11 For a good, popular overview of the term's genealogy, see Carolina A. Miranda's "How the Art of Social Practice Is Changing the World, One Row House at a Time," *Artnews*, April 7, 2014, http://www.artnews.com/2014/04/07/art-of-social-practice-is-changing-the-world-one-row-house-at-a-time/.

12 The two books that explore this art most cogently and that I turn to throughout are by Shannon Jackson and Claire Bishop. While both Jackson and Bishop make reference to social practice, they themselves do not use the term to categorize the works they discuss, preferring instead their own idioms. That all of these works, as Jackson herself notes, rely on tropes of theatricality and performativity is surely important with regard to the situation of interpersonal relationality. Both Jackson and Bishop provide their own versions of the genealogy from relational aesthetics to the present: for Jackson's see *Social Works: Performing Art, Supporting Publics* (New York: Routledge, 2012), 46–48; for Bishop see *Artificial Hells: Participatory Art and the Politics of Spectatorship* (London: Verso, 2011), 2–3, which also provides a genealogy of the terminology, its differentiation from "relational aesthetics," and its up-to-now institutionalization.

13 Thus I do not include forms of slavery and other regimes of servitude. For the long discussion of whether or how slavery should be considered capitalist in terms of the debate's impressive historiography, see Walter Johnson, *Soul by Soul: Life Inside the Antebellum Slave Market* (Cambridge, MA: Harvard University Press, 2000).

14 Karl Marx, *Capital*. Vol. 1, *The Process of Production of Capital* (London: Penguin, 1976), 376–77.

15 Marx, *Capital*, 377.

16 This according the U.S. Fair Labor Standards Act: U.S. Department of Labor, Wage and Hour Division, "Fact Sheet #71: Internship Programs under the Fair Labor Standards Act," updated January 2018, https://www.dol.gov/whd/regs/compliance/whdfs71.pdf/.

17 For the class-based cruelness of reality television, see Anna McCarthy, "Reality Television: A Neoliberal Theatre of Suffering," *Social Text* 93, 25, no. 4 (winter 2007): 17–42. Tanner Mirrlees, "Reality TV's Low-Wage and No-Wage Work," *Alternate Routes* 27 (2016): 187–212.

18 Jordan Sargent, "Urban Outfitters' Fall Strategy: Asking Employees to Work for Free," *Gawker*, October 7, 2015, http://gawker.com/urban-outfitters-fall-strategy-asking-employees-to-wor-1735228986/.

19 See *Girls*, "All Adventurous Women Do," season 1, episode 4, directed by Lena Dunham, written by Lena Dunham and Lesley Arfin, aired April 29, 2012, on HBO.

20 See Dave Beech in *Art and Value* (London: Brill, 2015), 142. He writes that art could be considered as in need of decommodification. I look at Beech's work more closely toward the end of this introduction; Beech ultimately rejects decommodification as a useful rubric.

21 Jackson, *Social Works*, 18.

22 Roberts, *Revolutionary Time*. His location of a "second economy" is perhaps the closest approximation currently available to the claim I am making. Yet, for him, "second economy" is not a heuristic.

23 Silvia Federici, *Revolution at Point Zero* (Oakland: PM Press, 2012) contains a reprint of the essay with Federici's retrospections.

24 Peter Linebaugh, *The London Hanged* (London: Verso, 1991), 319.

25 See Leigh Claire La Berge, *Scandals and Abstraction: Financial Fiction of the Long 1980s* (New York: Oxford University Press, 2014).

26 Marx, *Capital*, vol. 1, 176.

27 Marx, *Capital*, vol. 1, 176.

28 Thus in *Postmodernism, or the Cultural Logic of Late Capitalism* (Durham, NC: Duke University Press, 1991), 34, Fredric Jameson singles out "nature"—not only art—as one the last footholds to have been absorbed into capitalism.

29 Terry Eagleton, *The Ideology of the Aesthetic* (London: Verso, 1990), 3.

30 Lambert Zuidervaart, *Artistic Truth* (Cambridge: Cambridge University Press, 2010), 58.

31 See Peter Osborne, *Anywhere or Not at All: A Philosophy of Contemporary Art* (London: Verso, 2012), 4. Jaleh Mansoor exclaims more forcefully: "It is . . . evident that 'art' is neither a site of autonomy [nor] an exceptional site of 'free play'—in the tradition of Baumgarten, Kant, and most significantly, Schiller." Jaleh Monsoor, "Ayreen Anastas's M*Bethlehem and Pasolini Pa Palestine," *Journal of Aesthetics and Protest* 8 (winter 2011), http://joaap.org/issue8/mansoor.htm. Yet also note that the very title of the journal here, *"Aesthetics and Protest"* shows how deeply contradictory the use of the term "aesthetic" is.

32 Eagleton, *Ideology of the Aesthetic*, 9.

33 See Tithi Bhattacharya, ed., *Social Reproduction Theory: Remapping Class, Recentering Oppression* (London: Pluto, 2017).

34 In Yve-Alain Bois, *Painting as Model* (Cambridge, MA: MIT Press, 1990), 236.

35 Dave Beech's *Art and Value* traces the exceptional nature of art in the discourse of the political economy from Adam Smith to Keynes and the neoliberals.

36 The full text from Kant reads "Pleasure in aesthetic judgement [. . .] is merely contemplative [. . .]. The very consciousness of a merely formal purposiveness in the play of the subject's cognitive powers, accompanying a presentation by which an object is given, is that pleasure. For this consciousness in an aesthetic judgement contains a basis for determining the subject's activity regarding the quickening of his cognitive powers, and hence an inner causality (which is purposive) concerning cognition in general, which however is not restricted to a determinate cognition. Hence it contains a mere form of the subjective purposiveness of a presentation."

Immanuel Kant, *Critique of Judgment*, trans. Werner Pluhar (Indianapolis, IN: Hackett, [1790] 1987), §12, 68, Ak. 222.

37 Theodor Adorno, *Aesthetic Theory* (Minneapolis: University of Minnesota Press, 1997), 227.

38 Michael Denning, "Wageless Life," *New Left Review* 66 (November/December 2010), https://newleftreview.org/II/66/michael-denning-wageless-life/.

39 Kathi Weeks, *The Problem with Work* (Durham, NC: Duke University Press, 2011), 224.

40 I am indebted to Moishe Postone's interpretation of Marx's labor theory of value in *Time, Labor and Social Domination: A Reinterpretation of Marx's Critical Theory* (Cambridge: Cambridge University Press, 1996), wherein labor itself is conceived of as a socially produced form of abstract domination.

41 David Harvey's *The Limits to Capital* (London: Verso, 1982) is still the best text on how the time- and space-bound nature of capitalist value production remains crucial.

42 Kant, *Critique of Judgment*.

43 Jacques Rancière quoted in Yates McKee and Jaleh Mansoor, eds., *Communities of Sense* (Durham, NC: Duke University Press, 2009), 43.

44 Jacques Attali, *Noise: The Political Economy of Music* (Manchester: Manchester University Press, 1985), 47.

45 Boris Groys, *Art Power* (Cambridge: MIT Press, 2008), 6.

46 Maria Gough, *The Artist as Producer* (Berkeley: University of California Press, 2005), 8.

47 Defined by the *New York Times* (and there taken from the academic blog "Marginal Utility") as the "increasingly blurred distinction between online play and labor." "Playbor," *New York Times*, "Schott's Vocab" blog, March 12, 2010, http://schott.blogs.nytimes.com/2010/03/12/playbor/?_php=true&_type=blogs&_r=0/.

48 See Julia Bryan-Wilson, "Occupational Realism," *TDR: The Drama Review* 56, no. 4 (winter 2012): 32–48.

49 Marina Vishmidt, "Situation Wanted: Something about Labour," *Afterall: A Journal of Art, Context, and Enquiry* 19 (autumn/winter 2008): 20–34, 23.

50 For example, Sarah Brouillette notes that "as the worker has been imagined in definitively aesthetic terms, management thought has also become particularly attentive to the aesthetic as a means of addressing the problem of creating the conditions for good work. For decades now, of course, businesses have looked to the arts and culture for a variety of expedient services." See Sarah Brouillette, "Creative Labor," *Mediations* 24, no. 2 (spring 2009): 140–49, 145.

51 Andrea Fraser, *Museum Highlights: The Writings of Andrew Fraser*, ed. Alexander Alberro (Cambridge, MA: MIT Press, 2005), 251.

52 As Jasper Bernes states: "Luc Boltanski and Éve Chiapello have called 'the artistic critique,' a challenge to labor which focuses on alienation rather than exploitation, on the conditions of work rather than the wage and its share of total product, counter-posing to routinized, deadening labors the free, playful, self-directed and

mutable activity embodied by art and artists." Jasper Bernes, "Art, Work, Endlessness: Flarf and Conceptual Poetry among the Trolls," *Critical Inquiry* 42, no. 4 (summer 2016): 760–82.

53 As John Locke states: "Though the Earth, and all inferior Creatures be common to all Men, yet every Man has a "Property" in his own "Person." This no Body has any Right to but himself. The Labour of his Body, and the "Work" of his Hands, we may say, are properly his." John Locke, *The Second Treatise on Government* (London: Thomas Tegg, 1821), 209.

54 Marx, *Capital*, vol. 1, 169.

55 I have extensively explored this transformation and its cultural logics. See my *Scandals and Abstraction*; see also my "The Rules of Abstraction: Methods and Discourses of Finance," in "The Fictions of Finance," eds., Aaron Carico and Dara Orenstein, special issue, *Radical History Review*, no. 118 (winter 2014): 93–103.

56 Roberts, *Revolutionary Time*, Kindle location 208–09.

57 Helen Molesworth, *Work Ethic* (State College, PA: Penn State University Press, 2003), 25.

58 In some respects this demand is not new; see Michael Denning's *The Cultural Front* (New York: Verso, 2003). But while the cultural workers Denning tracks wanted to (and did) get hired and paid, this new group of organizations is less interested in getting paid than in critiquing the structures of their nonpayment. For Arts & Labor's statement of purpose, see http://artsandlabor.org/wp-content /uploads/2011/12/AL-Statement.pdf.

59 Diarmuid Costello, "Kant after LeWitt: An Aesthetics of Conceptual Art," In *Philosophy and Conceptual Art*, ed. Peter Goldie and Elisabeth Schellekens (Oxford: Oxford University Press, 2007), 92.

60 Raymond Williams, *Marxism and Literature* (London: Oxford, 1977).

61 Adorno quoted in Peter Bürger, "The Institution of Art as a Category for the Sociology of Literature," *Cultural Critique*, no. 2 (winter 1985–1986): 5–33, 22.

62 Stewart Martin, "The Absolute Artwork Meets the Absolute Commodity." *Radical Philosophy* 146 (November–December 2007): 15–25, 23.

63 Adorno, *Aesthetic Theory*, 146.

64 Denning, "Wageless Life." See also Lisa Adkins, "What Are Post-Fordist Wages? Simmel, Labour Money and the Problem of Value," *South Atlantic Quarterly* 14, no. 2 (2015): 331–53.

65 Tania Bruguera, "Introduction on Useful Art," April 23, 2011, http://www.tania bruguera.com/cms/528-0-Introduction+on+Useful+Art.htm (accessed August 12, 2016).

66 Adorno, *Aesthetic Theory*, 1.

67 Braverman, *Labor and Monopoly Capital*, 37.

68 Lauren Weber, "The End of Employees," *Wall Street Journal*, February 2, 2017, https://www.wsj.com/articles/the-end-of-employees-1486050443/.

69 Bethany Moreton, "The Future of Work: The Rise and Fall of the Job," *Pacific Standard*, October 22, 2015. Also of note, throughout the 1990s there were predic-

tions of "the end of work," whose primary cause was located in technology. See, for example, Stanley Aronowitz and William DiFazio, *The Jobless Future* (Minneapolis: University of Minnesota Press, 1994).

70 We are reminded of Ernest Mandel's great comment: "The thesis that Keynesianism will ultimately provoke a serious economic crisis by inflation, which [Hayek] has put forward with remarkable obstinacy for years[,] seems to be unchallengeable in the long-run. The only point is that for Hayek this leads to the familiar alternative between the devil and the deep blue sea: to prevent a serious economic crisis in the long-run, [Hayek] has consistently advocated an economic policy which would have unleashed the same economic crisis in the short-run. A retrospective look at the world of 1945–50 is all that is needed to understand why the governments of the victorious imperialist powers could not have regarded such an alternative as realistic . . . Keynes' classic answer to his critics [was]: 'in the long-run we are all dead.' It was an outlook of a class condemned by history. " Ernest Mandel, *Late Capitalism* (London: Verso, 1975), 415n23.

71 La Berge, *Scandals and Abstraction*, 4.

72 Arrighi, *The Long Twentieth Century*, 1.

73 Fredric Jameson, *Value: The Representation of Labor* (London: Verso, 2011).

74 Neil Larsen, Mathias Nilges, Josh Robinson, and Nicholas Brown, eds., *Marxism and the Critique of Value* (Chicago: MCM Press, 2014).

75 "Without diminishing the actuality (in Hegel's sense) of the problem of inequality, I would suggest that the cynic is on to something, and an equally cynical assessment of the degree to which 'inequality' has become a cause célèbre, especially among Keynesians, would confirm it." Geoff Mann, *In the Long Run We Are All Dead: Keynesianism, Political Economy, and Revolution* (London: Verso, 2017), Kindle locations 5038–40.

76 Weeks, *The Problem with Work*, 11.

77 Quinn Slobodian and I explore the genealogy of neoliberalism more fully in our "Reading for Neoliberalism, Reading Like Neoliberals," *American Literary History* 29, no. 3 (2017): 602–14, https://doi.org/10.1093/alh/ajx016.

78 Michel Foucault, "Truth and Juridical Forms," in *Power: Essential Works of Michel Foucault, 1954–1984: Volume Three*, ed. James D. Faubion, trans. Robert Hurley et al. (New York: New Press, 2000), 86.

79 From the history of the concept in *Endnotes 2*: "In the 1970s—in the midst of the historical break with the programmatic epoch of class struggle—the concept of 'subsumption' emerged in Marxist discourse in the process of a general return to Marx, and in particular to the drafts of *Capital*." "The History of Subsumption," *Endnotes 2*, "Misery and the Value Form," April 2010, https://endnotes.org.uk /issues/2/en/endnotes-the-history-of-subsumption/.

80 Postone, *Time, Labor and Social Domination*, 283.

81 Jason Read, "A Genealogy of Homo-Economicus: Neoliberalism and the Production of Subjectivity," *Foucault Studies* , no. 6 (2009): 25–36, 29.

82 English translation from *Telos*, no. 17 (fall 1973): 98–121. Originally published as

"Il Piano del capitale," in *Quaderni Rossi*, no. 3 (1963): 44–73. Reprinted in Mario Tronti, *Operaie Capitale* (Turin, Italy: Einaudi, 1971), 267–311.

83 Michel Foucault, *The Birth of Biopolitics: Lectures at the Collège de France, 1978–1979* (London: Palgrave, 2009), 224.

84 Postone offers a different account of real subsumption, one that also undercuts the power accorded to labor; he focuses on relative and absolute surplus value. "The fundamental contradiction of capitalist society . . . refers not to one between industrial production and capitalism, but to one within the capitalist mode of production itself. This, obviously, undermines the traditional conception of the role accorded the working class in the transition from capitalism to socialism." Postone, *Time, Labor and Social Domination*, 283–84.

85 Silvia Federici, *Caliban and the Witch* (New York: Autonomedia, 2004).

86 George Caffentzis, "Immeasurable Value: An Essay on Marx's Legacy," *The Commoner*, no. 10 (spring/summer 2005): 87–114, 97.

87 Melinda Cooper offers one suggestion as to what this reconciliation might look like. "Ultimately, what Foucault is pursuing here is the genealogy of the mid-twentieth-century welfare or social state—the constitutional form that most successfully brings together the administration of demographics with that of economic growth." See Cooper, *Life as Surplus: Biotechnology and Capitalism in the Neoliberal Era* (Seattle: University of Washington Press, 2008), 7.

88 Esping-Andersen, *The Three Worlds of Welfare Capitalism*, 22. While he never uses the term "decommodified labor," he does suggest that labor's decommodification may be found when "a service is rendered as a matter of right, and when a person can maintain a livelihood without reliance on the market" (22).

89 Vail lists five schemes under which non-market-based social reproduction might be possible: "boundary protection [of markets]; enhanced public good provision, decommodified economic circuits, social protection and market transparency." John Vail, "Decommodification and Egalitarian Political Economy," *Politics & Society* 38, no. 3 (September 2010): 310–46, 319.

90 Karl Marx, *Grundrisse* (New York: Penguin, 1993), 159.

91 Bruce G. Carruthers, "Financial Decommodification: Risk and the Politics of Valuation in U.S. Banks," working paper, Department of Sociology, Northwestern University, Evanston, IL, and Wissenschaftskolleg zu Berlin, May 2014. http://www.maxpo.eu/Downloads/Paper_BruceCarruthers.pdf, accessed October 2018.

92 The key text here is Viviana Zelizer, *Pricing the Priceless Child* (Princeton, NJ: Princeton University Press, 1985).

93 Antonio Negri, *Time for Revolution* (New York: Continuum, 2003), 27.

94 Jonathan Crary, *24/7: Late Capitalism and the Ends of Sleep* (New York: Verso, 2013).

95 "The Social Artwork Revisited," *October* 142 (fall 2012): 74–85.

96 See Grant Kester's introduction to the journal, FIELD, at http://field-journal .com/about (accessed October 2018).

97 Jasper Bernes and Daniel Spaulding, "Truly Exceptional," *Radical Philosophy* 195 (January/February 2016): 51–54, 51.

98 Martin, "Absolute Artwork Meets the Absolute Commodity," 15.

99 For an empirical survey of the possibility of a global history of unemployment—parts of which could configured as "decommodified labor"—see the fascinating dissertation by Aaron Benanav, *A Global History of Unemployment: Surplus Populations in the World Economy, 1949–2010* (PhD diss., University of California Los Angeles, 2014), http://escholarship.org/uc/item/7r14v2bq#page-9/.

100 Katherine Reynolds Lewis, "Unpaid Jobs: The New Normal?" March 25, 2011, http://fortune.com/2011/03/25/unpaid-jobs-the-new-normal/ (accessed August 4, 2014).

101 Kester, *The One and The Many: Contemporary Collaborative Art in a Global Context* (Durham, NC: Duke University Press, 2012), 102 and 15, respectively.

102 Pablo Helguera, Caroline Woolard, Mammalian Diving Reflex, Temporary Services, Tania Bruguera, Mierle Laderman Ukeles, Zachary Gough, Thomas Gokey, and Cassie Thornton have, through their own writings, all sought to contribute to the discussion about the production and purchase of socially engaged art.

103 See Kester, *The One and The Many*, 15.

104 Jackson, *Social Works*, 18

105 Bishop, *Artificial Hells*.

106 Lane Relyea, *Your Everyday Art World* (Cambridge, MA: MIT Press, 2014), Kindle location 221. Several other recent books offer what amounts to a compendium of art practices and artist interviews. Here the force of the critique must be taken to include the act of the collecting itself. Yates McKee's *Strike Art: Contemporary Art and the Post-Occupy Condition* (New York: Verso, 2016) offers an investigation of what he terms "post-occupy" (as in Occupy Wall Street, the 2011 uprising in lower Manhattan) art practices. Indeed, what is striking about the genealogy McKee offers is, quite simply, that it is not aesthetic. Rather, his foundation is found in the radical democracy practices of the 1990s—terms such as "creative direct action," which he claims resignifies art in terms of "direct action, collective affect and political subjectification" (Kindle locations 2646–49). See also *Collectivism after Modernism: The Art of Social Imagination after 1945*, edited by Gregory Sholette and Blake Stimson (Minneapolis: University of Minnesota Press, 2007), and Tom Finkelpearl's *What We Made: Conversations of Socially Engaged Art* (Durham, NC: Duke University Press, 2013). Both volumes seek to secure a kind of institutional place for such art through the act of collation itself.

107 See Bryan-Wilson, "Occupational Realism," 32–48, 85.

108 Julia Bryan-Wilson, *Art Workers* (Berkeley: University of California Press, 2009).

109 Bryan-Wilson, "Occupational Realism."

110 John Roberts, *Intangibilities of Form* (London: Verso, 2011), 32.

111 John Roberts, "Art After Deskilling," *Historical Materialism* 18 (2010): 77–96, 78.

112 Roberts, *Revolutionary Time and the Avante-Garde*.

113 See Nicholas Brown, "The Work of Art in the Age of Its Real Subsumption under

Capital," nonsite.org, March 13, 2012, https://nonsite.org/editorial/the-work-of
-art-in-the-age-of-its-real-subsumption-under-capital (accessed December 12, 2014).

114 Steven Shaviro, "Accelerationist Aesthetics: Necessary Inefficiency in Times of
Real Subsumption," *e-flux*, no. 46 (June 2013), https://www.e-flux.com/journal
/46/60070/accelerationist-aesthetics-necessary-inefficiency-in-times-of-real
-subsumption/.

115 Beech, *Art and Value*, 152.

116 Timothy Mitchell, *Carbon Democracy* (London: Verso, 2011).

Chapter 1. Art Student, Art Worker

Michel Foucault, *The Birth of Biopolitics: Lectures at the Collège de France,
1978–1979*, trans. Graham Burchell (Palgrave Macmillan, 2008), 229.

1 Robert Filliou, *Teaching and Learning as Performing Arts* (Koln: Gerstenberg Verlag, 1970), np.

2 Howard Singerman, *Art Subjects: Making Artists in the American University*
(Berkeley: University of California Press, 1999), 187.

3 Hannah Higgins, *Fluxus Experience* (Berkeley: University of California Press,
2002) 187.

4 Sharon Zukin, *Loft Living: Culture and Capital in Urban Change* (New Brunswick, NJ: Rutgers University Press, 1986), 97–98.

5 Zukin, *Loft Living*, 97–98.

6 Mark McGurl, *The Program Era* (Cambridge, MA: Harvard University Press,
2009).

7 Singerman, *Art Subjects*.

8 Marc Bousquet, *How the University Works: Higher Education and the Low-Wage
Nation* (New York: New York University Press, 2008), chapter 4, "Students Are
Already Workers."

9 David Graeber, "Army of Altruists," *Harper's Magazine*, May 2007, 31–38.

10 These demands continue to be long-going, and as recently as 2015 the National
Labor Relations Board asserted—this time in the name of "labor stability"—that
"student" and "worker" are mutually exclusive categories. The worker seeks an "income"; the student seeks an "education."

11 After one issue, the editorial board fractured. After two issues, the board decided
to cease publication. For the history of the getting together and falling apart by
Harry Cleaver, see "General Introduction to Zerowork," http://zerowork.org/o
.GenIntro.html (accessed July 2016).

12 In August 2016, Common Notions re-released a Spanish and English edition of the
text edited by Jakob Jakobsen with an introduction by George Caffentzis. Wages
for Students et al., *Wages for Students - Sueldo Para Estudiantes - Des Salaires Pour
Les Etudiants*, ed. Jakob Jakobsen, Maria Berrios, and Malav Kanuga, Mul edition
(Brooklyn: Common Notions, 2016).

13 The Wages for Students Students, "Wages for Students," 1975, http://zerowork
.org/WagesForStudents.html (accessed July 2016).

14 See Silvia Federici, *Revoultion at Point Zero* (Brooklyn, NY: Autonomedia, 2012).

15 George Caffentzis, "Throwing Away The Ladder: The Universities in the Crisis," *Zerowork*, no. 1 (December 1975).

16 Melinda Cooper, *Family Values* (Brooklyn, NY: Zone Books, 2017), 218.

17 Cooper, *Family Values*, 219.

18 Yates McKee, "Debt: Occupy, Postcontemporary Art, and the Aesthetics of Debt Resistance," *South Atlantic Quarterly* 112, no. 4 (September 21, 2013): 784–803. Critics Silvia Federici and George Caffentzis were involved in Strike Debt as well.

19 Ruth Simon and Rob Barry, "A Degree Drawn in Red Ink," *Wall Street Journal*, February 18, 2013, www.wsj.com/articles/SB10001424127887324432004578306610055834952/.

20 For Benjamin, the artist was famously a "producer"; for Foster, the artist is, less famously, an "ethnographer"; see Hal Foster, *The Return of the Real: The Avante-Garde at the End of the Century* (Cambridge, MA: MIT University Press, 2006).

21 McKee, "Debt."

22 For a range of statistics on who pays for various kinds of MFAs and how, see Juliana Spahr and Stephanie Young, "The Program Era and the Mainly White Room," *Los Angeles Review of Books*, September 20, 2015, https://lareviewofbooks.org/article/the-program-era-and-the-mainly-white-room/#. See also "Artists Report Back, Animated" at bfamfaphd.com (accessed June 2016).

23 John Roberts, *Revolutionary Time and the Avant-Garde* (London: Verso, 2015), Kindle location 126.

24 Claire Bishop, *Artificial Hells: Participatory Art and the Politics of Spectatorship* (London: Verso, 2011), 243.

25 Hart Business Research Group, http://hartbusinessresearch.com/2012/02/has-the-number-of-art-students-increased/ (accessed July 2016). This group has since shut down and archived parts of its website; the link I cite no longer functions.

26 The Federal Reserve Bank of New York has recently confirmed this again: David O. Lucca, Taylor Nadauld, and Karen Shen, "Credit Supply and the Rise in College Tuition: Evidence from the Expansion in Federal Student Aid Programs," staff report no. 733, July 2015, revised February 2017, https://www.newyorkfed.org/medialibrary/media/research/staff_reports/sr733.pdf (accessed July 2016).

27 Marx famously said of value: "value is a social relation"; Karl Marx, *Capital*, vol. 1, *The Process of Production of Capital* (London: Penguin, 1976), 179.

28 Maurizio Lazzarato, *The Making of the Indebted Man: An Essay on the Neoliberal Condition*, trans. Joshua David Jordan, reprint (Los Angeles: Semiotext(e), 2012); David Graeber, *Debt: The First 5,000 Years* (New York: Melville House, 2011). See also Richard Dienst, *The Bonds of Debt* (London: Verso, 2011) and Miranda Joseph, *A Debt to Society* (Minneapolis: University of Minnesota Press, 2014). In his much-cited *The Making of the Indebted Man*, Lazzarato deploys debt as both a metaphor and a concept. He labels it "an archetype of social relations" that, through the course of his treatise, becomes endowed with ever greater philosophical, if not economic, specificity. "Debt constitutes the most deterritorialized and

most general power relation through which the neoliberal power bloc institutes its class struggle," he writes (xx).

29 Joseph, *A Debt to Society*, x.

30 See their conference, "The Artist as Debtor," held at Cooper Union, January 23, 2015; materials are available at http://artanddebt.org/, (accessed July 2016).

31 Rea McNamara, "Should I Get an MFA? The 2016 Edition," *Art F City*, January 21, 2106, http://artfcity.com/2016/01/21/should-i-get-an-mfa-the-2016-edition/.

32 All citations to Cassandra Thornton, MFA Thesis Project, *Application to London School of Economics*, California College of the Arts, May 2012, cassiethornton.com (accessed March 2, 2013). All links and images are used with the permission of the author. Thornton's work was on view at "To Have and To Owe" at the Elizabeth Foundation for the Arts in New York City, September 22 to October 21, 2012, curated by Leigh Claire La Berge and Laurel Ptak; documentation is available at http://to-have-and-to-owe.tumblr.com/.

33 This is what I have been referring to as "socially engaged art." Thornton's own institution defines "Social Practice" as that which "incorporates art strategies as diverse as urban interventions, utopian proposals, guerrilla architecture, 'new genre' public art, social sculpture, project-based community practice, interactive media, service dispersals, and street performance. The field focuses on topics such as aesthetics, ethics, collaboration, persona, media strategies, and social activism, issues that are central to artworks and projects that cross into public and social spheres. These varied forms of public strategy are linked critically through theories of relational art, social formation, pluralism, and democracy. Artists working within these modalities either choose to co-create their work with a specific audience or propose critical interventions within existing social systems that inspire debate or catalyze social exchange." In 2012, Portland State University launched a journal devoted exclusively to Social Practice artwork in connection with its own MFA program.

34 Nicolas Bourriaud, *Relational Aesthetics* (Paris: Presses Du Reel, 2002).

35 Bourriaud, *Relational Aesthetics*, 21.

36 Jeremy Deller, quoted in Claire Bishop, "Relational Antagonism," *October* 110, (fall 2004): 51–79, 54.

37 W. J. T. Mitchell, *What Do Pictures Want? The Lives and Loves of Images* (Chicago: University of Chicago Press, 2006), 198.

38 Andrea Fraser, "From the Critique of Institutions to an Institution of Critique," *Artforum* 44, no. 1 (2005): 278–85. Consider, for example, Fraser's own "Museum Highlights: A Gallery Talk" (1989), delivered at the invitation of the Philadelphia Museum of Art; Fred Wilson's critical curatorial work at the Maryland Historical Society for "Mining the Museum" (1992–93); and Mark Dion's residencies at London's Natural History Museum, the American Philosophical Society, and other institutions.

39 See Jeffrey Williams, "Debt as Pedagogy," in the Edu-Factory collective's *Towards A Global Autonomous University*, (Brooklyn: Autonomedia, 2009), pp, 89–96.

40 See Brian Whitener and Dan Nemser, "Circulation and the New University," *Reclamations*, Fall 2010, http://www.reclamationsjournal.org/blog/?p=596/.

41 See http://wageforwork.com/calculator/ for the W.A.G.E calculator for minimum standards of compensation.

42 Cassie Thornton, *Fedora Archive*, http://feministeconomicsdepartment.com/fedora-archive/.

43 Thornton, *Fedora Archive*.

44 Thornton, *Fedora Archive*.

45 Rosalind E. Krauss, *A Voyage on the North Sea: Art in the Age of the Post-Medium Condition* (London: Thames and Hudson, 2000).

46 Diarmuid Costello, "Kant after LeWitt: An Aesthetics of Conceptual Art," in *Philosophy and Conceptual Art*, ed. Peter Goldie and Elisabeth Schellekens (Oxford: Oxford University Press, 2007), 96.

47 Adorno quoted in Peter Bürger, "The Institution of Art as a Category for the Sociology of Literature," *Cultural Critique*, no. 2 (winter 1985–1986): 5–33, 22

48 Stewart Martin, "The Absolute Artwork Meets the Absolute Commodity." *Radical Philosophy* 146 (November–December 2007): 15–25, 21.

49 Roberts, *Revolutionary Time*, Kindle locations 1622–26.

50 Rosalind Krauss contends that "the abandonment of the specific medium spells the death of serious art." See Rosalind Krauss, *A Voyage on the North Sea: Art in the Age of the Post-Medium Condition.* (London: Thames and Hudson, 2000) 33.

51 Nicholas Brown, "The Work of Art in the Age of Labor's Real Subsumption to Capital," nonsite.org, March 13, 2012, https://nonsite.org/editorial/the-work-of-art-in-the-age-of-its-real-subsumption-under-capital/ (accessed February 2014).

52 Rosalind E. Krauss, *Perpetual Inventory* (Cambridge, MA: MIT Press, 2013), 33.

53 Singerman, *Art Subjects*, 3.

54 Yve-Alain Bois, Hal Foster, and David Joselit, "Recessional Aesthetics: An Exchange," *October* (January 1, 2011): 93–116, 100.

55 Bois, Foster, and Joselit, "Recessional Aesthetics," 100.

56 Shannon Jackson, *Social Works: Performing Art, Supporting Publics* (New York: Routledge, 2012); for Creative Time, see Nato Thompson's *Living as Form* (Cambridge, MA: MIT Press, 2012).

57 *October* Roundtable, "The Social Artwork."

58 For a wonderful reading of Thornton and her debt work, see Annie McClanahan, *Dead Pledges: Debt, Crisis, and Twenty-First-Century Culture* (Stanford, CA: Stanford University Press, 2016).

59 Thornton, *Application*, 2.

60 Thornton, *Application*, 21.

61 Gary S. Becker, *Human Capital* (Chicago: Chicago University Press, 1994).

62 Foucault, *Birth of Biopolitics*, 223–24.

63 Foucault, *Birth of Biopolitics*, 229.

64 From an edited transcript of a conversation held at the University of Chicago on May 9, 2012, in Foster Hall 505, the seminar room of the Committee on Social

Thought. The video recording of the open seminar can be viewed online at http://vimeo.com/43984248. It may seem odd to find Gary Becker here where one might expect to find Nietzsche, but as the transcript of this conversation reveals, Becker has deep sympathy with Michel Foucault on the constitution of neoliberalism.

65 Thornton, *Application*, 50.

66 Thornton, *Application*, 50.

67 Michelle White, Bernice Rose, and Gary Garrels, eds., *Richard Serra Drawing: A Retrospective* (Houston: The Menil Collection, 2011), 82–83.

68 Thornton, *Application*, 21.

69 White, Rose, and Garrels, *Richard Serra Drawing*, 82–83.

70 Thornton, *Application*, 38.

71 See Giovanni Arrighi, *The Long Twentieth Century: Money, Power and the Origin of our Times* (London: Verso, 1994).

72 For a good overview of some of the econometrics of this transition, see Greta R. Krippner, "The Financialization of the American Economy," *Socio-Economic Review* 3, no. 2 (May 1, 2005): 173–208.

73 Hal Foster, ed., *October Files: Richard Serra* (Cambridge, MA: MIT Press, 2000), 45.

74 For the classic articulation of this see Saskia Sassen, *Globalization and Its Discontents: Essays on the New Mobility of People and Money* (New York: New Press, 1999). Bishop considers a similar point in her discussion of Bourriaud: "It is important to emphasize, however, that Bourriaud does not regard relational aesthetics to be simply a theory of interactive art. He considers it to be a means of locating contemporary practice within the culture at large: relational art is seen as a direct response to the shift from a goods to a service-based economy. It is also seen as a response to the virtual relationships of the Internet and globalization, which on the one hand have prompted a desire for more physical and face-to-face interaction between people, while on the other have inspired artists to adopt a do-it-yourself (DIY) approach and model their own 'possible universes'" (Bishop, *Artificial Hells*, 56).

75 Personal communication with the artist, March, 2014.

76 White, Rose, and Garrels, *Richard Serra Drawing*, 14.

77 The full quotation reads, "Richard Serra's sculpture is about sculpture: about the weight, the extension, the density and the opacity of matter, and about the promise of the sculptural project to break through that opacity with systems which will make the work's structure both transparent to itself and to the viewer who looks on from outside," in Hal Foster and Gordon Hughes, eds. *October Files: Richard Serra*. Cambridge, MA: MIT Press, 2000), 18.

78 Marx, *Capital*, vol. 1, 923.

79 Fabien Tepper, "What's Next for Strike Debt and the Rolling Jubilee?" *Utne Reader*, March/April 2013, https://www.utne.com/politics/rolling-jubilee-strike-debt-zmoz 13mazlin/.

80 Gokey, Thomas, Zachary Gough, Max Haiven, and Cassie Thornton. *A Soft Spot*

in a Hard Place. Portland, OR: Portland State University, 2016. http://psusocial
practice.org/a-soft-spot-in-a-hard-place-by-thomas-gokey-zachary-gough-max
-haiven-cassie-thornton/, accessed July 2016.

81 Roberts, *Revolutionary Time*.

82 For a longer description of Rolling Jubilee, including continuously updated numerical figures, see http://rollingjubilee.org/, accessed October 2018.

83 Yates McKee, *Strike Art: Contemporary Art and the Post-Occupy Condition* (New
York: Verso, 2016), Kindle locations 2719–22.

84 Kraus quoted at http://artistsspace.org/programs/artists-after-occupy (accessed
June 2016).

85 Gokey et al., *A Soft Spot in a Hard Place*, 89.

86 Gokey et al., *A Soft Spot in a Hard Place*, 89.

87 Peter Osborne, "Imaginary Radicalism," *Pavilion Magazine*, n.d., http://pavilion
magazine.org/peter-osborne-imaginary-radicalisms/.

88 Here is McKee: "The Rolling Jubilee (RJ) originated as a para-artistic conceptual
project by the artist and organizer Thomas Gokey and was collectively developed
by Strike Debt over the course of five months." McKee, *Strike Art*, Kindle locations, 2719–22.

89 Gokey et al., *A Soft Spot in a Hard Place*, 27.

90 Benjamin H. D. Buchloh, "Conceptual Art 1962–1969: From the Aesthetic of
Administration to the Critique of Institutions," in *Conceptual Art: A Critical Anthology*, eds. Alexander Alberro and Blake Stimson (Cambridge, MA: MIT Press,
1999), 519.

91 Julia Bryan-Wilson, "Occupational Realism," *TDR: The Drama Review* 56, no. 4
(winter 2012): 32–48.

92 Bryan-Wilson, "Occupational Realism," 34.

93 Bryan-Wilson, "Occupational Realism," 38.

94 Gokey et al., *A Soft Spot in a Hard Place*.

95 Graeber, *Debt*, 381.

96 Joshua Clover, "Debtpop," *The Nation*, November 25, 2013, https://www.the
nation.com/article/debtpop/.

97 McKee, *Strike Art*, Kindle locations 2646–49.

98 Gokey et al., *A Soft Spot in Hard Place*, 82.

99 Geoffrey Wildanger reads Roberts as such in his "Autonomy, Negation, and
Space: The Leap of the Avant-Garde," *Los Angeles Review of Books*, August 5, 2016,
https://lareviewofbooks.org/article/autonomy-negation-space-leap-avant-garde/.

100 Andrew Ross and Astra Taylor, "Rolling Jubilee Is a Spark—Not the Solution," *The
Nation*, November 27, 2012, https://www.thenation.com/article/rolling-jubilee
-spark-not-solution/.

101 Costello, "Kant after LeWitt," 101.

102 http://strikedebt.org/The-Debt-Resistors-Operations-Manual.pdf/, accessed July
2016.

Chapter 2. Institutions as Art

Theodor Adorno, *Aesthetic Theory* (Minneapolis: University of Minnesota Press, 1997), 33.

1 For example, the New Museum recently organized a call for a conference on the theme of "Why Are Artists Starting Institutions?" See also the ambitious convention in Vancouver on "Institutions by Artists" at http://arcpost.ca/conference, accessed March 2017. *Afterall* reported on the conference. See Liz Park, "Pluralising the Institution: On the Conference 'Institutions by Artists,'" *Afterall*/Online, December 20, 2012, https://www.afterall.org/online/pluralising-the-institution -on-the-conference-institutions-by-artists#.WPDmXtwh5pY/.

2 *Artists Report Back*, available at bfamfaphd.com (accessed October 27, 2016).

3 Juliana Spahr and Stephanie Young have produced absolutely important demographic findings about similar race, gender, and class disparities in the field of creative writing. See Juliana Spahr and Stephanie Young, "The Program Era and the Mainly White Room," *Los Angeles Review of Books*, September 20, 2015, https:// lareviewofbooks.org/article/the-program-era-and-the-mainly-white-room/ (accessed May 1, 2017).

4 See Anton Vidokle, "Art without Market, Art without Education: Political Economy of Art," *e-flux Journal*, no. 43 (March 2013), http://www.e-flux.com/journal/43/60205 /art-without-market-art-without-education-political-economy-of-art.

5 Both concepts were discussed in my introduction. See Dave Beech, *Art and Value* (London: Brill, 2015); John Roberts, *Revolutionary Time and the Avant-Garde* (London: Verso, 2015).

6 See Peter Bürger, *Theory of the Avant-Garde* (Minneapolis: University of Minnesota Press, 1984).

7 Karl Marx, *Capital*, vol. 1, *The Process of Production of Capital* (London: Penguin, 1976), 167.

8 David Joselit, "Institutional Responsibility: The Short Life of Orchard," *Grey Room*, no. 35 (spring 2009): 108–15, 109.

9 There are many lineages of and requiems for institutional critique—what it wanted, what it succeeded in getting, how it failed, and how it was institutionalized. The most thorough collection is *Institutional Critique: An Anthology of Artists Writing*, edited by Alexander Alberro and Blake Stimson (Cambridge, MA: MIT Press, 2009). In a different register altogether, Gregory Sholette and Blake Stimpson write, in their wonderful history of artistic "collectivism after modernism," that "Modernist collectivism, as we will have it here, was the first real effort to develop a sustained alternative to commodified social life by cultural means, and it was full of the spirited and sometimes foolish ambition of youth." Gregory Sholette and Blake Stimson, eds., *Collectivism after Modernism: The Art of Social Imagination after 1945* (Minneapolis: University of Minnesota Press, 2007), 3.

10 The signal exception here is AWC, Art Workers Coalition, and their "Art Strike." See, of course, Julia Bryan-Wilson, *Art Workers* (Berkeley: University of Califor-

nia Press, 2009). As Gregory Sholette writes, "one of the AWC's demands was for the establishment of a trust fund that would provide living artists with 'stipends, health insurance, help for artists' dependents and other social benefits.'" Gregory Sholette, *Dark Matter* (New York: Pluto Press, 2010), 14. Note in particular his comparison between the AWC and the APT (Artist Pension Trust) (116–34). Note also that before the 1960s existed groups including Artists League of America and Artists Equity.

11 See the website, http://www.wageforwork.com/about/6/faqs, accessed June 2015. The group W.A.G.E. and its website is still active, however this specific link no longer functions.

12 Adorno, *Aesthetic Theory*, 33.

13 Personal conversation with the artist.

14 Tom Finkelpearl, *What We Made: Conversations on Art and Social Cooperation* (Durham, NC: Duke University Press, 2013), 12.

15 Joselit makes the important claim that one of the limits of institutional critique is that "institutions are run by people"; see "Institutional Responsibility," 113. He stops short, then, of looking at labor, what those people produce and exchange to run institutions, and instead introduces a Latourian notion of actors, agency, and networks. A nice response to that tendency is found in Chris Gilbert: "Why is it that most 'institutional critique' has remained satisfied with the easy target of bricks and mortar, while setting aside the more volatile flesh, bones, and brains that are just as much a part of an organization's equipment?" See Chris Gilbert, in Sholette and Stimson, eds., *Collectivism after Modernism*, chapter 3, "Art & Language and the Institutional Form in Anglo-American Collectivism," 77.

16 Maria Lind cited in Janet Marstine, *Critical Practice: Artists, Museums, Ethics* (New York: Routledge, 2017), 21. See also Claire Doherty, "The Institution is Dead, Long Live the Institution! Contemporary Art and the New Institutionalism," *Engage*, no. 15 (summer 2004): 1–6, 1. Note also Creative Capital's 2013 invitation to fund such bodies: "Over the years, Creative Capital has noticed that an increasing number of grantees have decided to start their own organizations. . . . These new institutions have focused on issues of social justice, food, product development and critical thinking skills." Lisa Dent, "The In-between: Artists Build New Frameworks for Institutions," Creative Capital blog, April 11, 2013, http://blog.creative-capital.org/2013/04/artists-build-new-frameworks-for-institutions/, (accessed January 2017).

17 Harry Braverman, *Labor and Monopoly Capital: The Degradation of Work in the Twentieth Century* (New York: Monthly Review Press, 1974).

18 Peter Frase, "De-commodification in Everyday Life," June 7, 2011, http://www.peterfrase.com/2011/06/de-commodification-in-everyday-life.

19 Images and descriptions are available at carolinewoolard.com; see also www.tradeschool.coop; ourgoods.org; and Exchange Cafe at "MoMA Studio: Exchange Café," http://www.moma.org/visit/calendar/exhibitions/1364. For an in-depth look at Woolard's work on the Real Estate Investment Cooperative, see Art21's

documentary production, "Caroline Woolard Flips the Real Estate Script," Art21, July 31, 2015, at https://art21.org/watch/new-york-close-up/caroline-woolard-flips-the-real-estate-script/, (accessed April 2017).

20 Donna M. Binkiewicz, *Federalizing the Muse: United States Arts Policy and the National Endowment for the Arts, 1965–1980* (Chapel Hill: University of North Carolina Press, 2004), 32.

21 Sharon Zukin, *Loft Living: Culture and Capital in Urban Change* (New Brunswick, NJ: Rutgers University Press, 1986), 98.

22 I am thinking of Gilbert's fantastic reading of Art & Language in "Art and the Language of Institutional Form." According to Gilbert, it marks the move from art collective to art institution in direct response to the British academic subsumption of art.

23 The piece was reviewed in Jillian Steinhauer, "Report Finds NYC's Art World 200% Whiter Than Its Population," *Hyperallergic*, June 30, 2014, http://hyperallergic.com/135474/report-finds-nycs-art-world-200-whiter-than-its-population.

24 Curated by Eugenie Tsai; see the show's catalogue: Eugenie Tsai, ed., *Crossing Brooklyn*, (Brooklyn: Brooklyn Museum, 2014.).

25 See Peter Schjeldahl, "Local Heroes," *New Yorker*, October 20, 2014, *http://www.newyorker.com/magazine/2014/10/20/local-heroes* (accessed March 2017).

26 Pierre Bourdieu, *Distinction: A Social Critique of the Judgment of Taste* (New York: Routledge, 1986).

27 The sociologist Mathieu Hikaru Desan makes this point in his wonderful article "Bourdieu, Marx, and Capital: A Critique of the Extension Model," *Sociological Theory* 31, no. 4 (September 2001): 318–42. He argues: "So whereas for Marx capital denotes the social relation of exploitation—that is, the extraction of surplus-labor—contained within the production of commodities, for Bourdieu capital designates an object insofar as, due to its unequal distribution within a field, it is capable of accruing benefits to its owner. In other words, capital, for Bourdieu, simply designates an exploitable object, not a social relation of exploitation" (332).

28 See Peter Plagens, "Ideology and Art from the Heart of Brooklyn," *Wall Street Journal*, November 7, 2014, http://www.wsj.com/articles/ideology-and-art-from-the-heart-of-brooklyn-1415408688, (accessed April 2017); see Ken Johnson, "The Artist Next Door," *New York Times*, October 2, 2014, https://www.nytimes.com/2014/10/03/arts/design/crossing-brooklyn-local-talent-at-brooklyn-museum.html?_r=0, (accessed April 2017).

29 Roberts, *Revolutionary Time and the Avant-Garde*, Kindle locations 567–69.

30 Peter Osborne would claim it *is* a de-aestheticizing, and that's OK. "Contemporary art is post-aesthetic," he argues. Indeed, it is unclear why Jackson needs to maintain the language of "aesthetics"; Osborne would sooner leave them behind to develop a new philosophical category for the analysis of art. See Peter Osborne, *Anywhere or Not At All: A Philosophy of Contemporary Art* (London: Verso, 2012), 48.

31 Shannon Jackson, *Social Works: Performing Art, Supporting Publics* (New York: Routledge, 2012), 28.

32 Jackson, *Social Works*, 16.

33 Roberts, *Revolutionary Time and the Avant-Garde*, Kindle locations 695–96.

34 See Hal Foster, "The Artist as Ethnographer," in *The Return of the Real: The Avant-Garde at the End of the Century* (Cambridge, MA: MIT Press, 1996), 306.

35 Foster, "The Artist as Ethnographer."

36 Claire Bishop, *Artificial Hells: Participatory Art and the Politics of Spectatorship* (London: Verso, 2011), 8.

37 In conversation with the artist.

38 The etymology of metaphor here includes "meta" or "over" and "pherein" or "to carry," that is, to carry over. A metaphor moves something, and not only does it contain a vehicle, but literary critics often refer to it as a vehicle.

39 Richard Halperin, *Shakespeare among the Moderns* (Ithaca, NY: Cornell University Press, 1997), 12.

40 Jackson here is discussing Mierle Laderman Ukeles's "maintenance artwork," which finds an easy aesthetic correlation in what it takes to maintain both an individual art practice (a wife) and an art institution and art world.

41 Guy Trebay, "Sex, Art and Videotape," *New York Times*, June 13, 2004, http://www.nytimes.com/2004/06/13/magazine/13ENCOUNTER.html

42 Peggy Phelan, "Marina Abramovic: Witnessing Shadows," *Theatre Journal* 26, no. 4, "Theorizing the Performer" (2004): 569–77, 571.

43 See "Monumental Garage Sale," http://www.moma.org/interactives/exhibitions/2012/garagesale/, (accessed May 2017).

44 A complete description of the project is available at http://www.harrellfletcher.com/projects/485 (accessed January 2017). See also Finkelpearl, *What We Made*, 152–73.

45 Caroline Woolard, "Dear Potential Trade School Organizer," *Social Text Online*, October 14, 2013, http://socialtextjournal.org/periscope_article/trade-school/, (accessed February 2016).

46 Nicolas Bourriaud, *Relational Aesthetics* (Paris: Presses Du Reel, 2002).

47 All citations to Marina Vishmidt, "'Mimesis of the Hardened and Alienated': Social Practice as a Business Model," *e-flux Journal*, no. 43 (March 2013), http://www.e-flux.com/journal/43/60197/mimesis-of-the-hardened-and-alienated-social-practice-as-business-model.

48 Ben Austen, "Chicago's Opportunity Artist," *New York Times Magazine*, December 20, 2013, http://www.nytimes.com/2013/12/22/magazine/chicagos-opportunity-artist.html.

49 That the University of Chicago itself has been partly responsible for the decimation of black areas of culture and business development is an omitted part of this narrative.

50 An example similar to Gates may be found in the work of the Houston-based artist Rick Lowe, whose residential development, *Project Row Houses*, is, by its self-description, "founded on the principle that art—and the community it creates—

can be the foundation for revitalizing depressed inner-city neighborhoods." Cited in Finkelpearl, *What We Made*, 132.

51 In conversation with the artist.

52 Michel Foucault, *Birth of Biopolitics: Lectures at the Collège de France, 1978–1979* (London: Palgrave, 2009), 224.

53 See Jason Read, "A Genealogy of Homo-Economicus: Neoliberalism and the Production of Subjectivity," *Foucault Studies*, no. 6 (2009): 25–36.

54 Stewart Martin, "The Absolute Artwork Meets the Absolute Commodity," *Radical Philosophy* 146 (November/December 2007), 18.

55 Marx, *Capital*, vol. 1, 377.

56 Finkelpearl, *What We Made*, 205.

57 The possibility of artists' wages is no doubt much better in the Western European countries in which Martens primarily works. Importantly, Grant Kester has linked the rise of "relational aesthetics" to the European welfare state—and here we see one case of how his claim could be supported.

58 Martens did an extensive presentation, including a panel and response, for several interlocutors at the De Balie Gallery in Amsterdam; it is available online here: https://vimeo.com/192262127, (accessed March 2017). Unless indicated otherwise, all quotations by Martens have been taken from this piece. As for the building of an actual gallery, as I write in October 2018, an OMA-designed structure has been erected in Lusanga, what Martens calls a "white cube" gallery.

59 See Miranda Joseph, *Against the Romance of Community* (Minneapolis: University of Minnesota Press, 2002).

60 For "Opera Village," see "Operndorf Afrika," http://www.operndorf-afrika.com /en/; for "The Art of Creating the State," see Jonas Staal, "To Make a World, Part II: The Art of Creating a State," *e-flux Journal*, no. 60 (December 2014), http://www .e-flux.com/journal/60/61062/to-make-a-world-part-ii-the-art-of-creating-a-state/.

61 See Grant Kester, *The One and the Many: Contemporary Collaborative Art in a Global Context* (Durham, NC: Duke University Press, 2012); Shollete and Stimson, *Collectivism After Modernism*. See also Jennifer Bajorek, *How to Write a Visual History of Liberation*, forthcoming.

62 Superflex have helped to develop and market the commercial beverage Guarana Power, an energy drink with "limited distribution [and] sold primarily at art openings of Superflex." Kester offers a critique of Superflex in his section, "The Limits of Ethical Capitalism" in *The One and the Many*, 124–40.

63 See Martens' website for *Enjoy Poverty*, http://www.enjoypoverty.com/, (accessed September 2017).

64 See Nicholas Brown, "Renzo Martens and the Institute for Human Activities," *c magazine* 122 (summer 2014): 24–29. (Note: this is a different Nicholas Brown than the one I have cited throughout).

65 All citations are to the film.

66 See the forthcoming work from Bajorek, *How to Write a Visual History of Lib-*

eration. Ashley Dawson, in conversation with Renzo Martens and Claire Bishop, CUNY Grad Center, May 16, 2014.

67 The best book on the workings of satire remains Steven Weisenburger's *Fables of Subversion* (Athens: University of Georgia Press, 1995).

68 All from IHA's website: http://www.humanactivities.org/, (accessed January 2017).

69 Gilbert, "Art and the Language of Institutional Form," 77–91.

70 T. J. Demos, "Gentrification after Institutional Critique," *Afterall: A Journal of Art, Context and Enquiry,* no. 40 (autumn/winter 2015): 76–89, 87.

71 Fran Ilich, on view at *To Have and To Owe,* curated by Leigh Claire La Berge and Laurel Ptak, Oct. 2012, at the Elizabeth Foundation for the Arts in New York City.

72 I return to children as artists in chapter 4; see Pooja Rangan's wonderful article "Immaterial Child Labor: Media, Advocacy, Autoethnography, and the Case of Born into Brothels," *Camera Obscura: Feminism, Culture, and Media Studies* 75, 25, no. 3 (December 2011), 143–77.

73 See Elizabeth Povinelli, *Economies of Abandonment* (Durham, NC: Duke University Press, 2011), chapter 1.

74 For an example of Povinelli giving the kind of performance lecture I am talking about in an art context, see her at Pérez Art Museum in Miami giving the lecture "Karrabing: An Indigenous Otherwise in the Late Liberal Australian Geontology," July 2, 2015, https://www.youtube.com/watch?v=vYS9NimnNZM.

75 Martens at De Balie.

76 He cites Simon Gikandi's *Slavery and the Culture of Taste* (Princeton, NJ: Princeton University Press, 2011).

77 Walter Benjamin, *On the Concept of History* (CreateSpace Independent Publishing Platform, 2009), VII.

78 It is a common misreading of the neoliberal perspective that the state needs to let the market do its thing; rather, neoliberals insist that the market needs constant supervision and attendance; the state needs to provide supports for it, frequently in undemocratic ways. Philip Mirowski has explored this extensively in his, *Never Let a Serious Crisis Go to Waste: How Neoliberalism Survived the Financial Meltdown* (London: Verso, 2014).

79 Mirowski, *Never Let A Serious Crisis Go to Waste,* 64.

80 Take perhaps the ur-definition of institutional critique offered by Alexander Alberro: "a juxtaposition that [seeks] to foreground the tension between the theoretical self-understanding of the institution of art and its actual practice of operation, and [that] summon[s] the need to a resolution of that tension or contradiction." Alberro and Stimson, *Institutional Critique,* 3.

81 The apotheosis of this understanding is found in the "efficient market hypothesis"—that price reflects all available information. If that is not possible, then the assumption is that a market is not properly constructed, *not* that the hypothesis itself should be questioned.

82 Mirowski, *Never Let A Serious Crisis Go to Waste,* 65.

83 Hayek quoted in Mirowski, *Never Let A Serious Crisis Go to Waste,* 65.

84 Martens in Demos, "Gentrification after Institutional Critique," 88.

85 See Beech, *Art and Value*, especially chapters 5 and 6.

86 Franco Moretti, *The Way of the World* (London: Verso, 1987), 17.

Chapter 3. Art Worker Animal

Donna Haraway, *When Species Meet* (Minneapolis: University of Minnesota Press, 2008), 72.

1 I learned about this piece from Meiling Cheng, whose terminology I borrow throughout the chapter. See her "Down and Under, Up and Over: Animalworks by Sun Yuan and Peng Yu," *Performance Paradigm* 4 (May 2008): 4. Yet it was subsequently planned to be shown—and after controversy and protest from animal rights activists, not shown—at the Guggenheim in New York in 2017.

2 Postone describes the movement of capital as a kind of ceaseless repetition through seemingly forward motion. He calls this process "the treadmill effect." Moishe Postone, *Time, Labor, and Social Domination: A Reinterpretation of Marx's Critical Theory* (Cambridge: Cambridge University Press, 1996), 218. At the same time, treadmills were quite literally developed in poor houses and animals were early participants.

3 Jacques Derrida, *The Animal That Therefore I Am (With More to Follow)* (New York: Fordham University Press, 2008).

4 But as Mel Chen notes in *Animacies*, neither Lippits nor Derrida includes the animal in the possible spectrum of linguistic interlocuters. Mel Y. Chen, *Animacies* (Durham, NC: Duke University Press, 2012), 90.

5 See the show's catalogue *Becoming Animal*, ed. Nato Thompson (Cambridge, MA: MIT Press, 2006). Now, perhaps another canonical work is emerging. MIT Press published in 2016 a new book in its Whitechapel: Documents of Contemporary Art Series edited by Filipa Ramos and simply called *Animals*.

6 But there will be soon. Indeed, animal studies itself—along with much object-oriented ontology—might be seen as a quite logical extension of neoliberalism. Quinn Slobodian and I have made this argument in more detail in our article, "Reading for Neoliberalism, Reading Like Neoliberals," where we draw on Hayek's theory of knowledge: "Learning from experience among men no less than among animals is a process not primarily of reasoning but of the observance, spreading, transmission and development of practices" (18). See Leigh Claire La Berge and Quinn Slobodian, "Reading for Neoliberalism, Reading Like Neoliberals," *American Literary History* 29, no. 3 (September 2017): 602–14.

7 Steve Baker, *The Postmodern Animal* (London: Reaktion Books, 2000).

8 Baker is here building on his previous and widely cited *The Postmodern Animal*.

9 Haacke reflects on chickens in his 1971 "Provisional Remarks," and he concludes that not only are they not artists, they aren't even unique as chickens: "Chickens growing up in a museum . . . are still the same kind of chickens that would have been born from these eggs on a chicken farm." In Albert Alberro and Blake Stimson, eds., *Institutional Critique* (Cambridge, MA: MIT Press, 2009), 121.

10 Steve Baker, *Artist Animal* (Minneapolis: University of Minnesota Press, 2012).

11 There is a tension already noticeable between animal studies and posthumanism; I prefer animal studies and will argue as to why that approach better serves my archive. For a counterargument, see Cary Wolfe, *What is Post-Humanism?* (Minneapolis: University of Minnesota Press, 2010). For the emergence of this field in the realm the literary and the theatrical, see, respectively, Cary Wolfe, "Human, All Too Human: 'Animal Studies' and the Humanities," PMLA 124, no. 2 (March 2009): 564–75; and Martin Harries, "Regarding the Pain of Rats: Kim Jones's Rat Piece," TDR: *The Drama Review* 51, no. 1 (T 193) (Spring 2007): 160–65. This is a huge field, one that includes philosophy, cognitive science, cultural studies, and so on. I cannot trace its genealogy here, but one of the leading figures in the field, Cary Wolfe, has done this kind of state-of-the-field work. See his "Human, All Too Human." See also the journals *Antennae* and *Humanimalia*.

12 By "cultural worker" I mean broadly someone who works in the culture industries, including the academy itself. See Sarah Brouillette's incisive "Creative Labor," *Mediations* 24, no. 2 (Spring 2009): 140–49. See also Andrew Ross, *Nice Work If You Can Get It* (New York: New York University Press, 2010). Both analyses argue that "the creative" is a prototypical forerunner of the precarious worker.

13 Julia Bryan-Wilson, *Art Workers* (Berkeley: University of California Press, 2009).

14 Nicole Shukin has meticulously traced this history. See Nicole Shukin, *Animal Capital* (Minneapolis: University of Minnesota Press, 2009), Kindle, which I will return to later in the chapter.

15 I pointedly use "material" instead of "medium," for it is part of my contention that animals have not yet become a "medium," an organization that requires a substantial discursive infrastructure to support it.

16 The Art Workers Coalition advocated for wages, for strikes, and for an end to the Vietnam war; see Bryan-Wilson, *Art Workers*. For Haacke and the use of natural processes in systems art, see Luke Skrebowski, "All Systems Go: Recovering Haacke's Systems Art," *Grey Room* 30 (winter 2008): 54–83.

17 Krauss herself notes that Marcel Broodthaers's "Museum of Modern Art, Eagles Department" was crucial in formulating the postmedium condition. See her *Voyage on the North Sea: Art in the Age of the Post-Medium Condition* (London: Thames and Hudson, 2000).

18 Richard Serra quoted in Giovanni Aloi, *Art and Animals* (London: Laurentis, 2012), 7.

19 For a wonderful article on Schneemann, performance art, and cats, see Thyrza Nichols Goodeve, "'The Cat is My Medium': Notes on the Writing and Art of Carolee Schneemann," 5–22, *Art Journal* 74, no. 1 (spring 2015): 4. The whole issue is of interest.

20 While Jones's burning of rats should be considered animal cruelty (and indeed it was by the state), my interests in this chapter are discursive, not ethical. For a discussion of Jones's piece that subsumes ethics into questions of art, see Martin Harries's excellent "Regarding the Pain of Rats."

21 Gilles Deleuze and Félix Guattari, "Becoming Animal," in *The Animals Reader: The Essential Classical and Contemporary Writings*, ed. Linda Kalof and Amy Fitzgerald (Oxford: Berg, 2007), 37–50. They also write, "art is continually haunted by the animal."

22 Sarah E. McFarland, "'The Animal' Is a Verb: Liberating the Subject of Animal Studies," *JAC* 30, nos. 3–4 (2010): 813–23.

23 Giorgio Agamben, *The Open: Man and Animal*, trans. Kevin Attell (Stanford, CA: Stanford University Press, 2002).

24 See Joseph Tanke, *Foucault and Aesthetics* (London: Bloomsbury, 2011).

25 Wolfe, "Human, All Too Human," 564–75.

26 See Teresa Heffernan, "Robots' Rights," work in progress, cited with permission of the author.

27 Broglio, *Surface Encounters: Thinking With Animals and Art* (Minneapolis: University of Minnesota Press, 2011), xix. His approach parallels the contemporary trend in literary studies of "surface reading." Stephen Best and Sharon Marcus, "Surface Reading: An Introduction," *Representations* 108, no. 1 (fall 2009): 1–21.

28 In the economic field, the poststructuralist project was different. In "Can the Mosquito Speak," Timothy Mitchell attempted to signpost an economic difference without an agent. Published in 1988, however, Mitchell's title now marks a difference. Of course it cannot speak, was Mitchell's answer. Then it was a joke, if an off-color one, in its dismissal of Gayatri Spivak's question, "Can the Subaltern Speak?" Today, however, one might say, yes, perhaps the mosquito can. Timothy Mitchell, *Rule of Experts: Egypt, Techno-Politics, Modernity* (Berkeley: University of California Press, 2002), 19.

29 Shukin, *Animal Capital*, Kindle locations 160–61.

30 *Animal Capital* is a wonderful book, but its own "cultural readings" of the representation of animals (i.e., its own aesthetics) are the weakest part of Shukin's argument. Because I concentrate on labor, I keep some distance from Shukin's excellent work on animal capital, which strangely neglects labor even as she argues that early "time-motion studies seized not only on the body of the animal but also on the body of the laborer, another of industrial capitalism's primary objects of 'intellectual scrutiny.'" Shukin, *Animal Capital*, Kindle locations 877–80.

31 See Jason Hribal, *Fear of the Animal Planet: The Hidden History of Animal Resistance* (New York: AK Press, 2010). I discuss Hribal's work more in depth later in the chapter.

32 Dawne McCance has used the phrase "the animal abstraction" in her *Critical Animal Studies: An Introduction* (Binghamton: SUNY Press, 2013), 58. However she uses it as a tool discuss the work of Derrida and Paola Cavalieri, and not as a process in itself, which is how I intend it. For animals as juridical subjects, see Hribal, *Fear of the Animal Planet*. Until the seventeenth century, animals were given legal counsel, put on trial, charged with crimes ranging from sodomy to petty thievery to matricide. Yet they were also given certain latitude, as animals. Could one really expect a rat not to eat a farmer's sacks of grain?

33 Derrida, *The Animal That Therefore I Am*.

34 I do not necessarily endorse this logic, from Foucault's *The Order of Things*, but it is helpful epistemologically. While Foucault would subsume all abstract/concrete dualities into this, I think they follow from "the real abstraction."

35 John Berger gives us a slightly different claim, but one governed by the same logic: "Public zoos came into existence," Berger notes, "at the beginning of the period which was to see the disappearance of animals from daily life. The zoo to which people go to meet animals, to observe them, to see them, is, in fact, a monument to their disappearance." John Berger, *Why Look at Animals* (New York: Penguin, 2009), 3.

36 Alfred Sohn-Rethel, *Intellectual and Manual Labor: A Critique of Epistemology* (London: Macmillan, 1978), 37.

37 As I elaborated in the introduction, work is the action and labor is the abstraction.

38 Thus I disagree with Mel Chen's reading of Marx as an archive of animacy. See her *Animacies*, 44–49.

39 Here is Stewart Martin explaining Adorno's notion of the "absolute" artwork along similar lines: "Adorno's elaboration of an aesthetics of abstraction derived from Marx's account of the value form faces a major problem: abstraction is not aesthetic." Martin, "The Absolute Artwork Meets the Absolute Commodity," *Radical Philosophy* 146 (November–December 2007): 21.

40 Postone, *Time, Labor, and Social Domination*, 152.

41 See my "The Rules of Abstraction: Methods and Discourses of Finance" in *Radical History Review*, no. 118 (winter 2014): 93–103.

42 Perhaps it is this fear that has led certain commentators to insist on "the real abstraction" or "lived abstraction." In attempting to stay close to the "real abstraction," I rehearse what abstract labor entails and what it generates, and I argue that abstract labor as opposed to "biopolitics" is an important intellectual constituency for a discussion of both "animal work" and "animalworks." Animals may only represent labor in a regime of abstract labor, a regime from which they are disqualified as workers; conversely, it is precisely this disqualification that produces them as an abstraction.

43 Sohn-Rethel, *Intellectual and Manual Labor*.

44 For a contemporary elaboration of the problem of materiality in literature and philosophy, see Christopher Breu, *The Insistence of the Material* (Minneapolis: University of Minnesota Press, 2014).

45 Chen, *Animacies*, 45.

46 Karl Marx, *Capital*, vol. 1, *The Process of Production of Capital* (London: Penguin, 1976), 219.

47 Brian Massumi, *What Animals Can Teach Us about Politics* (Durham, NC: Duke University Press, 2014).

48 That animals do not have abstract thought is a truism, one that is beginning to be challenged by the likes of theorists such as Massumi. But for the moment, that truism holds.

49 Braverman, *Labor and Monopoly Capital: The Degradation of Work in the Twentieth Century* (New York: Monthly Review Press, 1974), 54.

50 This is beginning to change in contemporary work such as Breu's; but consider, for example, Foucault's dictum on biopolitics in *Lectures from the College de France*: that the neoliberal amounts to a "breakdown in labor and capital into income." Labor, that is, loses its efficaciousness as a concept. See the section titled "Economies of Art Criticism" in the introduction to this volume for my more in-depth consideration of this trend.

51 Karl Marx, *Capital*, vol. 2, *The Process of Circulation of Capital* (New York: Penguin, 2009), 260, 292.

52 The dialogue between Smith and Marx over the animals, and the quotations found therein, are found in Jason Hribal, "'Animals are Part of the Working Class': A Challenge to Labor History," *Labor History* 44, no. 4 (2003): 435–53.

53 Aristotle, *The Politics* (New York: Penguin, 1981), 12.

54 Theodor Adorno, *Aesthetic Theory* (Minneapolis: University of Minnesota Press, 1987), 119.

55 Marina Vishmidt, "Situation Wanted: Something about Labour," *Afterall: A Journal of Art, Context, and Enquiry* 19 (autumn/winter 2008): 20–34.

56 Raymond Williams, "Culture." In *Keywords* (London: Oxford University Press, 1978), 87.

57 I have learned so much from Jason Hribal's many texts on animal resistance. See his *Fear of the Animal Planet*; in particular, the chapter on killer whale workactions at Sea World is invaluable.

58 Haraway, quoted in Chen, *Animacies*, 101.

59 Bob Torres, *Making a Killing: The Political Economy of Animal Rights* (Oakland, CA: AK Press, 2007), 39.

60 Animals still exist as commodities, of course, and there is a vast global industry in them.

61 See Michael Peterson's article "The Animal Apparatus" (*TDR: The Drama Review* 51, no. 1 (T 193) [Spring 2007]: 33–48) for his decidedly less avant-garde tradition of animals in circus acts, in which they have a long tradition as workers.

62 See Raymond Williams, *Marxism and Literature* (London: Oxford, 1977).

63 Jonathan Burt, "The Aesthetics of Livingness," *Antennae* 5 (2008): 5.

64 Krauss, *Voyage on the North Sea*. Broodthaers's was not a live animal, of course, but his fictitious "Department of Eagles" in his conceptual "Museum of Modern Art," circa 1968. See footnote 17.

65 Burt, "Aesthetics of Livingness," 5.

66 Aloi, *Art and Animals*.

67 Massumi, *What Animals Can Teach Us about Politics*, 1.

68 See Mary Kosut and Lisa Jean Moore, "Bees Making Art: Insect Aesthetics and the Ecological Moment," *Humanimalia* 5, no. 2 (2014): 1–13.

69 Baker, *Artist Animal*, 51–53.

70 "You have to enlarge the idea of art to include all creativity. And if you do that

it follows that every living being is an artist." Joseph Beuys, cited in Tom Finkel-pearl, *What We Made: Conversations on Art and Social Cooperation* (Durham, NC: Duke University Press, 2013), 29.

71 Deleuze and Guattari cited in Broglio, 107.

72 Deleuze and Guattari, *Becoming Animal*, 3–6.

73 Gilles Deleuze, *Difference and Repetition* (New York: Columbia, 1995).

74 Bijal P. Trivedi, "Painter-Explorers Turn Animals into Artists," *National Geo-graphic Today*, August 6, 2003, http://news.nationalgeographic.com/news/2003/08/0806_030806_tvanimalpainters.html/. Sharon Guynup, "Brooklyn Dog a Rising Star in New York Art Scene," October 21, 2002, *National Geographic Channel*, cited at: http://www.tillamookcheddar.com/bio/index.html, accessed October 2018; Hillary Mayell, "Painting Elephants Get Online Gallery," *National Geographic*, June 26, 2002, 2.

75 Heather Bush and Burton Silver, *Why Cats Paint: A History of Feline Aesthetics.* (Berkeley, CA: Ten Speed Press, 1994); Vitaly Komar and Alexander Melamid, *When Elephants Paint: The Quest of Two Russian Artists to Save the Elephants of Thailand* (New York: Harper, 2000).

76 See this book's introduction.

77 See chapter 2, of course, but also "Artists Report Back" at bfamfaphd.com.

78 "Arte povera, a term canonized mostly in the 1980s and 1990s, identifies an art trend, while arte povera (in Italian) refers to the tentative critical category devised by Celant in the summer of 1967," according to Nicholas Cullinan in "From Viet-nam to Fiatnam: The Politics of Arte Povera," *October* 124 (spring 2008): 12.

79 See Lucy Lippard's *Six Years: The Dematerialization of the Art Object* (Berkeley: University of California Press, 1997); Bryan-Wilson does use it in *Art Workers* but offers no conceptual unpacking; it appears as a fact, not a concept.

80 In *Kounellis*, catalogue retrospective, archived at the New York Public Library.

81 The key source here is, of course, Georg Lukacs. See his "Reification and the Con-sciousness of the Proletariat," in *Writer and Critic and Other Essays* (London: Mer-lin, 1983). For the transmutation of reification into an aesthetic form, one particu-larly concerned with vision, see Anita Chari's recent book, *A Political Economy of the Senses* (New York: Columbia University Press, 2016).

82 Anna Dickie, "Jannis Kounellis in Conversation," *Ocula*, January 21, 2014, http://ocula.com/magazine/conversations/jannis-kounellis/ (accessed January 2015).

83 *Kounellis.*

84 Nicolas Bourriaud, *Relational Aesthetics* (Paris: Presses Du Reel, 2002).

85 Cullinan, "From Viet-nam to Fiatnam."

86 Allison Meier, "The Calm and the Controversy of 12 Horses in an Art Gallery," *Hyperallergic*, June 26, 2015, http://hyperallergic.com/218248/the-calm-and-con troversy-of-12-horses-in-an-art-gallery/.

87 Lane Relyea, *Your Everyday Art World* (Cambridge, MA: MIT Press, 2014). Kindle.

88 Roberta Smith, "Art That Snorts," *New York Times*, May 26, 2016, https://www
.nytimes.com/2015/06/26/arts/design/review-art-that-snorts-from-jannis-kounellis
-at-gavin-browns-enterprise.html, (accessed Nov. 2016).

89 Eileen Kinsella, "Animal Rights Activists Protest 'Untitled (12 Horses)' at Gavin
Brown's Enterprise," *artnet News*, June 26, 2015, https://news.artnet.com/art
-world/animal-activists-protest-gavin-brown-312404/.

90 "Animal Rights Protestors Demonstrate against Gavin Brown's Restaging of Jannis Kounellis's Untitled (12 Horses)," *ArtReview, ArtReviewAsia*, June 30, 2015,
http://artreview.com/news/news_30_june_2015_animal_rights_protestors
_demonstrate_against_kounellis_12_horses/.

91 Meier, "Calm and the Controversy."

92 Smith, "Art That Snorts."

93 Lange in Kinsella, "Animal Rights Activists Protest."

94 Michael M. Grynbaum, "City Council Stands in Way of Carriage Horse Ban,
de Blasio Tells Activists," *New York Times*, August 19, 2015, http://www.nytimes
.com/2015/08/20/nyregion/city-council-stands-in-way-of-carriage-horse-ban-de
-blasio-tells-activists.html.

95 Regulations are available at http://www.banhdc.org/, (accessed September 2015).

96 The group lists the top sixteen reasons to ban them here: http://banhdc.org
/archives/ch-fact-reasons-6–4-11.shtml. As I was drafting this chapter, New York
City reduced the number of carriage horses for hire in Central Park, as well as the
number of hours those horses could work.

97 Broglio, *Surface Encounters*, xxiv.

98 Baker, *Artist Animal*, 8.

99 Massumi, *What Can Animals Teach Us about Politics*, 3.

100 Claire Bishop, *Artificial Hells Participatory Art and the Politics of Spectatorship*
(London: Verso, 2011); see all of chapter 8.

101 Bishop, *Artificial Hells*, 219.

102 Elizabeth Gurdus, "Gavin Brown's Enterprise Bids Farewell to Village with Live
Horse Installation" *Observer*, June 26, 2015, http://observer.com/2015/06/gavin
-brown-enterprise-bids-farewell-to-village-with-live-horse-installation/.

103 Bishop continues: "It should be clear by now that I am trying to argue for a more
complicated understanding of delegated performance than that offered by a Marxist framework of reification or a contemporary critical discourse rooted in positivist pragmatics and injunctions to social amelioration... all of which reduce these
works to standard-issue questions of political correctness" (Bishop, *Artificial Hells*,
238).

104 John Roberts, *The Intangibilities of Form* (London: Verso, 2011), xx: "The ready-
made's deflationary logic," he argues, "invites more than a critique of painting's
circumscribed sense of artistic craft. Duchampian deflation [at first] stands . . .
simply as a negation of the status of painting."

105 See the previous chapter for an in-depth examination of Peter Bürger's "the insti-

tution of art" in his *Theory of the Avant-Garde* (Minneapolis: University of Minnesota Press, 1984).

106 Braverman, *Labor and Monopoly Capital.*

107 Roberts, *Intangibilities of Form.*

108 Roberts, *Intangibilities of Form,* xx.

109 Sianne Ngai, "Theory of the Gimmick," *Critical Inquiry* 43, no. 2 (winter 2017): 466–505.

110 For a wonderful example of the necessity and historical specificity of the wage form as a money form, see Peter Linebaugh's *The London Hanged* (London: Verso, 1991), especially chapter 11 on the struggles to replace "chips" (wood cutoffs) with money as a form of payment in British shipyards in the eighteenth century.

111 See *Crossing Brooklyn*, curated by Eugenie Tsai at the Brooklyn Museum, October 2014,

112 Melena Ryzik, "Avian Artistry with Smuggled Cigars," *New York Times*, October 16, 2013.

113 Colin Jerolmack, *The Global Pigeon* (Chicago: University of Chicago Press, 2014).

114 Nichols cited in Jerolmack, *Global Pigeon*, 263.

115 Jerolmack, *Global Pigeon*, 9.

116 See Eben Kirksey, *The Multi-Species Salon* (Durham, NC: Duke University Press, 2015).

117 Jerolmack, *Global Pigeon*, 49.

118 Indeed, some have argued that lack of attention to race is a problem of animal studies per se. For a fascinating amendment to this problem that examines the relations between race, class, and animality in urban space, see Lisa Uddin's wonderful and wonderfully creative *Zoo Renewal: White Flight and the Animal Ghetto* (Minneapolis: University of Minnesota Press, 2015). While scholars in critical animal studies may be beginning to include race as an import constituent for analysis, that inclusion has not yet filtered into criticism about animals as artists. See also Chen, *Animacies.*

119 See R. T. Naylor, *Hot Money and the Politics of Debt* (Ithaca, NY: Cornell University Press, 1985).

120 "Interview with Artist Duke Riley, Magnan Metz Gallery at Armory Show 2013," YouTube, published March 24, 2013, https://www.youtube.com/watch?v=2voqF5uAztQ/.

121 Denise F. Blum, *Cuban Youth and Revolutionary Values: Educating the New Socialist Citizen* (Austin: University of Texas Press, 2011), 14.

122 "United States Embargo against Cuba," Wikipedia, n.d., https://en.wikipedia.org/wiki/United_States_embargo_against_Cuba - cite_note-State_Department-34/, (accessed March 2016).

123 Jonathan Crary, *24/7: Late Capitalism and the Ends of Sleep* (New York: Verso, 2013).

124 Antonio Negri, *Time for Revolution* (New York: Continuum, 2003), 27.

125 See Tania Bruguera, *Tatlin's Whisper #6*, http://www.taniabruguera.com/cms/.

126 Jonathan Eburne, *Surrealism and the Art of Crime* (State College: Penn State University Press, 2008).

127 "Hillary Mayell, "Painting Elephants Get Online Gallery," *National Geographic*, June 26, 2002, 2.

128 Cited in Jerolmack, *Global Pigeon*.

Chapter 4. The Artwork of Children's Labor

Karl Marx, *Grundrisse*, trans. Martin Nicolaus (Harmondsworth, 1979), 110.

1 Dave Sinclair, *Liverpool in the 1980s* (Liverpool: Amberley, 2014).

2 "Liverpool Biennial 2016 Announces Full Programme," Liverpool Biennial website, http://www.biennial.com/news/liverpool-biennial-2016-announces-full-programme (accessed September 2017).

3 These two prohibitions, no sex and no labor, ground definitions of the child in works as diverse as economic sociologist Vivian Zelizer's *Pricing the Priceless Child* (Princeton, NJ: Princeton University Press, 1985) and Kathryn Bond Stockton's, *The Queer Child: Moving Sideways in the Twentieth Century* (Durham, NC: Duke University Press, 2009). I return to both works throughout the chapter.

4 The great study of children inheriting the future is, of course, Franco Moretti's *The Way of the World* (London: Verso, 1987). Moretti notes that in the premodern epic, the hero is fully formed as an individual; he travels spatially through the world. In the modern novel, by contrast, the hero grows up; he travels through time to become an adult.

5 Hettie Judah, "Why Are Children Having Such a Bad Time in Today's Art?" *artnet News*, October 30, 2015, https://news.artnet.com/art-world/children-having-bad-time-in-art-350798 (accessed July 2017).

6 Shannon Jackson, *Social Works: Performing Art, Supporting Publics* (New York: Routledge, 2012), 241.

7 Ernesto Pujol quoted in Tom Finkelpearl, *What We Made: Conversations on Art and Social Cooperation* (Durham, NC: Duke University Press, 2013), 102: "I believe that every time we try to engage children or adolescents we should concentrate on them only and not treat them as merely another piece of the art education initiative. Capturing kids' attention presents too many challenges these days, with their attention deficit disorders, depression, obesity, alcohol and drug abuse, undisciplined behavior, guns, absentee and unemployed parents, etc." Claire Bishop, *Artificial Hells: Participatory Art and the Politics of Spectatorship* (London: Verso, 2011), 22.

8 Lee Edelman, *No Future: Queer Theory and the Death Drive* (Durham, NC: Duke University Press, 2004).

9 See Bond Stockton, *Queer Child*; see also José Muñoz, *Cruising Utopia: The Then and There of Queer Futurity* (New York: New York University Press, 2009).

10 Joseph Weiss, *The Idea of Mimesis: Semblance, Play, and Critique in the Works of*

Walter Benjamin and Theodor W. Adorno (PhD diss., DePaul University, 2012), http://via.library.depaul.edu/cgi/viewcontent.cgi?article=1131&context=etd (accessed June 2017).

11 Sianne Ngai, *Our Aesthetic Categories: Zany, Cute, Interesting* (Cambridge, MA: Harvard University Press, 2012), 13.

12 Ngai, *Our Aesthetic Categories*, 3.

13 Moretti, *Way of the World*, 4.

14 Zelizer, *Pricing the Priceless Child*, all of chapter 2. Zelizer's economic history is foundational for the history of child labor and its obsolescence—she notes that children were forced out of work by a wave of immigration in the 1920s.

15 Zelizer, *Pricing the Priceless Child*, 81.

16 Judah, "Why Are Children Having Such a Bad Time in Today's Art?"

17 Paolo Virno, "Childhood and Critical Thought," *Grey Room* 39, no. 21 (fall 2005): 6–12, http://www.mitpressjournals.org/doi/abs/10.1162/grey.2005.1.21.6?journalCode=grey#.WQxtstwh5pY/.

18 "Manifesto of the Communist Party," https://www.marxists.org/archive/marx/works/1848/communist-manifesto/ (accessed January 2016). Of course, the world over, children continue to work; their decommodification in the Global North is the exception, not the rule, on a global scale.

19 For a study of Kaprow's reliance on children's play in his practice, see J. Kelley, *Childsplay: The Art of Allan Kaprow* (Berkeley: University of California Press, 2004), 14.

20 Katarzyna Zimna, *Play in the Theory and Practice of Art* (PhD diss., Loughborough University, 2010), 120 and 122, respectively, https://dspace.lboro.ac.uk/2134/6277.

21 Zimna, *Play in the Theory and Practice of Art*, 115.

22 Thus Lambert Zuidervaart locates three polarities that he correctly claims have been foundational to all modern theories of aesthetics: "between play and work, between entertainment and instruction, and between expression and communication" (Lambert Zuidervaart, *Artistic Truth* [Cambridge: Cambridge University Press, 2010], 57).

23 Theodor Adorno, *Minima Moralia: Reflections on a Damaged Life* (London: Verso, 2006), 228.

24 Walter Benjamin, quoted in Weiss, *Idea of Mimesis*, 34.

25 Italics in the original. Images and text are courtesy of the artist, Caitlin Berrigan, caitlinberrigan.com (accessed July 2016).

26 See chapter 1 of this book for the complete etymology of the term.

27 "Mark-to-market" accounting is essentially the recording of profits as profits before they are made as profits. I have discussed this as a kind of writing in my article, Leigh Claire La Berge, "How to Make Money with Words: Finance, Performativity, Language," in "Pragmatics of Money," eds. Melinda Cooper and Martjin Konings, special issue, *Journal of Cultural Economy* 9, no. 1 (2016): 43–62.

28 Philip Mirowski, *Never Let a Serious Crisis Go to Waste: How Neoliberalism Survived the Financial Meltdown* (London: Verso, 2014), 205.

29 In creating a barrier to be overcome, here "play," capital creates a site of possible profit. The quotation is from Marx, *Grundrisse*, 712. See also David Harvey, *Limits to Capital* (London: Verso, 1982).

30 For a brief history of the term, see "Playbor," *New York Times*, "Schott's Vocab" blog, March 12, 2010, https://schott.blogs.nytimes.com/2010/03/12/playbor/ (accessed February 2015).

31 Walter Benjamin quoted in Susan Buck-Morss, *The Dialectics of Seeing* (Cambridge, MA: MIT Press, 1989), 273.

32 Buck-Morss, *Dialectics of Seeing*, 266.

33 Adorno, *Minima Moralia*, 228.

34 Virno, "Childhood and Critical Thought," 9.

35 Adorno, *Minima Moralia*, 228.

36 Benjamin quoted in Buck-Morss, *Dialectics of Seeing*.

37 I've learned so much from Kevin Floyd's wonderful article, "The Importance of Being Childish: Queer Utopias and Historical Contradiction," *Work and Days* 59/60, 30, nos. 1–2 (2012): 323–28.

38 Buck-Morss, *Dialectics of Seeing*, 262.

39 Bill Brown, *The Material Unconscious: American Amusements, Stephen Crane, and the Economies of Play* (Cambridge, MA: Harvard University Press, 1996), 132.

40 Philippe Ariès, *Centuries of Childhood: A Social History of Family Life* (New York: Penguin, 1960), 125. Ariès's argument regarding the "discovery" of childhood in the seventeenth century is predicated upon another, much-debated point: namely, his assertion that "in medieval society the idea of childhood did not exist."

41 Zelizer, *Pricing the Priceless Child*, chapter 5.

42 Julian Gill-Peterson has an excellent piece that looks at representation of work as a compensation for the deprivations of childhood. See their "The Value of the Future: The Child as Human Capital and the Neoliberal Labor of Race," *Women's Studies Quarterly* 43, nos. 1–2 (spring/summer 2015): 181–96.

43 Gary Becker and Gregg H. Lewis, "Interaction between Quality and Quantity of Children," in *Economics of the Family: Marriage, Children and Human Capital*, ed. Theodore W. Schultz (Chicago: University of Chicago Press, 1974), 81–90.

44 Michel Foucault, *The Birth of Biopolitics: Lectures at the Collège de France, 1978–1979* (London: Palgrave, 2009), 229.

45 Edelman, *No Future*, 4.

46 Julian Gill-Peterson has done a wonderful reading of neoliberal discourses of investment as directed toward children in which they argue that "childhood becomes a form of futures trading." What Gill-Peterson attends to, which I do not, is the manner in which race is a crucial site of potential profit or loss. Becker attends to this, of course, and unsurprisingly mistakes the effect (black wages are low) for the cause (there is not enough investment in black children). See Gill-Peterson, "Value of the Future," 186.

47 I saw Berrigan do a similar performance at Wellesley College in November 2015

with twenty-one- to twenty-two-year-old students who also produced question after question about their retirement strategies—class-based, of course, but still.

48 Bob and Roberta Smith is the working name of the British artist originally named Patrick Brill, who took the name Bob Smith in the 1990s and soon after added the name of his sister, Roberta.

49 All textual material from "Bob and Roberta Smith: Art Amnesty," MoMA PS1, October 2014, http://momaps1.org/exhibitions/view/391/ (accessed June 2017).

50 In all quotations, capitalization is set as in the original, from the MoMA PS1 website.

51 Directed by John Rogers (2012) and available to watch online at, https://makeyourowndamnfilm.com/ (accessed June 2017).

52 "Bob and Roberta Smith: Art Amnesty," Arts Initiative Columbia University, http://artsinitiative.columbia.edu/events/bob-and-roberta-smith-art-amnesty (accessed June 2017).

53 Benjamin quoted in Buck-Morss, *Dialectics of Seeing*.

54 Buck-Morss, *Dialectics of Seeing*, 276.

55 Adorno, *Minima Moralia*, 228.

56 Melinda Cooper, *Family Values* (Brooklyn: Zone Books, 2017), 23.

57 Joan Robinson, *Economic Philosophy* (New York: Routledge, 1962), 45.

58 For an overview of Tanaka's work, see *e-flux*'s retrospective: "Koki Tanaka: Artist of the Year 2015," *e-flux*, July 5, 2014, http://www.e-flux.com/announcements/30874/koki-tanaka-artist-of-the-year-2015/, (accessed May 30, 2017). In a profile, the artist is described as, "Tanaka, a global trotter, is also a savvy mobilizer of collective actions and encourages sharing and exchange among participants to produce a common sense of creativity and imagination while probing new rules of negotiation and collaboration."

59 Transcript available at https://www.margaretthatcher.org/document/106689, (accessed December 2017).

60 Thatcher, cited in David Harvey, *A Brief History of Neoliberalism* (New York: Oxford University Press, 2005), 23.

61 For an interesting take on the original event as well as the restaging, see Stuart Jeffries, "We Took on the Tories and Won! . . . Why Liverpool's Striking Schoolkids Are Back," *Guardian*, July 5, 2016, https://www.theguardian.com/artanddesign/2016/jul/05/we-took-on-the-tories-and-won-liverpool-striking-schoolkids/.

62 Dave Sinclair and Craig Atkinson, eds., *YTS Children's Strike Liverpool 1985* (Liverpool: Café Royal Books, 2016).

63 Koki Tanaka's video works are assembled and accessible on his website: https://vimeo.com/kktnk. For *Provisional Studies #6,* see: https://vimeo.com/177500375, (accessed October 2018).

64 Marx, *Grundrisse*, 111.

65 Kevin Floyd says, a bit more clearly, that "childhood figures a critical perspective on the lie of formal equivalence." Floyd, "Importance of Being Childish," 329.

66 Adorno, *Minima Moralia*, 228.

67 Donald Woods Winnicott, *Playing and Reality* (London: Routledge, 1970), 74.

68 Benjamin in Buck-Morss, *Dialectics of Seeing*, 262.

69 Virno, "Childhood and Critical Theory," 1.

70 All material and quotations about *Haircuts by Children* are taken from mammalian.ca (accessed February 2016) unless otherwise noted.

71 As it is with their piece "All the Sex I've Ever Had," in which a self-selecting group of "elderly" people speak publicly about their individual sexual histories.

72 In conversation with MDR member Jenna Winter, March 2016.

73 In conversation with MDR member Jenna Winter, March 2016.

74 Hannah Higgins, *Fluxus Experience* (Berkeley: University of California Press, 2002), 101–3.

75 Historical Materialism, "Gender and Capital Panel," New York City, April 2012.

76 Mammalian Diving Reflex, "The Mammalian Protocol for Collaborating with Children," 2011, http://www.mammalian.ca/pdf/MDR%20Protocol6Dec2011.pdf/.

77 Bond Stockton, *Queer Child*, 38.

78 Ariès, *Centuries of Childhood*.

79 Both quotations cited in Zelizer, *Pricing the Priceless Child*, chapter 3.

80 United Nations, chapter IV, "Human Rights," "11. Convention on the Rights of the Child," November 20, 1989, https://treaties.un.org/pages/ViewDetails. aspx?src=IND&mtdsg_no=IV-11&chapter=4&lang=en/.

81 James Kincaid, *Erotic Innocence: The Culture of Child Molesting* (Durham, NC: Duke University Press, 1998).

82 It is, of course, family members and intimates, teachers, coaches, and priests—those who are repeatedly in proximity to children—who are the danger; the closer the proximity, the greater the danger.

83 Jennifer Doyle, *Hold it Against Me: Difficulty and Emotion in Contemporary Art* (Durham, NC: Duke University Press, 2013), 3.

84 Conversation with Jenna Winter, March 2016.

85 Benjamin quoted in Buck-Morss, *Dialectics of Seeing*.

86 Conversation with Jenna Winter, March 2016.

87 Kester states, "I identify a series of elisions in recent critical theory that have led to a privileging of the un-worked and simultaneous over the labored and durational. I outline a new framework for the analysis of collaborative art practice rooted in the reinterpretation of labor." But that reinterpretation happens outside of an engagement with labor as a commodity. Grant Kester, *The One and The Many: Contemporary Collaborative Art in a Global Context* (Durham, NC: Duke University Press, 2011), 62.

88 Kester, *The One and the Many*, 69.

89 Kester, *The One and the Many*, 70.

90 Kester, *The One and the Many*, 76.

91 Jackson, *Social Works*, 242.

92 Alicia DeSantis, "At the Guggenheim, the Art Walked Beside You, Asking Questions," *New York Times*, March 12, 2010, http://www.nytimes.com/2010/03/13/arts/design/13progress.html.

93 Jackie Wullschlager, "Frieze Art Fair: The Best Piece of Theatre in Town," *Financial Times*, October 14, 2014, http://blogs.ft.com/photo-diary/2014/10/carsten-hollers-gartenkinder/.

94 "Carsten Höller Turns Frieze Booth into Children's Playground," artdaily.org, October 15, 2014, http://artdaily.com/news/73620/Carsten-H-ouml-ller-turns-Frieze-booth-into-children-s-playground#.WTlHCsm1vdQ/.

95 Weiss, *The Idea of Mimesis*, 187; Zuidervaart also claims this in *Artistic Truth*, 57.

96 Theodor Adorno, *Aesthetic Theory* (Minneapolis: University of Minnesota Press, 1987), 100.

97 Mammalian Diving Reflex, "Mammalian Protocol for Collaborating with Children."

98 Laura Fitzpatrick, "Should Students Be Paid for Good Grades?" *Time*, January 14, 2009, http://content.time.com/time/nation/article/0,8599,1871528,00.html (accessed November 2017).

Epilogue

Friedrich Nietzsche, *Also sprach Zarathustra, in Kritische Studienausgabe*, ed. Giorgio Colli and Mazzino Montinari (Berlin: de Gruyter, 1988), 295.

1 Jori Finkel, "Urs Fischer and 1,000 volunteers go big—and messy—at MOCA," *Los Angeles Times*, April 14, 2013, http://articles.latimes.com/2013/apr/14/entertainment/la-et-cm-urs-fischer-moca-20130414/2 (accessed November 10, 2017). Immediately after this comment, the article parenthetically notes that volunteers will be given free admission and be identified by name on a museum wall.

2 For my longer exploration of decommodified labor, see my article "Decommodified Labor: Conceptualizing Work after the Wage," *Lateral* 7, no. 1 (spring 2018), http://csalateral.org/issue/7-1/decommodified-labor-work-after-wage-la-berge/.

3 Karl Marx, *Grundrisse* (New York: Penguin, 1993), 611.

4 Thanks, John Munro, for this comment while showing me around Vancouver.

5 Immanuel Kant, *Critique of Judgment*, trans. Werner Pluhar (Indianapolis, IN: Hackett, 1987), introduction iv, vol. 5, 179.

6 Geoff Mann, *In the Long Run We Are All Dead: Keynesianism, Political Economy, and Revolution* (New York: Verso, 2017). Kindle.

7 Mann, *In the Long Run We Are All Dead*, Kindle locations 269–71.

8 Mann, *In the Long Run We Are All Dead*, Kindle location 282.

9 Marx, Karl. Writings of Young Marx on Philosophy and Society. New York: Hackett Publishing Company, 1997, 402.

10 See my "The Humanist Fix" in *Neoliberalism and Literary Culture,* eds. Rachel Greenwald Smith and Mitchum Huehls (Baltimore: Johns Hopkins University Press, 2017), 291–316.

11 John Roberts, *The Intangibilities of Form* (London: Verso, 2011), 32.

Bibliography

Adkins, Lisa. "What Are Post-Fordist Wages? Simmel, Labour Money and the Problem of Value." *South Atlantic Quarterly* 14, no. 2 (2015): 331–53.

Adorno, Theodor. *Aesthetic Theory*. Minneapolis: University of Minnesota Press, 1997.

Adorno, Theodor. *Minima Moralia: Reflections on a Damaged Life*. London: Verso, 2006.

Agamben, Giorgio. *The Open: Man and Animal*. Translated by Kevin Attell. Stanford, CA: Stanford University Press, 2002.

Alberro, Alexander, and Blake Stimson, eds. *Conceptual Art: A Critical Anthology*. Cambridge, MA: MIT Press, 1999.

Alberro, Alexander, and Blake Stimson, eds. *Institutional Critique*. Cambridge, MA: MIT Press, 2009.

Aloi, Giovanni. *Art and Animals*. London: Laurentis, 2012.

Ariès, Philippe. *Centuries of Childhood: A Social History of Family Life*. New York: Penguin, 1960.

Aristotle. *The Politics*. New York: Penguin, 1981.

Arrighi, Giovanni. *The Long Twentieth Century: Money, Power and the Origin of Our Times*. London: Verso, 1994.

Aronowitz, Stanley, and William DiFazio. *The Jobless Future*. Minneapolis: University of Minnesota Press, 1994.

Attali, Jacques. *Noise: The Political Economy of Music*. Manchester: Manchester University Press, 1985.

Bajorek, Jennifer. *How to Write a Visual History of Liberation*. Durham, NC: Duke University Press, forthcoming.

Baker, Steve. *Artist Animal*. Minneapolis: University of Minnesota Press, 2012.

Baker, Steve. *The Postmodern Animal*. London: Reaktion Books, 2000.

Barrett, G. Douglas. *After Sound: Toward a Critical Music*. New York: Bloomsbury, 2016.

Beech, Dave. *Art and Value*. London: Brill, 2015.

Becker, Gary S. *Human Capital*. Chicago: Chicago University Press, 1994.

Becker, Gary, and Gregg H. Lewis. "Interaction between Quality and Quantity of Children." In *Economics of the Family: Marriage, Children and Human Capital*, edited by Theodore W. Schultz. Chicago: University of Chicago Press, 1974.

Beckert, Sven. *Empire of Cotton: A Global History*. New York: Penguin, 2014.

Benanav, Aaron Seth. *A Global History of Unemployment: Surplus Populations in the*

World Economy, 1949–2010 (PhD diss., University of California Los Angeles, 2014), http://escholarship.org/uc/item/7r14v2bq#page-9/.

Benjamin, Walter. *On the Concept of History.* CreateSpace Independent Publishing Platform, 2009.

Berger, John. *Why Look at Animals?* New York: Penguin, 2009.

Bernes, Jasper. "Art, Work, Endlessness: Flarf and Conceptual Poetry among the Trolls." *Critical Inquiry* 42, no. 4 (summer 2016): 760–82.

Bernes, Jasper. *The Work of Art in the Age of Deindustrialization.* Stanford: Stanford University Press, 2017.

Bernes, Jasper, and Daniel Spaulding. "Truly Exceptional." *Radical Philosophy* 195 (January/February 2016): 51–54.

Best, Stephen, and Sharon Marcus. "Surface Reading: An Introduction." *Representations* 108, no. 1 (fall 2009): 1–21.

Bhattacharya, Tithi, ed. *Social Reproduction Theory: Remapping Class, Recentering Oppression.* London: Pluto, 2017.

Binkiwicz, Donna M. *Federalizing the Muse: United States Arts Policy and the National Endowment for the Arts, 1965–1980.* Chapel Hill: University of North Carolina Press, 2004.

Bishop, Claire. *Artificial Hells: Participatory Art and the Politics of Spectatorship.* London: Verso, 2011.

Bishop, Claire. "Relational Antagonism." *October* 110 (fall 2004): 51–79.

Blum, Denise F. *Cuban Youth and Revolutionary Values: Educating the New Socialist Citizen.* Austin: University of Texas Press, 2011.

Bois, Yve-Alain. *Painting as Model.* Cambridge, MA: MIT Press, 1990.

Bois, Yve-Alain, Hal Foster and David Joselit. "Recessional Aesthetics: An Exchange," *October* (January 1, 2011): 93–116.

Boltanski, Luc, and Eve Chiapello. *The New Spirit of Capitalism.* London: Verso, 2006.

Bond Stockton, Kathryn. *The Queer Child: Moving Sideways in the Twentieth Century.* Durham, NC: Duke University Press, 2009.

Bourdieu, Pierre. *Distinction: A Social Critique of the Judgment of Taste.* New York: Routledge, 1986.

Bourriaud, Nicolas. *Relational Aesthetics.* Paris: Presses Du Reel, 2002.

Bousquet, Marc. *How the University Works: Higher Education and the Low-Wage Nation.* New York: New York University Press, 2008.

Braverman, Harry. *Labor and Monopoly Capital: The Degradation of Work in the Twentieth Century.* New York: Monthly Review Press, 1974.

Breu, Christopher. *The Insistence of the Material.* Minneapolis: University of Minnesota Press, 2014.

Broglio, Ron. *Surface Encounters: Thinking With Animals and Art.* Minneapolis: University of Minnesota Press, 2011.

Brouillette, Sarah. "Creative Labor." *Mediations* 24, no. 2 (spring 2009): 140–49.

Brown, Bill. *The Material Unconscious: American Amusements, Stephen Crane, and the Economies of Play*. Cambridge, MA: Harvard University Press, 1996.

Brown, Nicholas. "The Work of Art in the Age of Labor's Real Subsumption to Capital." nonsite.org, March 13, 2012. https://nonsite.org/editorial/the-work-of-art-in-the-age-of-its-real-subsumption-under-capital/. Accessed February 2014.

Bryan-Wilson, Julia. *Art Workers*. Berkeley: University of California Press, 2009.

Bryan-Wilson, Julia. "Occupational Realism." *TDR: The Drama Review* 56, no. 4 (winter 2012): 32–48.

Buck-Morss, Susan. *The Dialectics of Seeing*. Cambridge, MA: MIT Press, 1989.

Bürger, Peter. "The Institution of Art as a Category for the Sociology of Literature." *Cultural Critique*, no. 2 (winter 1985–1986): 5–33.

Bürger, Peter. *Theory of the Avant-Garde*. Minneapolis: University of Minnesota Press, 1984.

Burt, Jonathan. "The Aesthetics of Livingness." *Antennae* 5 (2008): 4–11.

Bush, Heather, and Burton Silver. *Why Cats Paint: A History of Feline Aesthetics*. Berkeley, CA: Ten Speed Press, 1994.

Caffentzis, George. "Immeasurable Value: An Essay on Marx's Legacy." *The Commoner*, no. 10 (spring/summer 2005): 87–114.

Caffentzis, George. "Throwing Away The Ladder: The Universities in the Crisis." *Zerowork*, no. 1 (December 1975).

Carruthers, Bruce G. "Financial Decommodification: Risk and the Politics of Valuation in U.S. Banks." Working Paper, Department of Sociology, Northwestern University, Evanston, IL, and Wissenschaftskolleg zu, Berlin. May 2014. http://kenan.ethics.duke.edu/wpcontent/blogs.dir/2/files/2013/10/carruthers_final_1_22.pdf/.

Chari, Anita. *A Political Economy of the Senses*. New York: Columbia University Press, 2016.

Chen, Mel Y. *Animacies*. Durham, NC: Duke University Press, 2012.

Cheng, Meiling. "Down and Under, Up and Over: Animalworks by Sun Yuan and Peng Yu." *Performance Paradigm* 4 (May 2008): 4.

Clough, Patricia, ed. *The Affective Turn*. Durham, NC: Duke University Press, 2007.

Cooper, Melinda. *Life as Surplus: Biotechnology and Capitalism in the Neoliberal Era*. Seattle: University of Washington Press, 2008.

Cooper, Melinda. *Family Values*. Brooklyn, NY: Zone Books, 2017.

Costello, Diarmuid. "Kant after LeWitt: An Aesthetics of Conceptual Art." In *Philosophy and Conceptual Art*, edited by Peter Goldie and Elisabeth Schellekens. Oxford: Oxford University Press, 2007.

Crary, Jonathan. *24/7: Late Capitalism and the Ends of Sleep*. New York: Verso, 2013.

Cullinan, Nicholas. "From Viet-nam to Fiatnam: The Politics of Arte Povera." *October* 124 (spring 2008): 8–30.

Deleuze, Gilles. *Difference and Repetition*. New York: Columbia University Press, 1995.

Deleuze, Gilles, and Félix Guattari. "Becoming Animal." In *The Animals Reader:*

The Essential Classical and Contemporary Writings, ed., Linda Kalof and Amy Fitzgerald, 37–50 (Oxford: Berg, 2007).

Demos, T. J. "Gentrification after Institutional Critique." *Afterall: A Journal of Art, Context and Enquiry*, no. 40 (autumn/winter 2015): 76–89.

Denning, Michael. *The Cultural Front*. New York: Verso, 2003.

Denning, Michael. "Wageless Life." *New Left Review* 66 (November/December 2010). https://newleftreview.org/II/66/michael-denning-wageless-life/.

Derrida, Jacques. *The Animal That Therefore I Am (With More to Follow)*. New York: Fordham University Press, 2008.

Dienst, Richard. *The Bonds of Debt*. London: Verso, 2011.

Doherty, Claire. "The Institution is Dead, Long Live the Institution! Contemporary Art and the New Institutionalism," *Engage*, no. 15 (summer 2004): 1–6.

Doyle, Jennifer. *Hold it Against Me: Difficulty and Emotion in Contemporary Art*. Durham, NC: Duke University Press, 2013.

Eagleton, Terry. *The Ideology of the Aesthetic*. London: Verso, 1990.

Eburne, Jonathan. *Surrealism and the Art of Crime*. State College: Penn State University Press, 2008.

Edelman, Lee. *No Future: Queer Theory and the Death Drive*. Durham, NC: Duke University Press, 2004.

Esping-Andersen, Gøsta. *The Three Worlds of Welfare Capitalism*. Princeton, NJ: Princeton University Press, 1990.

Federici, Silvia. *Caliban and the Witch*. New York: Autonomedia, 2004.

Federici, Silvia. "Wages against Housework." In *Revolution at Point Zero*. Brooklyn: Autonomedia, 2012.

Filliou, Robert. *Teaching and Learning as Performing Arts*. Koln: Gerstenberg Verlag, 1970.

Finkelpearl, Tom. *What We Made: Conversations on Art and Social Cooperation*. Durham, NC: Duke University Press, 2013.

Floyd, Kevin. "The Importance of Being Childish: Queer Utopias and Historical Contradiction." *Work and Days* 59/60, 30, nos. 1–2 (2012): 323–28.

Foster, Hal, and Gordon Hughes, eds. *October Files: Richard Serra*. Cambridge, MA: MIT Press, 2000.

Foster, Hal. *The Return of the Real: The Avante-Garde at the End of the Century*. Cambridge, MA: MIT Press, 1996.

Foucault, Michel. *The Birth of Biopolitics: Lectures at the Collège de France, 1978–1979*. London: Palgrave, 2009.

Foucault, Michel. "Truth and Juridical Forms." In *Power: Essential Works of Michel Foucault, 1954–1984: Volume Three*, edited by James D. Faubion, translated by Robert Hurley et al. New York: New Press, 2000.

Fraser, Andrea. *Museum Highlights: The Writings of Andrea Fraser*, edited by Alexander Alberro. Cambridge, MA: MIT Press, 2005.

Fraser, Andrea. "From the Critique of Institutions to an Institution of Critique." *Artforum* 44, no. 1 (2005): 278–85.

Gikandi, Simon. *Slavery and the Culture of Taste*. Princeton, NJ: Princeton University Press, 2011.

Gill-Peterson, Julian. "The Value of the Future: The Child as Human Capital and the Neoliberal Labor of Race." *Women's Studies Quarterly* 43, nos. 1–2 (spring/summer 2015): 181–96.

Gokey, Thomas, Zachary Gough, Max Haiven, and Cassie Thornton. *A Soft Spot in a Hard Place*. Portland, OR: Portland State University, 2016. http://psusocial practice.org/a-soft-spot-in-a-hard-place-by-thomas-gokey-zachary-gough-max -haiven-cassie-thornton/.

Goodeve, Thyrza Nichols. "'The Cat is My Medium': Notes on the Writing and Art of Carolee Schneemann," *Art Journal* 74, no. 1 (spring 2015): 5–22.

Gough, Maria. *The Artist as Producer*. Berkeley: University of California Press, 2005.

Graeber, David. *Debt: The First 5,000 Years*. New York: Melville House, 2011.

Groys, Boris. *Art Power*. Cambridge, MA: MIT Press, 2008.

Halperin, Richard. *Shakespeare among the Moderns*. Ithaca, NY: Cornell University Press, 1997.

Haraway, Donna. *When Species Meet*. Minneapolis: University of Minnesota Press, 2003.

Hardt, Michael, and Antonio Negri. *Empire*. Cambridge, MA: Harvard University Press, 2000.

Harries, Martin. "Regarding the Pain of Rats: Kim Jones's Rat Piece." *TDR: The Drama Review* 51, no. 1, 193 (Spring 2007): 160–65.

Harvey, David. *The Limits to Capital*. London: Verso, 1982.

Harvey, David. *A Brief History of Neoliberalism*. New York: Oxford University Press, 2005.

Higgins, Hannah. *Fluxus Experience*. Berkeley: University of California Press, 2002.

Hikaru Desan, Mathieu. "Bourdieu, Marx, and Capital: A Critique of the Extension Model." *Sociological Theory* 31, no. 4 (September 2001): 318–42.

Hribal, Jason. "'Animals are Part of the Working Class': A Challenge to Labor History." *Labor History* 44, no. 4 (2003): 435–53.

Hribal, Jason. *Fear of the Animal Planet: The Hidden History of Animal Resistance*. New York: AK Press, 2010.

Jackson, Shannon. *Social Works: Performing Art, Supporting Publics*. New York: Routledge, 2012.

Jakobsen, Jakob, María Berríos, and Malav Kanuga, eds. *Wages for Students - Sueldo Para Estudiantes - Des Salaires Pour Les Etudiants*, Mul edition. Brooklyn: Common Notions, 2016.

Jameson, Fredric. *Postmodernism, or the Cultural Logic of Late Capitalism*. Durham, NC: Duke University Press, 1991.

Jameson, Fredric. *Value: The Representation of Labor*. London: Verso, 2011.

Jerolmack, Colin, *The Global Pigeon*. Chicago: University of Chicago Press, 2014.

Joselit, David. "Institutional Responsibility: The Short Life of Orchard." *Grey Room*, no. 35 (spring 2009): 108–15.

Joselit, David. "Roundtable: The Social Artwork" *October* 142 (fall 2012): 74–85.

Johnson, Walter. *Soul by Soul: Life Inside the Antebellum Slave Market.* Cambridge, MA: Harvard University Press, 2000.

Joseph, Miranda. *Against the Romance of Community.* Minneapolis: University of Minnesota Press, 2002.

Joseph, Miranda. *A Debt to Society.* Minneapolis: University of Minnesota Press, 2014.

Kant, Immanuel. *Critique of Judgment.* Translated by Werner Pluhar. Indianapolis, IN: Hackett, 1987.

Kelley, J. *Childsplay: The Art of Allan Kaprow.* Berkeley: University of California Press, 2004.

Kester, Grant. *The One and the Many: Contemporary Collaborative Art in a Global Context.* Durham, NC: Duke University Press, 2011.

Kincaid, James. *Erotic Innocence: The Culture of Child Molesting.* Durham, NC: Duke University Press, 1998.

Kirksey, Eben. *The Multi-Species Salon.* Durham, NC: Duke University Press, 2015.

Krauss, Rosalind. *Perpetual Inventory.* Cambridge, MA: MIT Press, 2013.

Krauss, Rosalind. "Sculpture in the Expanded Field." *October* 8 (Spring 1979): 30–44.

Krauss, Rosalind. *A Voyage on the North Sea: Art in the Age of the Post-Medium Condition.* London: Thames and Hudson, 2000.

Krippner, Greta R. "The Financialization of the American Economy." *Socio-Economic Review* 3, no. 2 (May 1, 2005): 173–208.

Komar, Vitaly, and Alexander Melamid. *When Elephants Paint: The Quest of Two Russian Artists to Save the Elephants of Thailand.* New York: Harper, 2000.

Kosut, Mary, and Lisa Jean Moore. "Bees Making Art: Insect Aesthetics and the Ecological Moment." *Humanimalia* 5, no. 2 (2014): 1–25.

La Berge, Leigh Claire. "Decommodified Labor: Conceptualizing Work after the Wage." *Lateral* 7, no. 1 (spring 2018), http://csalateral.org/issue/7-1/decommodified-labor-work-after-wage-la-berge/.

La Berge, Leigh Claire. "How to Make Money with Words: Finance, Performativity, Language." In "Pragmatics of Money," edited by Melinda Cooper and Martijn Konings, special issue. *Journal of Cultural Economy* 9, no. 1 (2016): 43–62.

La Berge, Leigh Claire. "The Humanist Fix." In *Neoliberalism and Literary Culture,* edited by Rachel Greenwald Smith and Mitchum Huehls, Baltimore: Johns Hopkins University Press, 2017.

La Berge, Leigh Claire. "The Rules of Abstraction: Methods and Discourses of Finance." In "The Fictions of Finance," ed., special issue, *Radical History Review,* no. 118 (winter 2014): 93–103.

La Berge, Leigh Claire. *Scandals and Abstraction: Financial Fiction of the Long 1980s.* New York: Oxford University Press, 2014.

La Berge, Leigh Claire, and Quinn Slobodian. "Reading for Neoliberalism, Reading Like Neoliberals." *American Literary History* 29, no. 3 (2017): 602–14.

Larsen, Neil, Mathias Nilges, Josh Robinson, and Nicholas Brown, eds. *Marxism and the Critique of Value.* Chicago: MCM Press, 2014.

Lazzarato, Maurizio. *The Making of the Indebted Man: An Essay on the Neoliberal Condition*. Translated by Joshua David Jordan, reprint. Los Angeles: Semiotext(e), 2012.

Linebaugh, Peter. *The London Hanged*. London: Verso, 1991.

Lippard, Lucy. *Six Years: The Dematerializaiton of the Art Object*. Berkeley: University of California Press, 1997.

Locke, John. *The Second Treatise on Government*. London, 1821.

Lukacs, Georg. *History and Class Consciousness*. Cambridge, MA: MIT Press, 1972.

Lukacs, Georg. *Writer and Critic and Other Essays*. London: Merlin, 1983.

Mandel, Ernest. *Late Capitalism*. London: Verso, 1975.

Mann, Geoff. *In the Long Run We Are All Dead: Keynesianism, Political Economy, and Revolution*. London: Verso, 2017. Kindle.

Marstine, Janet. *Critical Practice: Artists, Museums, Ethics*. New York: Routledge, 2017.

Martens, Renzo. *Enjoy Poverty, Episode III*. Renzomartens.com. Accessed February 2016.

Martin, Stewart. "The Absolute Artwork Meets the Absolute Commodity." *Radical Philosophy* 146 (November–December 2007): 15–25.

Marx, Karl. *Capital*. Vol. 1, *The Process of Production of Capital*. London: Penguin, 1976.

Marx, Karl. *Capital*. Vol. 2, *The Process of Circulation of Capital*. New York: Penguin, 2009.

Marx, Karl. *Grundrisse*. New York: Penguin, 1993.

Marx, Karl. "The Manifesto of the Communist Party." https://www.marxists.org/archive/marx/works/1848/communist-manifesto/. Accessed January 2016.

Marx, Karl. *Writings of Young Marx on Philosophy and Society*. New York: Hackett Publishing Company, 1997.

Massumi, Brian. *What Animals Teach Us about Politics*. Durham, NC: Duke University Press, 2014.

McCance, Dawne. *Critical Animal Studies: An Introduction*. Binghamton: State University of New York Press, 2013.

McCarthy, Anna. "Reality Television: A Neoliberal Theatre of Suffering," *Social Text* 93, 25, no. 4 (Winter 2007): 17–42.

McClanahan, Annie. *Dead Pledges: Debt, Crisis, and Twenty-First-Century Culture*. Stanford, CA: Stanford University Press, 2016.

McFarland, Sarah E. "'The Animal' Is a Verb: Liberating the Subject of Animal Studies." *JAC* 30, nos. 3–4 (2010): 813–23.

McGurl, Mark. *The Program Era*. Cambridge, MA: Harvard University Press, 2009.

Mckee, Yates. "Debt: Occupy, Postcontemporary Art, and the Aesthetics of Debt Resistance." *South Atlantic Quarterly* 112, no. 4 (September 21, 2013): 784–803.

Mckee, Yates. *Strike Art: Contemporary Art and the Post-Occupy Condition*. New York: Verso, 2016. Kindle.

McKee, Yates, and Jaleh Mansoor, eds. *Communities of Sense*. Durham, NC: Duke University Press, 2009.

Mirowski, Philip. *Never Let a Serious Crisis Go to Waste: How Neoliberalism Survived the Financial Meltdown*. London: Verso, 2014.

Mirrlees, Tanner. "Reality TV's Low-Wage and No-Wage Work." *Alternate Routes* 27 (2016): 187–212.

Mitchell, Timothy. *Carbon Democracy*. London: Verso, 2011.

Mitchell, Timothy. *Rule of Experts: Egypt, Techno-Politics, Modernity*. Berkeley: University of California Press, 2002.

Mitchell, W. J. T. *What Do Pictures Want? The Lives and Loves of Images*. Chicago: University of Chicago Press, 2006.

Molesworth, Helen. *Work Ethic*. State College: Penn State University Press, 2003.

Monsoor, Jaleh. "Ayreen Anastas's M*Bethlehem and Pasolini Pa Palestine." *Journal of Aesthetics and Protest* 8 (winter 2011). http://joaap.org/issue8/mansoor.htm.

Moretti, Franco. *The Way of the World*. London: Verso, 1987.

Muñoz, José. *Cruising Utopia: The Then and There of Queer Futurity*. New York: New York University Press, 2009.

Naylor, R. T. *Hot Money and the Politics of Debt*. Ithaca, NY: Cornell University Press, 1985.

Negri, Antonio. *Time for Revolution*. New York: Continuum, 2003.

Ngai, Sianne. *Our Aesthetic Categories: Zany, Cute, Interesting*. Cambridge, MA: Harvard University Press, 2012.

Ngai, Sianne. "Theory of the Gimmick." *Critical Inquiry* 43, no. 2 (winter 2017): 466–505.

Nietzsche, Friedrich. *Also sprach Zarathustra, in Kritische Studienausgabe*. Edited by Giorgio Colli and Mazzino Montinari. Berlin: de Gruyter, 1988.

Osborne, Peter. *Anywhere or Not at All: A Philosophy of Contemporary Art*. London: Verso, 2012.

Peterson, Michael. "The Animal Apparatus." *TDR: The Drama Review* 51, no. 1, T 193 (Spring 2007): 33–48.

Phelan, Peggy. "Marina Abramovic: Witnessing Shadows." *Theatre Journal* 26, no. 4, "Theorizing the Performer" (2004): 569–77.

Polanyi, Karl. *The Great Transformation*. Chicago: University of Chicago Press, 1944.

Postone, Moishe. *Time, Labor, and Social Domination: A Reinterpretation of Marx's Critical Theory*. Cambridge: Cambridge University Press, 1996.

Povinelli, Elizabeth. *Economies of Abandonment*. Durham, NC: Duke University Press, 2011.

Purves Ted, and Shane Selzer, eds. *What We Want Is Free: Exchange and Generosity in Recent Art*. Binghampton: State University of New York Press, 2009.

Ramos, Filipa, ed., *Animals*. Cambridge, MA: MIT Press, 2016.

Ranciere, Jacques. *Aisthesis*. London: Verso, 2013.

Rangan, Pooja. "Immaterial Child Labor: Media, Advocacy, Autoethnography, and the Case of Born into Brothels." *Camera Obscura: Feminism, Culture, and Media Studies* 25 (December 1, 2011): 143–77.

Read, Jason. "A Genealogy of Homo-Economicus: Neoliberalism and the Production of Subjectivity." *Foucault Studies*, no. 6 (2009): 25–36.

Relyea, Lane. *Your Everyday Art World*. Cambridge, MA: MIT Press, 2014. Kindle.

Roberts, John. "Art After Deskilling." *Historical Materialism* 18 (2010): 77–96.

Roberts, John. *The Intangibilities of Form*. London: Verso, 2011.

Roberts, John. *Revolutionary Time and the Avant-Garde*. London: Verso, 2015.

Robinson, Joan. *Economic Philosophy*. New York: Routledge, 1962.

Ross, Andrew. *Nice Work If You Can Get It*. New York: New York University Press, 2010.

Sassen, Saskia. *Globalization and Its Discontents: Essays on the New Mobility of People and Money*. New York: New Press, 1999.

Shaviro, Steven. "Accelerationist Aesthetics: Necessary Inefficiency in Times of Real Subsumption." *e-flux*, no. 46 (June 2013)., http://www.e-flux.com/journal /accelerationist-aesthetics-necessary-inefficiency-in-times-of-real-subsumption/, accessed April 2015.

Shaviro, Steven. *Without Criteria: Kant, Whitehead, Deleuze and Aesthetics*. Cambridge, MA: MIT Press, 2010.

Sholette, Gregory. *Dark Matter*. New York: Pluto Press, 2010.

Sholette, Gregory, and Blake Stimson, eds. *Collectivism after Modernism: The Art of Social Imagination after 1945*. Minneapolis: University of Minnesota Press, 2007.

Shukin, Nicole. *Animal Capital*. Minneapolis: University of Minnesota Press, 2009. Kindle.

Sinclair, Dave. *Liverpool in the 1980s*. Liverpool: Amberley, 2014.

Sinclair, Dave, and Craig Atkinson, eds. *YTS Children's Strike Liverpool 1985*. Liverpool: Café Royal Books, 2016.

Singerman, Howard. *Art Subjects: Making Artists in the American University*. Berkeley: University of California Press, 1999.

Skrebowski, Luke. "All Systems Go: Recovering Haacke's Systems Art." *Grey Room* 30, (winter 2008): 54–83.

Sohn-Rethel, Alfred. *Intellectual and Manual Labor: A Critique of Epistemology*. London: Macmillan, 1978.

Tanke, Joseph. *Foucault and Aesthetics*. London: Bloomsbury, 2011.

Thompson, Nato, ed. *Becoming Animal*. Cambridge, MA: MIT Press, 2006.

Thompson, Nato. *Living as Form*. Cambridge, MA: MIT Press, 2012.

Thorton, Cassie. *Application to London School of Economics*. Cassiethornton.com. Accessed Jan. 2016.

Torres, Bob. *Making a Killing: The Political Economy of Animal Rights*. Oakland, CA: AK Press, 2007.

Tronti, Mario. *Operaie Capitale*. Turin, Italy: Einaudi, 1971.

Tsai, Eugenie, ed. *Crossing Brooklyn*, (Brooklyn: Brooklyn Museum, 2014).

Uddin, Lisa. *Zoo Renewal: White Flight and the Animal Ghetto*. Minneapolis: University of Minnesota Press, 2015.

Vail, John. "Decommodification and Egalitarian Political Economy." *Politics and Society* 38, no. 3 (September 2010): 310–46.

Virno, Paolo. "Childhood and Critical Thought." *Grey Room* 39, no. 21 (fall 2005): 6–12. http://www.mitpressjournals.org/doi/abs/10.1162/grey.2005.1.21.6?journal Code=grey#.WQxtstwh5pY/.

Vishmidt, Marina. "Situation Wanted: Something about Labour." *Afterall: A Journal of Art, Context, and Enquiry* 19 (autumn/winter 2008): 20–34.

Weeks, Kathi. *The Problem with Work.* Durham, NC: Duke University Press, 2011.

Weisenburger, Steven. *Fables of Subversion.* Athens: University of Georgia Press, 1995.

Weiss, Joseph. *The Idea of Mimesis: Semblance, Play, and Critique in the Works of Walter Benjamin and Theodor W. Adorno* (PhD diss., DePaul University, 2012). http://via.library.depaul.edu/cgi/viewcontent.cgi?article=1131&context=etd. Accessed June 2017.

White, Michelle, Bernice Rose, and Gary Garrels, eds. *Richard Serra Drawing: A Retrospective.* Houston: Menil Collection, 2011.

Williams, Raymond. *Keywords.* London: Oxford University Press, 1978.

Williams, Raymond. *Marxism and Literature.* London: Oxford University Press, 1977.

Winnicott, Donald Woods. *Playing and Reality.* London: Routledge, 1970.

Wolfe, Cary. "Human, All Too Human: 'Animal Studies' and the Humanities." PMLA 124, no. 2 (March 2009): 564–75.

Wolfe, Cary. *What is Post-Humanism?* Minneapolis: University of Minnesota Press, 2010.

Woolard, Caroline. "Complete Works." carolinewoolard.com. Accessed March 2016.

Zelizer, Viviana. *Pricing the Priceless Child.* Princeton, NJ: Princeton University Press, 1985.

Zimna, Katarzyna. *Play in the Theory and Practice of Art* (PhD diss., Louborough University, 2010). https://dspace.lboro.ac.uk/2134/6277.

Zuidervaart, Lambert. *Artistic Truth.* Cambridge: Cambridge University Press, 2010.

Zukin, Sharon. *Loft Living: Culture and Capital in Urban Change.* New Brunswick, NJ: Rutgers University Press, 1986.

Index

Art and Value (Beech), 32
art criticism, 13
Art Daily, 196
arte povera, 134–37, 230n78
arte util, 18
Artificial Hells (Bishop), 140
Art Institute of Chicago, 64–65
artist-activists, 30, 37, 63–64
Artist Animal (Baker), 120, 124, 131
artists: animals as, 124, 132–44; animals
    as artistic collaborators, 123; animals
    as art-workers, 144–55; as artivists, 30,
    37, 63–64; avoidance as a career and,
    172–76; as collateral, 45–47, 51, 55, 61,
    66; collectivization of labor and, 75;
    constructivism and, 14; decommodi-
    fication of other fields of labor by, 90;
    expansion of the art-labor force and,
    4; the exploited as, 108; institutions
    and, 82; MFA as debt and, 40; money
    and, 1, 3, 93, 131, 133; the new-economy
    and, 15; percent who are paid, 2, 133;
    percent who earn a living from their
    art, 75–76, 77, 133; play and, 161–63;
    race and, 76, 83; relationships to
    decommodified labor and, 4; resale
    rights and, 1–2; unionization and,
    30; universities and, 34–35; the wage
    system and, 76. See also decommodi-
    fied labor
artists and, 1, 3, 93, 131, 133
Artists Report Back: findings in, 75–76,
    77; installation and critique of, 84–86;
    physical presentation of, 83–84; social-
    scientific presentation of, 88–90.
    See also BFAMFAPhD; Woolard,
    Caroline
Art & Language, 83
artnet News, 137
The Art of Creating the State (Staal), 102
ArtPrize, 64
Art Review, 137
Arts & Labor, 17

Art Subjects (Singerman), 143
"Art That Snorts," 133
artwork: children and, 167; commodifi-
    cation and, 17–18, 76; as a commodity,
    13–14, 32, 93–94, 98–99; critique and,
    78; institutions as, 79; Marx on, 76;
    opposition to waged-work and, 12–14;
    relational, 41; uselessness and, 11, 18
"Art Work," 78
Art Workers (Bryan-Wilson), 30, 120
Art Workers Coalition, 17, 121
Asher, Michael, 42
Attali, Jacques, 13
autonomy, 11–12, 17, 46–48, 67, 77,
    87–88, 96, 130, 142, 156
the avant-garde, 14–17, 72, 131, 138, 172,
    206
"Avian Artistry, with Smuggled Cigars,"
    146, 154

Baker, Steve, 120, 131, 140, 143
Baldessari, John, 174
Ball, Hugo, 162
Barry Callebaut, 106, 107
barter, 91–95, 98–99. See also decom-
    modified labor
The Battle of Orgreave (Deller), 153, 178
Becker, Gary, 21, 54, 113, 171
Beckert, Sven, 32
"Becoming Animal," 119, 132–33
Beech, Dave, 7, 32, 76, 114, 207n20
BeeSpace, 116
Benjamin, Walter, 38, 163, 168, 170, 175, 184
Berlin, 2, 2, 3
Bernes, Jasper, 15, 28, 208n52
Berrigan, Caitlin, 163–72, 188
Beuys, Joseph, 39, 120–21, 132
BFAMFAPhD, 75, 82, 85–86, 88–89. See
    also Artists Report Back; Woolard,
    Caroline
Binkiewicz, Donna M., 82–83
Bishop, Claire, 7, 30, 39, 48, 89, 100,
    140–41, 159, 206n12, 217n74

Blu, 2, *2*, 3
Boatto, Alberto, 135
Bois, Yve-Alain, 47–48, 64
Bond Stockton, Kathryn, 160, 189, 191
Born into Brothels (Briski), 108
Bourdieu, Pierre, 85–86
Bourriaud, Nicolas, 41, 96
Bozhkov, Daniel, 15
Bradford, Mark, 27
Braverman, Harry, 19–20, 80, 127–29, 142
Breitz, Candice, 163
Breton, Andre, 162
Briski, Zana, 108
Broglio, Ron, 123, 140
Broodthaers, Marcel, 50
Brooklyn Museum, 84, 144
Brouillette, Sarah, 15, 208n50
Brown, Bill, 169
Brown, Gavin, 136, 138
Brown, Nicholas (critical theorist), 31–32, 67, 87–88, 202
Bruguera, Tania, 18, 152–53, *153*
Bryan-Wilson, Julia, 14, 30, 69–70, 120
Buchanan, James M., 36
Buchloh, Benjamin, 68
Buck-Morss, Susan, 169
Bürger, Peter, 77, 202
Burt, Jonathan, 132

Caffentzis, George, 23–24, 36, 40
California College of the Arts, 41–42, 44, *49*
capital: cultural, 85–86; human, 7, 23–24, 54–55, 170; manipulation of its own value and, 72; real subsumption and, 27; relation to labor and, 23; Rolling Jubilee and, 72–73; value composition of, 98; workers time and, 19. *See also* the aesthetic; commodification; labor
Capital (Marx), 13, 129
capitalism: cars and, 169; children and,

169–70, 188–89; deskilling of work under, 142; financialization of, 20; labor and, 10, 16–17, 77, 127, 177; *Lessons in Capitalism* and, 164–72; Marx and, 126–27; mass indebtedness and, 64; value generation and, 126. *See also* commodification; labor
Carbon Democracy (Mitchell), 32
Carruthers, Bruce, 25
Castro, Fidel, 152, *152*
cats. *See* animals
Celant, Germano, 135
Cercle d'Art des Travailleurs de Plantation Congolaise (CATPC), 105
Chaudhuri, Una, 122
Cheng, Meiling, 118, 225n1
Chevron, 99
Chickens Hatching (Haacke), 120–21, 144
Child Art Piece (Knowles), 162
children: the aesthetic and, 196–97; *Art Amnesty* and, 172–76; critical theory and, 159, 162; cuteness and, 159–60; decommodified labor and, 160–61, 163–64, 170, 172, 174, 176–77, 181–85, 189, 191–97; exclusion of shared sexuality and, 191–93; *Haircuts by Children* and, 186–96; as investments, 171–72, 235n46; labor and, 26, 160; labor prohibitions and, 188–90; *Lessons in Capitalism and,* 164–72; money and, 160, 171, 190; neoliberalism and, 164–76; play and, 161–76, 184; playgrounds and, 169; playing at work and, 163, 166–67, 172, 175–76, 184; real subsumption and, 176–96; rights of, 190–91; socially engaged art and, 1, 158–62, 172, 197; strike against the Youth Training Scheme and, 157–58, 177–85; as waged workers, 6, 26, 159–61, 163, 186–96
Children of Unquiet 2013–14 (Karikis), 163
chimpanzees. *See* animals
Citibank, 108

"Interaction between Quantity and Quality of Children" (Becker), 171
internship, 6
intersubjectivity, 41, 96
In the Long Run We Are All Dead (Mann), 201

Jackson, Shannon, 7, 30, 48, 86–87, 92, 158, 195, 206n12
Jameson, Fredric, 20
Javits, Jacob, 82
Jerolmack, Colin, 146–47
job enlargement, 19
Jones, Kim, 121
Joselit, David, 78–79, 105
Joseph, Miranda, 40
Judah, Hettie, 158

Kant, Immanuel, 12, 45, 47, 73
Kaprow, Allan, 162
Karikis, Mikhail, 163
Karrabing, 108–9
Kennedy administration, 83
Kester, Grant, 28, 30, 194, 237n87
Keynes, John Maynard, 20
Keynesian economics, 9, 19–20, 22–24, 34, 36, 210n70
"Kids with Cameras," 108
Kimbell, Lucy, 132
Kincaid, James, 191
Kinmont, Ben, 14, 69, 101
Kirksey, Eben, 147
Knowles, Alison, 162
Komar, Vitaly, 4, 155
Kosut, Mary, 132
Kounellis, Jannis, 4, 134–43
Kraus, Chris, 66–67
Krauss, Rosalind, 38, 63, 121, 132
Kreuzberg neighborhood. *See* Berlin

labor: abstract human, 124–31; activism and, 30; the aesthetic and, 74; affective, 4, 7–8, 62; animals and, 123; capitalism and, 10, 16–17, 77, 127, 177; commodification of, 4, 8, 101; debt and, 73; deskilling and, 142; education as a form of, 36; financial instruments and, 61; humanization of, 19; immaterial, 62; money and, 9, 12, 24; neoliberalism and, 23–24, 31, 33, 56, 98, 111, 129, 172, 185; opposition to artwork and, 12–15; real subsumption and, 22–24, 56; self-reflexivity of, 131; shift in the category of, 23; unfreedom and, 200
labor (artistic). *See* decommodified labor
Labor and Monopoly Capital (Braverman), 19, 127, 142
labor power: capitalism and, 77; as a commodity, 10, 15–17; decommodification of, 18–19; decommodified labor and, 24; devaluation of, 16, 19
Lange, Lisa, 138–39
L'Attico, 134
Lerner, Ben, 173
Lessons in Capitalism (Berrigan), 163–72, *167*
Levi Strauss and Co., 97
liberalism, 201–2
Lind, Maria, 79, 83, 220n16
Linebaugh, Peter, 8
Lippit, Akira Mizuta, 118, 125
Little John (coyote), 120
Liverpool Biennial (2016), 157
Liverpool in the 1980s (Sinclair), 157
loans. *See* student loans
Locke, John, 209n54
London, 155–56
Los Angeles Times, 198–99
Lowe, Rick, 99, 223n50
Lozano, Lee, 174
Lusanga International Research Centre for Art and Economic Inequality (LIRCAEI), 105
Lyft, 97–98